African Philosophical Illuminations

John Murungi

African Philosophical Illuminations

 Springer

John Murungi
Towson University
Towson, Maryland, USA

ISBN 978-3-319-52559-4   ISBN 978-3-319-52560-0   (eBook)
DOI 10.1007/978-3-319-52560-0

Library of Congress Control Number: 2017935446

© Springer International Publishing AG 2017
This work is subject to copyright. All rights are reserved by the Publisher, whether the whole or part of the material is concerned, specifically the rights of translation, reprinting, reuse of illustrations, recitation, broadcasting, reproduction on microfilms or in any other physical way, and transmission or information storage and retrieval, electronic adaptation, computer software, or by similar or dissimilar methodology now known or hereafter developed.
The use of general descriptive names, registered names, trademarks, service marks, etc. in this publication does not imply, even in the absence of a specific statement, that such names are exempt from the relevant protective laws and regulations and therefore free for general use.
The publisher, the authors and the editors are safe to assume that the advice and information in this book are believed to be true and accurate at the date of publication. Neither the publisher nor the authors or the editors give a warranty, express or implied, with respect to the material contained herein or for any errors or omissions that may have been made. The publisher remains neutral with regard to jurisdictional claims in published maps and institutional affiliations.

Printed on acid-free paper

This Springer imprint is published by Springer Nature
The registered company is Springer International Publishing AG
The registered company address is: Gewerbestrasse 11, 6330 Cham, Switzerland

Preface

A preface is anticipatory. It anticipates what is to come. Anticipating what is to come poses a problem for anticipation. Because what is to come is out of hand, it cannot be comprehended wholly. If it were to be comprehended wholly, it would not be anticipated. It would be already present. Nevertheless, there must be an awareness of what is anticipated, for, if this were not the case, its arrival would not be recognized. The anticipator must somehow be aware of what he or she anticipates and, at the same time, be not fully aware of what he or she anticipates. This is the case not only with the reader of a preface but also with the author of the preface. As the author of this preface, this is where I find myself. I am not fully aware of what is being prefaced. When I started writing this preface, I was not fully aware of what was to follow. I did not fully have in hand what I wanted to preface. Accordingly, this preface remains incomplete and, most likely, will remain so, for what it prefaces is likely to be incomplete. A philosophical work is, of necessity, incomplete.

Because this is a philosophical work, it deserves a philosophical preface. What makes a preface philosophical is that, in it, there is prefigured what is philosophical. In other words, what is true of philosophy's preface is true of philosophy. What is philosophical about philosophy is both in hand and out of hand. It is present and also what is to come. One does not comprehend fully what is philosophical about philosophy. I take this to be a central element in composing a philosophical work. This is how African philosophical illumination is to be understood. I do not have a fully predetermined idea about the nature of this illumination. It comes into being as I think and write about it. I have offered myself to it to guide me as I speak about it. One is to make sense of what I am speaking about under its guidance even if what guides is not fully at hand.

To think or write about philosophy is to do so creatively. This applies also to a reader of a philosophical work. One must read creatively. In other words, the reader coauthors what he or she reads. One must read a philosophical work philosophically to get its philosophical sense. How to read it this way must remain a philosophical issue until a philosophical work is no longer philosophical. I must point this out to the reader so that he or she does not anticipate what ought not to be anticipated.

The preface paves the way for the chapters that follow. In paving the way for them, it imparts what it is to them. Otherwise, it would be an improper preface. What is true of the preface is true of them. None of them is fully what it is, and should be read as such. Each of them opens with an image of an African work of art, and each image is inherent in other images if only because each is sensuous. The images are intended to provide an aesthetic (sensuous) source of philosophical illumination. The goal here is to shift the focus of philosophical illumination away from reason, mind, soul, or spirit as the only sources of illumination and to focus on the corporeal, and charge it or recognize it as charged with illuminating power. In his studies of the body, the French phenomenologist Maurice Merleau-Ponty has contributed to this shift—a shift that takes us to the African world, a world in which corporeal illumination is at home.[1] African works of art exemplify this illumination and invite us to embrace it. In doing so, at the same time, we embrace ourselves, since we too are sensuous. The images are images of what we are. To see them is to see ourselves. What works itself out in African works of art is the African and all that is entailed by, and in, being African. Moreover, since being African is being human, in these images, one ought to find what is human in all of us whether we are or are not African. Every human being is sensuously a path to every other human being. The sensuous is the site of what we are and is where we intrinsically connect with each other as human beings. The sensible unifies us in our being.

Under the assumption that what a philosopher does is different from what an artist does, and that the audience of each is different from the audience of the other, associating philosophy with a work of art may appear unwarranted. This assumption, however, is precisely what must be contested. It is possible that it rests on a misconception of the work of philosophy and on a misconception of a work of art. If it is recognized that in both works what is human is constituted and illuminated, philosophical work and a work of art are not at odds with each other. When adequately understood, each is a site for the appearance of the other. Each illuminates the other. Both are equal sources of illumination.

Each chapter in the book opens with an image of the sensuous, and because the image in each chapter is sensuous, every chapter opens to every other chapter and is the site of every other chapter. The image of the drum is placed in the introductory chapter to announce other chapters and to bring readers to attention. The belonging together of the images and their chapters is inaugurated by the African drum. It is what the drum drums into existence. It is illuminated as what it is in drumming, and it is illuminated as an illuminator. As is evident, it is a sculptured African drum. Sculpturing illuminates. It sensuously ingathers us and illuminates this ingathering. It sensuously opens each one of us to each and every one of us, and it illuminates the world in which we live. The world that is illuminated is sensuous and is inhabited by sensuous beings. These beings are not exclusively human. They encompass every being whether it is or is not human. Sensuousness finds its limit in nothing if only because nothing is nothing.

The projection of a drum as an image could generate an unintended error—the error of viewing it as if it were a copy or an image of something—an error of thinking that there is something that is behind or beneath it. This error is to be noted and avoided. The drum is also not to be seen or viewed primarily as an instrument. To avoid this error, the word "image," as used here, has nothing behind it. It does not represent. It is presence. The image and that of which it is the image are one and the same. It is an image that is what it is by effacing itself as an image. In effacing itself, it allows what is to show itself. As a version of the illuminated illuminating the sensuous, it is not opaque. It is exhaustively translucent, utterly as clear as crystal. The drum is presence and is illuminated as such. As presence, it illuminates.

The apparently normal belief that an image is an image of something is predicated on the false belief that there exists a thing out there, independent of its image, and the image is the image of that thing. It is a copy of it. The drum is not an image in this sense. It is the site of the sensuousness. It shows itself as belonging to the sensuous. It is a showing of the sensuous by the sensuous. Moreover, it should not be forgotten that the drum is a work of art and, as such, there is nothing thingly about it. A work of art exhausts itself in illuminating. It is an illuminated illuminating. In a work of art, what works out itself is illumination.

There are traditions in the world, such as the Western European tradition, where the sensuous has largely been disparaged. In such traditions, we are warned against corruption by the sensuous. For example, this is a warning that René Descartes calls to our attention in his Meditations.[2] Apparently, the sensuous has a corrupting effect and is an obstacle to the perception and the understanding of what is truly real. As presented here, the sensuous is the site for the constitution and illumination of what is truly real. Self and everything else that is, is exhaustively sensuous, and so is truth. Truth is not added to phenomena. It belongs to them. It inhabits them. Sensuous phenomena are truthful. It is in sensuousness that the truth of self and the truth of everything else are illuminated and, hence, become accessible. The sensuous is not to be confused with, or mistaken for, material or for the sensuous of the empiricist. It is not the subject for physicalists. It is what is presupposed by materialists and by physicalists. It is the necessary condition for the emergence of being. It lights up what is. It is not apart from what is. It inhabits what is. In this way, it is in a position to light it up. It lights itself up as it lights what is.

The book is addressed to the sensuous if only because there are no others to be addressed. It addresses them as sensuous and seeks to illuminate them as such. Accordingly, the author is a part of the addressed, since he too is sensuous. A philosophical journey begins and ends at home. This is the uncanny aspect of this sensuous journey. It is inescapably a singular journey, as well as a communal journey. Also, it is more than a human journey if only because a human being is what he or she is by being more that what he or she is. A human being does not have a monopoly on sensuousness. He or she is a part of everything else that is sensuous. Accordingly, his or her journey is a journey of the sensuous in its entirety, and it is a journey that is constituted and illuminated as such.

This book is uncanny in that, as one who reads it, one reads not only oneself but also reads all that is. It is not a book in front of a reader, as if it were an object that is other than the reader. It is intended to sensuously absorb the reader in such a way that in reading it, one reads oneself—a self that is a part of everything else that is. What one reads is freely self-composed. Ultimately, it is authored by the reader—

the reader who experiences himself or herself as multiple. If there is credit to be extended for the authorship of this book, it is extended to all. The authorship is shared by both the animate and the inanimate. I am grateful for their collaboration. Beings author themselves. Gratitude is like rain; it rains on all.

What is said in this book may come across as visceral anti-Eurocentrism. If what is said comes across as such, in part, it is indeed so. It is a reflection of the depth into which the projection of Africans as outcasts in the domain of what is human has reached. The outcasting of the African in this domain is an integral aspect in the process subjecting the African to slavery, colonization, and apartheid. Moreover, it is a subjection that is inseparable from racism. Racism is visceral in that it touches the nerve center of human corporeality. It is among the deepest and the most widespread assaults on human dignity. The African viscera have been adversely affected by it. Consequently, Africans stand in need of a philosophy that is going to diagnose and pave the way for the cure of this visceral illness. It is also an invitation to Euro-Westerners to examine their own viscera. What they have viscerally done to Africans they have viscerally done to themselves. Those who have enslaved, colonized, or subjected Africans to apartheid and to racism have a visceral disease. If they do not recognize this, they are in self-denial. They need a psychiatrist to bring to the conscious level what is pushed into their unconscious. For them, philosophy must entail a diagnosis of their viscera and a visceral therapy. In his preface to Frantz Fanon's book *The Wretched of the Earth*—a classic text on colonialism and on anticolonial struggle, Jean Paul Sartre, in reference to fellow Europeans, pointed out that Europeans "must confront an unexpected sight: the striptease of our humanism."[3] A successful process of decolonization must bring colonizers face to face with themselves to help them discover what colonialism did to them. As Aimé Césaire, an Afro-Caribbean thinker, pointed out in his "Discourse on Colonialism":

> First we must study how colonization works to decivilize the colonizer, to *brutalize* him in the true sense of the word, to degrade him, to awaken him to buried instincts, to covetousness, violence, race hatred and moral relativism; and we must show that each time a head is cut off or an eye is put out in Vietnam and in France they accept the fact, each time a little girl is raped and in France they accept the fact, each time a Madagascan is tortured and in France they accept the fact, civilization acquires another dead weight, a universal regression takes place, a gangrene sets in, a center of infection begins to spread; and that at the end of all these treaties that have been violated, all these lies that have been propagated, all these punitive expeditions that have been tolerated, all these prisoners who have been tied up and "interrogated," all these patriots who have been tortured, at the end of all the racial pride that has been encouraged, all the boastfulness that has been displayed, a poison has been instilled into the veins of Europe, and slowly but surely, the continent proceeds toward *savagery*.[4]

Although Césaire made this observation more than a half a century ago, the process of decolonization is not over yet. In this process, the role played by philosophy has been largely marginal. Today, it is important to bring philosophy to the center, both in African and in the Euro-West. It has also become increasingly clear that our time needs a philosophy that is psychiatric—a philosophy that undertakes the archaeology of the body, that diagnoses the ongoing corporeal illness, and that explores the appropriate therapy. Postcolonial African philosophy has yet to fully engage itself in this endeavor, and Euro-Western philosophy is yet to fully acknowledge that this endeavor is its endeavor too. For better or for worse, the destinies of these two philosophies necessarily have to work together to rid humanity of the scourge generated by racist colonialism. This book invites this collaboration.

What comes across as visceral anti-Eurocentrism could be construed as contrary to philosophy. Taken this way, what is said could lead to an erroneous belief that what is said is in defiance of reason, since the convention view is that reason lies at the heart of philosophy. One could be led to an erroneous belief that visceral anti-Eurocentrism is nothing more than an emotional or instinctive reaction to Euro-Westerners and to philosophy as understood in the Euro-West. What is contested in this book is the prevailing Euro-Western version of reason—a version of reason in which Africans have been projected as outcasts in philosophy, a version that finds in a human being a polarization of reason and emotion. African philosophy contributes to the healing of this rift in being human. Healing takes place when the emotion–reason dichotomy dissolves and is replaced by a unified sense of being human. Philosophy is an expression of this unified sense. It is where one is to find African philosophy and where African philosophy is illuminated as African philosophy.

It may be argued that in postcolonial Africa, the negative projection of the African has ceased and that philosophical space has opened to the point at which Africans are no longer projected as outcasts in the domain of the human and in the domain of philosophy. I will readily concede that this is indeed the case, but I do so grudgingly because the motives for projecting Africans as outcasts in these domains may be implicitly alive. It is indeed true that overt degradation of Africans is not as fashionable as it used to be. It makes sense not to flog dead horses, but some horses play at being dead. If philosophical life were to be taken as a life of reason, what has been taken as philosophy might have harbored an irrational element. That is, what has been taken as philosophical might have harbored an antiphilosophical or unphilosophical element. Reason is yet to be immunized against irrationality, and perhaps it will never be permanently immunized. Moreover, philosophical life is more than a life of reason. It is the life of the whole person. It is not to be assumed that reason and emotion are mutually exclusive or that they can be sharply distinguished from each other. Reason that is in opposition to emotion is not philosophical reason, and adding one to the other does not constitute philosophy. As an instantiation of what being human is, philosophy is an irreducible whole. This is a part of what African philosophy must illuminate.

Opening space for Africans in the domain of philosophy calls for a re-examination of the nature of this domain—that is, a re-examination of the nature of philosophy. In this re-examination, it should not be forgotten that, like every other human being, a philosopher is an embodied being. The domain of philosophy is a corporeal landscape. To philosophize is to philosophize from the standpoint of one's body—not the body as a biophysical entity but as a lived body that is the bearer of multiple significance. Inevitably, philosophy is philosophy of the lived body. Today, authentic African philosophy must be a philosophy that reclaims the humanity of the African's body and, in reclaiming it, it must reclaim non-African bodies too, for they, too, are human bodies. A human body is a body of all human bodies. No human body is what it is in isolation from other human bodies. In its bodily rootedness, African philosophy, appropriately understood, has a universal reach. One of the absurdities of racism is the attempt to segregate and enclose the African's body in itself and thereby cut it off from the European's body and from other human bodies. The European perpetrator of this absurd project attempts to do this with his own body: to cut it off and enclose it within itself, shutting out all other human bodies, especially the body of the African. African philosophy must illuminate this absurdity and call for a unitary human embodiment. It calls for an end to the alienation of human bodies from each other.

In postcolonial Africa, the African body must be decolonized. This book responds positively to this call. In African philosophy, today, the African body matters. By the African body, I do not mean the black body. The African body is the African body—a body that European modernity has blackened. It is not a black body. Being black is largely a construction of European modernity—a modernity that is also responsible for the construction of the white body. There is need for a radical divorce of the African body from the black body. One of the achievements of European modernity is the blackening of the African's body. It is this modernity that constituted Africa as the Dark Continent—a continent of dark bodies. This modernity is the Dark Age of the African body. Today, African philosophy must play a key role in the renaissance of the African body. This book makes a contribution to this endeavor—an endeavor that radicalizes somatology. It is a call for a new logos of the body. This book fuels this endeavor.

Paulin Hountondji has warned fellow African philosophers and African intellectuals against projecting themselves as the spokespersons of all of Africa or as spokespersons of all Africans, especially since Africans have not given them permission to do so.[5] Similarly, one can imagine a warning that they stay clear from speaking about all of Europe or about all Europeans, especially since Europeans have not given them permission to do so. Readers of this book may conclude that I have ignored this warning; consequently, I have injected into it words that are without referents. In other words, one can imagine an allegation that the book contains noxious generalizations and ignores concrete particulars and nuances that could assure more secure and sounder ontological and epistemological foundations for the claims that are made in the book. This conclusion may be unwarranted. Hountondji takes the position that philosophizing is an individual undertaking, and it is on the basis of this position that he denounces the pseudophilosophy that he refers to as ethnophilosophy—a bogus, concocted, unconscious "unthinking, spontaneous collective system of thought common to all Africans."[6] However, what he says must be understood contextually. Words that appear to be generalizations or devoid of referents have to be taken contextually. In some contexts, it is indeed true that they are bogus and without referents. It could be pointed out that in colonial Africa, the African or the Negro that the colonizers had in mind was a product of their own imagination. The uncivilized, primitive, savage African or Negro had no real existence in the African world. Africans did not think of themselves this way. Yet the colonizers took this fictional character as if it were truly real. In fictionalizing Africans, they thereby also fictionalized themselves and demanded that Africans treat their fictional characters as if they were truly real. The abstract was made real, and the real was made abstract. Colonialism attempted to bring about a reciprocal ontological revolution, revolutionizing the being of the African and the being of the European, presenting each as though it were other than what it was. The anticolonial revolution was an attempt to undo this revolution. It was an attempt to demythologize the African and, at the same time, to demythologize the European. This process is not over yet. This book serves as a reminder that this is indeed the case.

It should not be forgotten that colonialism did not target isolated African individuals. It targeted the community of Africans. It is indeed true that individual Africans bore the brunt of colonial violence. However, it should not be forgotten that these individuals were individuals in the community of Africans. Ultimately, it is this community that was under colonial assault. Although the anticolonial revolution was waged by individual Africans, it was more than an individual struggle. Ultimately, it was a revolution that engaged, or that had to engage, the entire African community. One does not colonize alone, and one does not get colonized alone. Fanon has noted that:

> The colonized intellectual who decides to combat these colonialist lies does so on a continental stage.... Colonialism, little troubled by nuances, has always claimed that the "nigger" was a savage, not an Angolan or a Nigerian, but a "nigger." For colonialism, this vast continent was a den of savages, infested with superstitions and fanaticism, destined to be despised, curses by God, a land of cannibals, a land of "niggers." Colonialism's condemnation is continental in scale. Colonialism's claim that the precolonial period was akin to a darkness of the human soul refers to the entire continent of Africa. The colonized's endeavors to rehabilitate himself and escape the sting of colonialism obeys the same rule of logic.[7]

It is also Fanon who reminds us that:

> The colonialist bourgeoisie hammered into the colonized mind the notion of a society of individuals where each is locked up in his subjectivity, where wealth lies in thought. But the colonized intellectual who is lucky enough to bunker down with the people during the liberation struggle, will soon discover the falsity of this theory.[8]

As a colonized person, an African philosopher participates in this people's endeavor. By referring to himself or herself as an African philosopher, he or she presupposes that in being himself or herself, he or she is more than an individual. He or she positions himself or herself in the community of Africans, not just in the community of African philosophers but in the community of all Africans. Hountondji is correct in denouncing ethnophilosophy, but he would be wrong to denounce the community of African philosophers or the community of African people. Were he to do so, he would problematize his standing as an African philosopher. To lay a claim that one is an African philosopher is to lay a claim to membership in the community of Africans. As developed by Mogobe Ramose, a South African philosopher, Ubuntu is a concept that captures this sense of being African.[9]

In my case, for example, I fully embrace my singularity, my individuality. As such, I stand out as different from other singularities, from other individuals. I am unique, and other individuals are similarly unique. Individuals *qua* individuals are not fungible. However, I also recognize that I am an African and I am a human being. As such, my existence is bound to fellow Africans and to fellow human beings. I have an organic relation with fellow Africans and with fellow human beings. What could be fictional is an African who is isolated from the community of Africans or an individual who is isolated from the community of human beings. To think of oneself as an African is to think of oneself as a member of the community of Africans, and to think of oneself as a human being is to think of oneself as a member of the community of human beings.

In this book, it is tempting to dismiss references to "the African," "the European," "the Westerner," "European or Western philosophy," or "African philosophy" as concepts that are devoid of intuition and, hence, empty concepts. What should not be forgotten is that these references are significant in reading and making sense of modern relations between Africans and Europeans. They illuminate important aspects of these relations. If all general concepts were to be avoided, it would be difficult to make sense of particulars. Most likely, language would be indistinguishable from silence. It makes sense to me to be what I am by being a member of the African community and, at the same time, to be a member of the human community. It also makes sense to see other individuals as members of their respective communities and as members of the human community. Philosophy illuminates these modes of human existence.

It is very difficult to challenge the construction of "the European" as the absolute other of "the African" or the construction of "the African" as the absolute other of such a European. The difficulty is largely a product of European modernity—a modernity that seeks in every way to convert all human beings to the cult of individualism. If this is indeed the creed of modernity, modernity could not be true to itself, since it is precisely modernity that fathered colonialism and racism, both of which deny individuality to the victims it has generated. It is European modernity that has generated the African as the absolute other and, in otherizing the African, it has otherized the European at the same time. That is, the European has generated himself as the other of the African and has also generated the African as the other of the European. In either case, the African is not to be held entirely responsible for this otherizing process. He or she is more or less its victim. To be sure, in response to this negative process of otherization, the African can easily fall prey to responding in kind—that is, he or she can construct the African as the negative other of the European or can construct the European as the negative other of the African. The reversal of these constructions does not do away with the negation that is operative here—a negation that is to be overcome. It should also be noted that within Africa, as is the case within Europe, there are otherizations. These otherizations, however, should not obscure the otherization that has taken place between Africans and Europeans. What it should call to our attention are the dynamics and nuances within the world of otherizations. Contrary to what might appear to be the case, it is not my intention in this book to construct negating constructions, but it may be fruitful to acknowledge that, in some contexts, generalizations are needed to counter other generalizations. Let it also not be forgotten that in a philosophical engagement, straw men are needed to counter other straw men. It is not easy to uproot unphilosophical or antiphilosophical weeds from the garden of philosophy. African philosophy is not immunized against this difficulty, and no other philosophy is immunized against it. The difficulty could be more bearable if all philosophers (African and non-African) could cooperate in identifying and uprooting the weeds that are toxic in a philosophical garden. Accordingly, this book is addressed to all philosophers. It is also addressed to all human beings, since the work of philosophy is the work of humanity. It is not anti-African philosophy when an African philosopher acknowledges the contribution made to philosophy by non-African philosophical colleagues. One cannot philosophize in a historical vacuum or in a societal or cultural vacuum. One cannot philosophize alone. Solipsistic philosophizing is a chimera.

In his resignation from the French Communist Party in 1954, Césaire correctly pointed out that "there are two ways to lose oneself: walled segregation in the particular or a dilution in the universal."[10] In this book, African philosophical illumination sheds light on these ways of losing oneself and also illuminates possibilities for avoiding them. It affirms the autochthony of the African while, at the same time, it affirms its kinship with all other philosophies. A philosophy that is absolutely cut off from other philosophies is not a philosophy.

It is very tempting to claim that this is a postcolonial period of African history and that it is senseless to fight a battle that is already over. In other words, colonialism is over now. To avoid making an erroneous and hasty conclusion, it is important to bear in mind that one cannot truly let the past be the past if one does not fully understand it. In some significant way, the past informs the present and paves the way for the future. One of the inescapable tasks for a self-conscious African philosopher is to undertake a hermeneutic study of colonialism, for it is only in the context of such an undertaking that he or she can move forward intelligently. There is a Kiswahili saying—"Haraka haina Baraka"—which may be translated as "Hurry hurry has no blessing." In philosophy, patience pays.

Being African is consciousness of being African. What is said in this book is intended to contribute to the generation of this consciousness. African philosophy is a part of this process. Carrying out this process does not take place in an African cave. Being African is a public mode of being. African philosophy is a public philosophy. The audience of African philosophy is both African and non-African. Contributors to this philosophy are equally both African and non-African. Accordingly, when the author refers to non-African philosophers or to non-African philosophy, the reference is not a diversion. It is a recognition of the fact that philosophy is an activity that is common to all human beings. African philosophy is a part of the planetary landscape of philosophy. No sector of the human community has a monopoly on this landscape.

Towson, MD, USA   John Murungi

Contents

1	Introduction/Initiation	1
2	African Grounding of Philosophy	11
3	To Be Received or Not to Be Received	35
4	On the Notion of the African History of Philosophy	43
5	The African Body as an Ethico-aesthetic Site	65
6	Seeing: An African Way	83
7	Chiwara: The African Antelope Speaks	99
8	The Way of Trees in Africa	109
9	Robben Island Is Not an Island: Introducing No-Geography	127
10	Conclusion	141
	Notes	149

Chapter 1
Introduction/Initiation

> *There once was a bird that died so long ago that no one can recall when it died or how it died. When it died, it went into the womb of the dead. Since then, what is known about it is that every now and then, it would spring up unexpectedly from the womb of the dead and then, after an indefinite period, it would unexpectedly die. The length of its sojourn in the womb of death was as unpredictable as the length of its life once it sprung up. Today, it is not known when it will spring up or where it will spring up again. It could spring up from any part of the earth at any time. Whenever it springs up and wherever it springs up, it illuminates the entire earth. When the entire earth is illuminated, everything in it, on it, above it, below it, and about it is illuminated. Day and Night, they call it in Africa. In other places, it has different names, but all the names refer to the same bird. It is also believed that the entire earth is its graveyard. Ancestors say knowledge too has its limits. The wise understand this. They do not seek knowledge where there is no knowledge. Knowledge and wisdom are not one and the same. The distinction is a matter of wisdom; so, the ancestors say. Drumming is the site of this saying. Ancestors say that if you want to understand the way of the bird, listen to drumming.*

The more the peoples of the world connect with each other, the more they become aware of their differences, and also the more they become aware of what they have in common. The same can be said about individual human beings. The more they connect with each other, the more they become aware not only of their differences but also of what they have in common. Whether as a people or as individuals, connectivity is not juxtapositional and, likewise, awareness is not juxtapositional. Awareness brings into being what a people are and what an individual is. In and by bringing into being, it illuminates what it brings into being. Awareness is illumination. This is precisely what an African drum calls to our attention. This is what the drum drums, provided that we do not stand in its way. To stand in its way is to stand in the way of our being, and it is also to stand in the way of the being of everything that is.

To hear and see what the drum drums, we must take it to be more than a musical instrument. It is more than an object forged out of the material provided by nature and destined for social or cultural uses. Primarily, it illuminates itself as an illuminator. As an illuminator, it illuminates not only what it is but also both what is human and what is not human. It illuminates not only the difference between what is human and what is not human but also what they have in common. In this way, it earns its ontological and existential place. It effaces itself as it illuminates, as a way of being itself. Human beings, as is the case with all other beings, belong to it and, by belonging to it, they become endowed with the ability to illuminate. To illuminate is not to illuminate what is already there. What is already there is already there as being illuminated. Accordingly, illuminating is a creative event. Nothing precedes it. Before it takes place, there is nothing to be illuminated. To be in the presence of the drum is to be in the presence of philosophy, for philosophy is precisely at home where there is an illuminating process. It is where it is and what it is.

We open this book with an image of an African drum. This image sets the background for the images that head every chapter. It gathers all of the images into itself and charges them with what it is. They are illuminators that derive their illuminating possibilities from it. It charges what they are with what it is: with illuminating power. To see and truly experience their sensuousness, it is important that the images not be viewed as objects of sense, and one should resist the temptation to look behind them to see what they are images of. Behind them, there is nothing. They are images that cease being images once they are seen the way they ought to be seen and are experienced the way they ought to be experienced. They are works of art that work out what they are by ceasing to be objects. They are what they are by exhausting themselves as they illuminate. As they are called to our attention, we ourselves are called to the attention of our being. We share their sensuousness. To see them is to see ourselves, and to experience them is to experience ourselves. This seeing or this experiencing is enabled by and in African drumming.

By African philosophical illumination, one should not have before oneself this illumination as if it were an object that one seeks to understand. On the face of it, this claim may come across as absurd. After all, it is assumed that what one seeks to understand lies before oneself as what is to be understood. What is understood by the expression "before oneself" could be diversionary if it is assumed that the conventional sense of this expression is its only sense. The proper hermeneutics of this expression illuminates its multiple senses. At issue here is the spatiality of this expression. In the conventional sense, it is assumed that one is apart from what is presented, and that what is presented is other than what one is. Although this is a legitimate sense of this expression, it is not the only one. Often overlooked or likely to be overlooked is the phenomenological sense in which a lived space opens up, whereby one is a part of what is presented and in which what is presented is a part of what one is. In the African drum, where what is essential about the drum lies in drumming, there lies this sense of presentation. Drumming presents and illuminates presencing.

In the light of what has been said above, it should be relatively clear that African philosophical illumination is not entirely subject to reflection. It is not entirely what one represents to oneself or what is represented or presented by others. Normally, reflection distances what is to be understood, and it also distances him or her who seeks to understand from himself or from herself. In its elemental sense, African philosophical illumination is prereflective and is brought to life by what is prereflective. It calls for an intersubjective presence. There is a blending of subject and object which, at the same time, founds their being. If this comes across as a contradiction, it should not be forgotten that there are experiences where logic is put out of commission. This is especially the case where an elemental sense of philosophical illumination is at stake. One should have an internal relation to it if it is to make sense, and one should not take it to be an "it" to which one is related. The subject–object relation does not reign here. Here, elemental illumination gets illuminated.

In the expression "African philosophical illumination," what is meant by "African" is not entirely a matter of reflection. If it were, it would be entirely subject to normal reflection. It would fall under the regime of objective science. What a deceptive concept "reflection" is! It obfuscates the collapse of the subject into the object and the collapse of the object into the subject. In the regime of science, the subject–object dichotomy has sway over thinking and perception. In it, everything is illuminated either as a subject or as an object. This is the regime of classical science. Likewise, what is "philosophical" should not be taken primarily as a matter of reflection. It is not an "object" that is called to one's attention. What is philosophical is on one's side, not in opposition to it. Being on one's side is at the same time being on the other's side and vice versa. It is a part of one's lived experience. The word "illumination" in the expression "African philosophical illumination" is to be similarly understood. It is not an "object" to be understood by a "subject." It does not allow for the subject–object dichotomy. Illumination illuminates itself in what it illuminates. It cannot have an independent existence apart from what it does.

African philosophical illumination must be Africanly and philosophically illuminated if it is to be truly understood. Anyone who seeks a true understanding of this illumination must be situated where this illumination is illuminating and be conscious that this is where he or she is situated. In other words, one must have a preunderstanding of what one seeks to understand. To be sure, one could ask, what is the point of trying to understand what one already understands? That is, if what is being illuminated is already illuminated and hence already understood, what is the point of seeking what illumination is? A provisional answer, which must remain as such, is that this positioning is proper to philosophical illumination. It is the way in which philosophical illumination is illuminated and in which it is to be understood. It is also the way it illuminates. One understands philosophical illumination horizontally. One never ceases to understand what one understands. African philosophical illumination is not an exception.

As a philosophical work, this book illustrates a philosophical illumination of what constitutes a philosophical work. Philosophy works its truth in its work. That is, philosophy constitutes and illuminates itself in its work. This is what should be expected from a book on African philosophical illumination. It should be taken as an introduction to philosophy. This is not an exception. Every philosophical work is an introduction to philosophy. Accordingly, African philosophical illumination introduces African philosophy and introduces it in such a way that it necessarily bears on the introduction to non-African philosophy. It is an introduction to philosophy as such. In its diversity, philosophy retains its unity. Its unity is just as essential as its diversity. In the pursuit of the universality of philosophy, one may be tempted to focus attention on an introduction to philosophy as such—an introduction that ignores the context of introduction to philosophy—but such a temptation should be resisted if only because nothing philosophical is thereby introduced. An introduction to philosophy is necessarily contextual and noncontextual at the same time.

1 Introduction/Initiation

The word "philosophy" appears in European languages and is said to be of Greek origin. It is not found in African languages. Because it does not appear in them, an erroneous impression may be given, suggesting that the meaning associated with it is exclusively a European meaning or a Greek meaning. In this case, what is referred to as African philosophical illumination is likely to be construed exclusively in a European or Hellenic sense of philosophical illumination. Today, many Africans are more likely to fall into this temptation because they have been exposed to academic philosophy in European languages—for example, in the English, French, and German languages. In this case, a question may arise as to whether there is something linguistically distinctive about African philosophical illumination. If the answer is yes, one may ask whether it is it possible to do justice to it if it is expressed in a European language rather than in an African language. Can what is African about philosophy and, hence, what is African about philosophical illumination be expressed in an African language? The answer to this question depends on what is understood by philosophy and on how human languages stand in relation to each other in their ability to express philosophy or its illumination. There is also the question of whether human languages are so indistinct from each other that what the word "philosophy" means in one language can be expressed in another language without doing an injustice to this meaning. It appears that an answer to this question cannot be given without a philosophical understanding of all human languages, and who among us can profess to have such an understanding? Is such an understanding possible? This latter question cannot satisfactorily be understood until the multiple senses of understanding are philosophically illuminated.

Provisionally, what can be pointed out is that insofar as each language is a human language, each and every one of them necessarily has an internal relation with each and every other human language. Otherwise, it would not be a human language. If this is granted, it must equally be granted that, as a human language, the language of philosophy is immanent in every human language. An African language is not an exception. Of course, it would follow that writing about African philosophical illumination in English or in any other language does not necessarily do an injustice to it. What ought to be evident is that for such writing to truly matter, a philosophical understanding must guide it and illuminate it as such. A philosophical illumination of African philosophical illumination must be so guided, and so must every other philosophical illumination.

Historically, it is clear that European thinkers have privileged their own languages above all other human languages in philosophical illumination. It should be equally clear that there is a need for a historic revision in the way they understand philosophical illumination and in the way they understand their own languages. Meeting this need is essential if they are to recognize and affirm the internal linkage their own sense of philosophical illumination ought to have with all other philosophical illuminations. It is particularly important not to succumb to an obsession with an alienated sense of the language of philosophy. There is a "prelingual" sense of philosophy—a sense in which every human language is rooted and that is ultimately served by every language. It is indeed true that philosophy expresses itself in language, but language is more than the spoken or a written word. It its essential sense, language is the language of the lived world. It is in such a world that language is to be secured and safeguarded from possible distortion. Differently stated, the lived world is the flesh of language. In its elemental sense, language does not represent such a world. It inhabits it. It is also important not to experience language as what sets human beings apart from other beings. Primordially, language is more than a human phenomenon. There is a place for language in everything that is. Everything that is speaks. It is in language that everything that is, is.

African universities have been, and continue to be, largely Europhonic. The language of philosophy has been, and continues to be, Eurocentric. African languages have been projected as having no place in this language. Students of philosophy have been socialized and acculturated into a Eurocentric philosophical illumination and into the belief that only European languages are the languages of philosophy. Although it is not a European language, the Greek language has been projected by Europeans as a European language. The belief that philosophy has a home only in the European and Greek languages is essentially a European belief, and it is both erroneous and unphilosophical. It falsifies what philosophy is and where its home is. It misconstrues what the language of philosophy is and, hence, is a misconception of philosophy's home. In part, African philosophical illumination illuminates and corrects this misconstruction and this misconception—not by claiming that it has a monopoly on the understanding of philosophy or the understanding of philosophical illumination, but in experiencing what it has in common with other understandings of philosophy and other philosophical illuminations. Philosophy's home is in every language and in all languages.

To be philosophical, an African does not have to step out of his or her African language. In what is philosophical, a non-African ought not to adopt a missionary attitude toward an African who aspires to be philosophical. Aspiration to be philosophical is indigenous to whoever aspires to be philosophical. Missionarism is incompatible with philosophical discourse. An African should not expect to learn what philosophical illumination is from non-Africans, and he or she should not expect to teach a non-African what it is to be philosophical or what philosophical illumination is. Philosophical illumination is indigenous to Africa, as it is elsewhere.

Another eccentric and questionable Eurocentric belief is that philosophy has its basic home in the academy. With the institutionalization of this belief, there has been a loss of memory. What has been forgotten is that the academy is not the exclusive home of philosophy or the exclusive home of philosophical illumination. There was philosophy and philosophical illumination before the founding of the academy, and there will be philosophy and philosophical illumination after the academy ceases to exist. There is no philosophical basis to believe that the academy will necessarily last forever. Because it is a historical fact that contemporary Africans have been subjected to European academic philosophy, it is important that what is viewed by European philosophical illumination be taken into account in preparing a site for the emergence of an African philosophical illumination. In doing so, it should not be forgotten that a fuller picture of the African philosophical illumination soon or later has to take into consideration other non-European philosophical illuminations, lest one become hostage to an erroneous European philosophical illumination. It should not be forgotten that the academy is not the exclusive site for philosophy or for philosophical illumination. One should be disabused of the belief that it is only at an African academy that one can be exposed to African philosophy or to African philosophical illumination.

For the most part, in Western European thinking, philosophical illumination has largely been taken to be the work of the soul, of reason, or of the mind. The soul, reason, or the mind have been taken to be divine-like or as deriving their illuminating power from the divine. Consequently, the divine has been understood to be the ultimate source of illumination. In other words, illumination is ultimately divine illumination. The divine has not only been taken as the ultimate source of illumination but also has been taken as illumination itself. It is because it is itself illumination that it illuminates. This view of illumination and its source is understood as such by the soul, reason, or the mind. Senses have nothing to do with it. Divine illumination, as is the case with the illumination process, has nothing to do with the senses. It is inaccessible to the senses. Accordingly, divine illumination and the divine itself are incorporeal. Apparently, sense organs cannot grasp this claim. It can only be grasped by the soul, reason, or the mind. In short, for the most part, in Western European thinking, an inquiry into the nature of philosophical illumination has been a theological process whose ultimate goal is to illuminate the divine and secondarily to illuminate the soul, reason, or the mind. Put differently, illumination is essentially a divine process mediated by human beings insofar as they are taken to be incorporeal. This is the case, notwithstanding the profession of atheism in European thinking. In European thinking, theism is so deeply rooted in atheism that any pretension to atheism should be considered suspect. That is, one should be deeply suspicious of Europeans who profess to be atheists.

What is remarkable—almost magical—is how, in the European tradition of philosophy, the concepts of God, soul, spirit, reason, and mind have been reified and, having been made real, they have been used as weapons by Europeans to eliminate anything and everything about them or in them that makes them natural beings. They have been used to uproot them from nature. There is what is suicidal about the way Europeans have used these concepts. Having been quasi-successful in this undertaking, they have used them as arrows, bullets, or missiles in the racist war against Africans and other non-European peoples. The possibility that Europeans have fetishized these concepts is not entertained. These concepts could be considered as products of European witchcraft or European sorcery. They have been mistaken for evidence illustrating the superiority of European civilization. One can imagine Africans seeing God, the soul, reason, and the mind as European idols or as European invisible fetishes. These idols or fetishes exemplify the European uprootedness from nature. According to European modernity, anyone who remains rooted in nature is a savage and is not human. The view that philosophy is rational knowledge is a part of this assault, and Africans have borne its brunt. They are projected as paradigmatic of those who are naturally devoid of such knowledge. In the mad rush to acquire such knowledge, Africans are contributing to their demise as natural beings. Under pressure from the agents of European civilization, they too want to be civilized in the same way that Europeans are civilized.

It is undeniable that Western European modernity has courted secularism especially because of the pressure exerted by "reason" or by science. But the soil in which secularism has grown remains watered by the Western European divine—divine in a Judeo-Christian sense—the sense that truly matters for Western Europeans since, in their eyes, it is the one and only true divine. The divine is their divine. When philosophical activity is projected in the West as a rational activity, as an activity of the soul, or as an activity of the mind, one should read between the lines and take note of the theo-religious assumption. Of note, is the setting aside from the body under the direction of reason, of the soul, or of the mind, since it is viewed as an obstacle to true philosophical illumination? The body is illuminated by the soul/reason/mind as dark, as a source of darkness, and as a negation of light. In the light of this illumination, the body darkens. In the philosophical landscape, reason, the soul, and the mind are projected as the supreme rulers. Regardless of how deeply this regime is entrenched, to do justice to philosophy and to its illumination, this regime must be contested. A liberation from this regime is in order. Provided that it is adequately understood, African philosophical illumination can contribute to this effort.

What, one may ask, does what has been said above have to do with African philosophical illumination? Isn't what has been said above a digression or a diversion from African philosophical illumination? Is African philosophical illumination solely a reaction to what Westerners have claimed to be the nature of philosophical illumination? A provisional response could be that what has been said above arises from an African philosophical illumination—an illumination that, at the same time, refers back to African philosophical illumination and that illuminates it. What is illuminated about this illumination differs from what has been provisionally associated with the conventional European notion of illumination. In African philosophical illumination, the body is not set aside. The senses are not set aside. Philosophical illumination is the work of the senses. Philosophical illumination is sensorial. Illumination is not ultimately the work of the divine. It is by viewing it as divine that led Europeans to view Africa as the Dark Continent—a continent without a place for the soul, for reason, or for the mind. The European assumption of the godlessness and the heathenism of Africans lies at the root of the misconception that the African continent is a continent without philosophy. In Africa, the divine is not immunized against the sensorial. It is thoroughly and exhaustively sensorial. From the African standpoint, it is not absurd to share the food that human beings eat with their gods. The gods have stomachs, just as humans do. They belch as we and other animals do. They fight among themselves, as we do. If this is viewed as superstitious, it is likely that it is viewed thus from an opposing superstition.

The European projection of Africa as the Dark Continent is not solely thus because it is a continent without civilization. It has been projected as a continent that is heathen, godless, and without divine illumination. As such, it is projected as an ideal place for missionary activity. In Africa, there prevails a view planted by Europeans that civilization is essentially Christian civilization. The linkage of heathenism and the savagery of paganism is a European product. Europeans have constructed and projected the European continent as the land of light and as the source of illumination. In European eyes, the greatest contrast among the peoples of the world has been the contrast between Europeans and Africans. Europe, where Europeans live, is the land of light, and Africa, where Africans live, is the land of darkness. Illuminating the falsehood of this contrast and shedding light on how to get rid of it ought to be, and should be, the work of philosophy. Re-establishment of the unity of humankind ought to be, and should be, a part of this work. Europe has projected itself as the sole source of the global philosophical illumination of this unity. Philosophy should contest this projection and restore the view that the unity of humankind is the work of all human beings. And the work of all branches of philosophy of necessity must include the African branch.

Development is another aspect of illumination by which Africa has been judged. In the light of this idea, Africa again appears philosophically undeveloped or philosophically underdeveloped. It is still in a state of darkness, not fully illuminated. Again, the source of illumination is Europe and, as is the case with religion, Africa is in a state of darkness in matters that pertain to philosophy and stands in need of the missionaries of philosophy. Apparently, development appears on the radar of the European concept of philosophical illumination to be in need of missionaries of philosophical illumination. It is utterly unphilosophical to create such a need in the African or in anyone else.

The African renaissance must be a renaissance that rediscovers philosophical illumination within Africans and must rediscover it in a way indicating that this illumination is a part of global human illumination. It has to be discovered in a way that does not privilege Africans among other human beings but, rather, an instantiation of the philosophical illumination that is to be found among all peoples.

Normally, when we think of illumination, we think of the eye and what enables the eye to see. In the philosophical domain, one should suspend this thinking by turning not to the intellect or to the mind but to the entire sensorial mode of illumination, to that mode of illumination that enables sensing to sense. In this sensorial mode, all senses are united in sensing. Sensing is the sensing of the entire person and of everything that senses—which is everything. Everything senses. The claim that there is what is outside sensing is absurd and erroneous. Sensorial illumination illuminates the veracity of this claim. Philosophical illumination is at home in holistic seeing, in holistic sensing. Being philosophical, this sensing is beyond the sensing that biology offers us. It is a lived sensing. It is a sensing that animates biological life. The distinction between what is animate and what is not animate, however, rests on a nondistinction. It is out of nondistinction that distinction arises. Ultimately, logic fails to illuminate this insight. This illumination is a matter of philosophy.

Chapter 2
African Grounding of Philosophy

> *I am a woman just as you are. I am a daughter of a woman just as you are. Women give birth to both female and male children. Without us there would be no children and, without children, there would be no human race. And without human race there would be nothing, for all that is, is for the human race and the human race is for it. As birthers, we are a part of all else that gives birth: insects, fish, birds, animals, and plants. We are a part of nature which is the birther of everything that is. Nature gives birth to everything that gives birth. Even the non-living are given birth by nature. Giving birth is the other name for nature.* (An African mother to her daughter)

And there was Osiris—the restorer and sustainer of life. And there is Osiris—the restorer and sustainer of life. And there will be Osiris—the restorer and sustainer of life. Osiris—the holder of the key of life and the key of death. Osiris—the bearer of our ancestral history—the bearer of our current history and the bearer and sustainer of our future history—that without whom there would be no time and no history. Time—the illuminator without which nothing could come to be or cease to be and without whom nothing would be understood. Time—Osiris's nickname. Source of poesy—poesy that gave birth to Kofi Awoonor and to which he has returned after being claimed by Osiris. By being claimed by her, he too has become the restorer and the sustainer of African life.

> Moon, moon shine on our way
> Shine bright for us to go home
>> The return is tedious
>> And the exiled souls gather on the beach
>> Arguing and deciding their
>>> Future
>> Should the return home
>> And face the fences the termites had eaten
>> And see the dunghill that has mounted their
>> Birth place
>> But their journey homeward done the sea scapes
>>> birth place
>> But their journey homeward done on the sea scapes
>>> roar
>> Their final stokes will lead them on
>> Forgotten shores
>> They committed the impiety of self-deceit
> lashed cut and wounded their souls
> And left manacles
> Before the Sacred cock
> Whose crow woke the night sleepers at dawn
> The moon, the moon is our father's spirit
> All the stars entrance night
> Revelers gather

> To sell their carter and inhuman seat to
>   the gateman
> And shuffle their feet in agonies of birth
> Lost soul, lost souls, lost souls that re still
>   at the gate[11]
>
> -Kofi Awanoor, a Ghanian poet

Poetry is the mother of philosophy and, as is the case with all poetic generations, philosophy remains poetic. One bears the genes of one's parents. However, it is a mistake to confuse oneself with one's mother. One is not one's mother. Philosophy's mother is its mother. Its mother is its mother, and it is what it is. And it is itself what it is. Poetry is poetry, and philosophy is philosophy. In Africa, another word for poetry is "proverb." The grounding of African philosophy is proverbial, and so is every other grounding of philosophy. For the Greeks, the proverb was the oracle. To move away from the proverbial is to move away from African philosophy and from Africa. Africa too is a proverb. Whatever is said about the grounding of African philosophy is, and must remain, proverbial. Chinua Achebe said it all when he said that proverbs are the palm-oil with which words are eaten.[12] Although he was referring to an Ibo conversation, he was at the same time speaking for Africans. The colonial language that the colonizing Europeans sought to impose on Africans as a replacement for African languages amounted to the declaration of war against African proverbialism. The colonizers demanded clarity in language, and the clarity they demanded was in opposition to clarity of the proverb. They demanded a language that was readily transparent. They did not see that the proverb reserves and conserves a higher sense of clarity by irreducibly being what it is. To speak clearly is not to shun proverbs. Colonizers believed that proverbs cloud language and hence are obstacles to unobstructed seeing and unobstructed understanding. Accordingly, language, they believed, must be purged of proverbs if it is to deliver to us clear meaning and clear understanding.

Proverbs impregnate thinking so that thinking can carry out its work—the work of thinking. To carry out its work of thinking and remain what it is, it must remain rooted in proverb. Thinking too is proverbial. Proverbs illuminate, sustain illumination, and preserve what is illuminated in a state of illumination. Thinking that is proper to philosophy constitutes and reveals philosophy as illuminating. In this way, philosophy is rendered proverbial and, accordingly, whatever philosophy itself generates is of necessity proverbial. The child bears the genes of the parent. Otherwise, there would be no children, and without children, there would be no parents.

Africa is often projected as a continent without indigenous philosophy and, other than the African philosophers who have been gloomed by Westerners, Africa is projected as a continent without indigenous philosophers. Accordingly, the African grounding of philosophy is likely to be viewed as the work of Westerners. The Africa so projected is not an African Africa, and the Africans so projected are not African Africans. The projections are products of Western imagination. It may come as news to some of us, but there are many Africas, and there are many Africans.

There is a European Africa, and there is an African Africa. There are European Africans, and there are African Africans. The African grounding of philosophy I seek to illuminate here is a grounding by African Africans. This entails the difficult task of setting aside the European Africa and also the setting aside of European Africans. It also entails an equally difficult task of identifying African Africans. It is an act of liberation from the grounding of philosophy that Westerners have exported and still export to Africa. It is an act of resisting the imposition on Africans of a sense of a philosophy that does not have African African roots. What is to guide these processes is a question that remains to be answered by African African philosophers. Moreover, what these African Africans are is primarily a matter for African Africans. African philosophical illumination illuminates these Africans.

Ordinarily, when we think about grounding, we often think of something being placed on something else. That on which it is placed is often thought of as being other than what is being placed. That is, what is being placed is construed as other than that on which it is placed. Here, otherness prevails. In what follows, grounding is not to be construed or understood this way. Here, the "on" displays the absence of otherness. There is no external relation between what is being placed and that on which it is placed. The commonsensical belief that to ground is to place something on something else or to have something placed on something else does not rule here. If grounding is taken as placing, that which is being grounded is not being grounded on what is other than itself. It is being grounded on itself. It is precisely this kind of grounding that befits a philosophical grounding. Accordingly, by the phrase "African grounding of philosophy," one is to understand philosophy grounding itself on itself. Evidently, this is not a normal sense of grounding—a sense that allows for a distinction between what is grounded and that on which it is grounded. If this defies logic, defiance is built into the very nature of philosophy, and logic should not be allowed to overstep its limits by trespassing into a territory that does not belong to it. When logic engages in this transgression, it fails the test it sets for itself. It contradicts itself. That logic can be a danger to philosophy has been noted by Martin Heidegger, a pre-eminent twentieth-century German philosopher. He points out that logic:

> ... began when Greek philosophy was drawing to an end and becoming an affair of the schools, organization and technique. It began when *eon*, the being of the essent was represented as *idea* and such became the object of episteme, Logic arose in the curriculum of the Platonic–Aristotelian schools. Logic is an invention of school teachers, not of philosophers. Where philosophers took it up it was always under more fundamental impulsions, not in the interest of logic.[13]

Mentioning Heidegger here is tricky. There is nothing I know of in his philosophical work that would lead one to believe that there a place for African philosophy in his conception of the landscape of philosophy. In his eyes, the landscape of philosophy is exclsuivey Greco-European. The African grounding of philosophy is a philosophical grounding and has to be illuminated as such. It is to be understood and assessed by the standard that philosophy sets for itself and not by an extraneous standard. Accordingly, when the grounding of philosophy is qualified by the word "African," this qualification belongs to philosophy and is to be understood philosophically. Assuming that this is the case, the inevitable question to be asked here is, what does the word "African" open up in our understanding of the grounding of philosophy? In other words, what is the substantive significance of the word "African" if it is more than mere cosmetics or a mere ornament? As we think through the answer, what is essential is that we be guided by philosophical questioning—a questioning that is intrinsically African.

It is indeed the case that the above topic calls attention to a qualified grounding of philosophy. As should be obvious, this qualifier suggests that there are other qualifiers. That is, philosophy can be grounded or is grounded in other ways. If this implication is in order, one of the questions that ought to be raised is how this qualifier is to be distinguished from other qualifiers? That is, what sets the African African grounding of philosophy apart from other groundings of philosophy? This question cannot be satisfactorily and adequately understood, let alone answered, if the question regarding the nature of philosophy is not raised and adequately answered. The answer to this latter question contributes to the understanding of all of the questions that are raised in every branch of philosophy. It is what is to guide us as we look for answers to any question that bears on philosophy. Differently stated, if one is to conduct an inquiry into the African grounding of philosophy, one must have an understanding of what is to be grounded—namely, philosophy. To be sure, there is also the question of whether philosophy is subject to grounding, a question that cannot be dealt with satisfactorily if the question on what philosophy is, is not aswered. The grounding of philosophy is itself a philosophical issue and must remain as such.

The African grounding of philosophy or any other grounding of philosophy is not an objective process that is subject to knowledge. It cannot be known and does not call for a knower. The primary reason for this is that philosophy is itself not subject to knowledge. It is not an object of knowledge. This is a major obstacle faced by the students who enroll in an introductory course in philosophy. Their normal expectation is that they will acquire knowledge about philosophy in the course. If one were to ask what the process of African grounding of philosophy is, or what it is being grounded, or who is grounding it—expecting information—one would be engaging in diversionary questioning. A philosophizing process or philosophical questioning has its own interrogative ecology whereby what the question is, is implicated in what is questioned, as well as in the questioner. We do not have here a subject–object dichotomy. Dichotomous thinking has no place here. Today, dichotomous thinking holds sway over thinking generally, and it is a formidable obstacle on the path of African African grounding of philosophy.

The prevailing notion that knowledge requires an object that is to be known, and a subject that is to know such an object, has been in place for such a long time that we have forgotten that the knowing subject has been constructed *ex nihilo*. There was a time when it did not exist, and there may come a time when it will cease to exist. Once constructed, it assumed a granite mode of being and is assumed to be eternally permanent. It is difficult to imagine a time when it was not or to imagine a time when it will cease to be. The very possibility of such imagination strikes us as absurd, if not contradictory, for it presupposes the existence of what is being denied. Imagination, after all, requires an imaginer. We are to imagine against such imagination. We live under the absolutist dictatorship of the subject that allegedly is responsible for knowing. The end of this dictatorship calls for a Copernican-like revolution. Grounding African African philosophy requires a Copernican-like revolution, but this revolution must be African, not Copernican. If taken seriously, philosophy compels us to say yes to such a revolution. The African African grounding of philosophy is a central part of this revolution. Philosophy comes alive and remains alive only in such a revolution. Otherwise, it is reduced to being nothing more than the knowledge of philosophy that professors of philosophy teach in school and students learn from them.

If one were to ask whether, in talking or writing about philosophy, one is not intending to convey knowledge and positing others as recipients of this knowledge, the proper answer would be that one should be sensitive to the diverse senses of speaking and writing. Neither of them is exclusively a matter of communicating or disseminating information. Hampâté Bâ of Mali, West Africa, reminds us that:

> "speaking" and "listening" refer to realities far more than those we usually attribute to them. The speech of Maa Ngala is seen, is heard, is smelled, is tasted is touched. It is a total perception, a knowing in which the entire being is engaged.[14]

What speaking or listening is, is not to be taken for granted. Neither of them has a frozen meaning. Neither of them is exclusively a human activity. Both are native to every entity whether it is human or non-human, whether it is or is not alive. Human beings are inescapably a part of everything that is, if only because they are. They are cut from the same ontological fabric as everything else. The claim that speaking and listening are attributes that exclusively belong to human beings reflects a misunderstanding of these attributes and also a misunderstanding of both what is and what is not human. If one disagrees with this claim, one has an enviable task of providing evidence for the counterclaim. It is indeed the case that this claim should not be embraced dogmatically. But the search for supporting evidence must be guided by what one is after. Argumentation, it must be pointed out, does not exhaust philosophical thinking or philosophical seeing. What should be evident is that most of us rarely question what speaking or listening is. Normally, we do not question who we are or what it is for anything to be. We take for granted that answers to these questions are self-evident and do not call for serious critical assessment.

In the attempt to understand what philosophy is, one can easily be seduced by epistemology, especially in today's world where all questions are assumed to be exclusively matters of epistemology. Thus, it appears normal to seek to know what philosophy is and to know how it is grounded. In so doing, however, one runs the risk of subordinating philosophy to epistemology. Epistemology is a branch of philosophy. Contrary to what appears to be the case today, philosophy is not a branch of epistemology. Epistemology is not the tree of philosophy. It makes sense only in the context of philosophy. Epistemology, like other branches of philosophy, receives its nourishment from philosophy and not vice versa. Today, the reverse appears to be the case. It is assumed that epistemology nourishes philosophy. Here, there is more than a reversal. Philosophy appears to dissolve into epistemology, and whoever seeks to contest this cannibalism or to seek a divorce between the two is likely to be viewed as barbaric, as anti-philosophical, or as engaging in an activity that is other than philosophy.

Scientific thinking has become so aggressive that to think in non-scientific ways is not to think at all. With this kind of attitude, violence has been done to thinking. To the extent that scientific epistemology has become hegemonic in the empire of epistemology, philosophy has been banished from its realm or is confined to the dustbin of history, or it has been reduced to being the handmaiden of science—similar to the role that philosophy was compelled to play in Medieval Christian thinking. This is what happened to philosophy at the hands of Wittgenstein in his *Tractatus Logico-philosophicus*. He tells us:

> The right method in philosophy would be to say nothing except what can be said using sentences such as those of natural science—which of course have nothing to do with philosophy—and then, to show those wishing to say something metaphysical that they failed to give any meaning to certain signs in their sentences. Although they would not be satisfied—they would feel you weren't teaching them any philosophy—this would be the only right method.[15]

His objective was to reduce philosophers to being nothing more than janitors of science or to the janitors of scientists. He ought to be charged with a crime against the friends of philosophy and for committing an offense against philosophy. It is indeed the case that Wittgenstein—for example, in his *Philosophical Investigation*—later shifts from the view expressed in *Tractatus*, but it should not be forgotten that hegemonic empirical epistemology has impoverished the philosophical method. The spirit of positivism, which is the umbrella under which empirical epistemology flourishes, has had disastrous effects not only on philosophy but also on the social sciences.[16] The success of science is not necessarily the success of philosophy. One should not mistake what philosophers do for what scientists do. What Wittgenstein says is particularly harmful to African philosophers, since it reduces them to being parasites of Westerner philosophers, since—by attuning philosophy to the spirit of science—the latter appear to be more advanced in philosophy than their African counterparts. Apparently, the spirit of science is yet to be firmly rooted among Africans, and African philosophers are yet to fully emancipate themselves from non-scientific thinking.

Today, genuine investigation of the African African grounding of philosophy appears to take place at the margins of the conventional understanding of philosophy—an understanding that is essentially Eurocentric. The African landscape appears to be flourishing with the missionaries of epistemology whose goal is to spread the gospel on the superiority of scientific epistemology, stamping out whatever stands in the way. What is not assimilable into scientific thinking is to be cast aside as superstitious. Kwasi Wiredu of Ghana, an important African philosopher, comes close to joining these missionaries when he asserts:

> In practice the contemporary African philosopher will find that it is the philosophies of the West that will occupy him most, for it is in that part of the world that modern developments in human knowledge have gone the furthest and where consequently, philosophy is closest touch with conditions of the modernization which he urgently desires of his continent.[17]

The knowledge that Wiredu has in mind is logical, mathematical, analytical, and scientific knowledge—knowledge that he takes to be the essential engine of modernization and that Africans noticeably lack, and without which they cannot develop or reach the stage of development that has already been reached in the West and in some parts of Asia. His view is shared by Paulin Hountondji, a fellow African philosopher from Benin, who has claimed that:

> Rather than pitting our culture against that of Europeans, we must, for the sake of our won real liberation take up European science and technology; and to attain this goal, we must begin putting to work the European concept of philosophy that goes hand in hand with the science and technology and by developing free and critical thinking on this subject to our present realities.[18]

Furthermore, Hountondji says:

> African philosophy is inseparable from African science, African scientific research, that it cannot exist as a specific form of literature except in is ordered difference, from and in articulation with scientific literature: that the only fruitful prospect for our philosophy today is to attach itself closely to the destiny of science by integrating itself with the immense of movement towards the acquisition of scientific knowledge that is now developing on the continent.[19]

According to both Wiredu and Hountondj (at least in their earlier writings), African philosophy must not only be guided by science. It has to be scientific. As Hountondji says, "philosophy belongs to scientific literature. Its livelihood and rhythm are the same as those of mathematics, physics, chemistry, biology and linguistics."[20] He also claims that:

> If the development of philosophy is in some way a function of the development of the sciences, then African philosophy cannot be separated from African science, and we will never have in Africa a philosophy in the strict since, philosophy articulated as an endless such until we have produced in Africa a history of science, a history of the sciences.[21]

It seems that in his mind, in Europe or in the West generally, philosophy is most developed because it is integrated into science—that is, because philosophy has become scientific. Hountondji appears to have compromised philosophical critical thinking. For him, scientific development appears to be synonymous with, or identical to, philosophical development. He does not demonstrate why philosophy ought to be subject to this development or to any other kind of development. In his way of thinking, one would have to accept the view that ancient philosophy is dinosauric or is prescientific. Why philosophy has to be placed within the history of science is an issue that disciples of science rarely raise and, clearly, to those who have been won over by scientific thinking, this is a non-issue. It is not to be accepted blindly that Africa is philosophically underdeveloped because it is scientifically underdeveloped. It is not clear whether or how the concept of development applies to philosophy. Hountondji and those who think like him have yet to provide us with a philosophical justification of why a philosophical path is a scientific path. It should not be assumed blindly that the two paths are identical or that the answer should be provided by science. Again, scientific justification is not synonymous with, or identical to, philosophical justification.

When one encounters problems in logic, one turns to logicians for solutions. When one encounters mathematical problems, one turns to mathematicians for solutions, and the solutions to scientific problems are for the scientist to solve. Now, for clarity's sake, a logician is not a philosopher; neither is a mathematician, nor a scientist. One turns to philosophers for solutions to philosophical problems. The point here is not that Africa does not need logicians, mathematicians, or scientists. It is that none of them should be mistaken for a philosopher. What philosophy does is not an obstacle to the development of logic, mathematics, or science, and none of them should stand in the path of philosophy. It is indeed true that Africa stands in need of development, as do other territories, and philosophy should not be an obstacle to such development. Such a need, however, has no place in the life of African African philosophy, just as it has no place in the life of any other branch of philosophy.

Where philosophy has been reduced to being the handmaiden of scientific epistemology, one is pressured to think of African African grounding of philosophy as an epistemological project. Today, African philosophers are pressured to participate in the building of the empire of epistemology. They have been reduced to being the proletariat in the empire of epistemology. Currently, to distinguish themselves as genuine philosophers, they are expected to be nothing more than junior partners by apprenticing themselves to Western masters, since it is taken for granted that the West is the headquarters of the empire of scientific epistemology. The achievement of scientific and technological thinking is so overpowering that philosophical thinking has largely been eclipsed, and by indulging in philosophical thinking, one is likely to be viewed as indulging in an activity that is analogous to resurrecting dinosaurs. African African philosophers are not the only ones under pressure. It is a pressure that is familiar to some Western philosophers, such as Heidegger, Friedrich Nietzsche, and Edmund Husserl. The latter's work, *The Crisis of European Sciences and Transcendental Phenomenology*,[22] attests to this. In Asia, philosophical thinking appears to be largely ignored, and some Asian thinkers attempt to keep up with the Joneses in the West by distilling epistemology from Hinduism, Buddhism, and other Asian traditions of philosophy.

Today, the danger that is not yet fully recognized is that of subordinating philosophy to epistemology instead of subordinating epistemology to philosophy. Epistemologists today stand accused of committing the crime of attempted patricide. They are the children of philosophy and seek the death of their father. What must not be forgotten is that philosophy is irreducible to modern epistemology. Philosophy has its own way of knowing—a way of knowing that is radically different from other ways of knowing. Its way is not to be confused with, or mistaken for, scientific knowing. Such confusion prevails in Africa, and it is largely a Western European export to Africa.

In Africa, it must be recalled that during European colonialism, European educators assumed that Africa was philosophically barren and that Africans were too dumb to benefit from the study of philosophy, or to appreciate it. The majority of these educators had already embraced the view that philosophy was synonymous with knowledge and more specifically with scientific knowledge. In their eyes,

Africans wallowed in superstitious beliefs and were deaf to the claims of scientific thinking. They were high on cognitive science and tended to reward those Africans who were deemed "smart" or "clever." Those who excelled in rote memory were identified and highly rewarded. At most, they viewed philosophy as an intellectual activity that amounted to no more than cleverness. Perhaps, nothing better could be expected of missionaries, for they knew no better. They were Christian missionaries and not philosophers. They were suspicious that philosophy would hinder their mission of converting Africans to Christianity. Philosophical knowing is a knowing that is subject to, and is guided by, wisdom. It is such a knowing that has been eclipsed and that continues to be eclipsed in what is presented as philosophy in Africa today.

In post-colonial Africa, there has been a duplication of the worship of knowledge—knowledge that is passed off as philosophy. In part, what is going on in Africa is an imitation of what is going in the Western European world. Philosophy is taken as an intellectual activity, as epistemology. The brightest and the most intellectual of Africans are nurtured and promoted as philosophers. It is not a surprise then that one readily assumes that the African African grounding of philosophy is the institutionalization of this trend. It is also not a surprise that African philosophers are creatures of the academy, since it is the academy that is the major factory that produces intellectuals. The academy is the factory of knowledge. It is a dangerous place for philosophy and for nurturing a philosopher.

There is a well-known statement by Aristotle, which appears at the beginning of his book *Metaphysics*, where he says "All men by nature desire to know."[23] This statement is subject to multiple interpretations. One could take it as a guiding light for modern epistemologists, who, for the most part, consist of intellectuals. The statement could also be interpreted philosophically in such a way that the desire to know is a philosophical desire. Were it to be interpreted this way, what passes as epistemology today would be subject to philosophy and not vice versa. What is obscured here is the difference between lovers of wisdom and lovers of knowledge. The former are philosophers, and the latter are epistemologists. Without recognizing the difference, one is likely to mistake one for the other. The difference has been called to our attention by Odera Oruka—an African philosopher who has done memorable work on Sage philosophy.[24]

It must be understood clearly that philosophers are not anti-epistemology. What must be resisted is the temptation to believe that philosophy is synonymous with epistemology. The African African grounding of philosophy is not same as the African African grounding of epistemology. How one is grounded is not identical with how the other is grounded. To avoid an error here, it is important to restrict each to its own province. The restriction presupposes an understanding of each. What should concern us here in the light of the above title is what is to be understood by philosophy. We want to make sure in the African African grounding of philosophy that we are not thereby undertaking an African African grounding of epistemology.

What then is one to make of the word "philosophy"? What does this word mean? The search for meaning is important if one is to be sure that in the African African grounding of philosophy, it is truthfully philosophy that is being grounded and not something else. The search is to be guided by philosophy and not by epistemology. Such guidance is not readily available, for today, the guidance of scientific epistemology forces itself on inquirers. Much can be gained in the understanding of proper guidance if one turns to indigenous African culture or to other indigenous cultures, or to other prescientific cultures, such as the Greek, Roman, Asian, and Native American cultures. The belief that the Moderns excel these cultures in understanding of philosophy is mostly a prejudice of the Moderns. Moreover, it must be understood that the turn to these cultures is not a cultural anthropological turn in its modern sense—a sense that is a product of modern scientific thinking. It must be a philosophical turn. One must turn to philosophical cultural anthropology—an anthropology that is informed by philosophy and not one that is informed by scientism.

If one seeks to understand what philosophy means, as it applies to cultural anthropology or to any other field of learning, it is very tempting to turn to a dictionary. Normally, one turns to a dictionary because it is taken to be a depository of what words mean. Dictionaries are language specific. If one seeks to find the meaning of an English word, one looks it up in an English dictionary. If one seeks the meaning of a Chinese word, one looks it up in a Chinese dictionary, and if it is a Kiswahili word, one looks it up in a Kiswahili dictionary. However, it worth recalling that before a word gets into a dictionary, most likely, it is already in social usage. In this regard, it can be said that it has a prelexical or an extralexical meaning. It is also important to note that dictionaries have not existed from time immemorial, and even today, there are cultures without them. In cultures where writing is not prominent, elders act as dictionaries. Even the meanings of the words that enter into a dictionary can change or become obsolete. Given this possibility, it may be unsatisfactory to look for the meaning of the word "philosophy" in the dictionary. Modernity seeks to confine nonlexical dictionaries to oblivion. In matters of meaning, elders do not count as much as they did in the past, and in Africa and elsewhere, they are ignored as disparaged sources of meaning. Just as there was a time when the "dictionary" did not exist, there may come time when it will cease to exist. Words, it must not be forgotten, ultimately have a lived meaning. In Africa, elders are living dictionaries. They are custodians of meaning. Today, it is unfortuatne that they are thought of as insignicant relics of the past.

Relying exclusively on a dictionary for the meaning of the word "philosophy" excludes its meaning from prelexical or extralexical spheres of language. It should also be noted that dictionaries confine what words mean to a written form. They are conservative. Although placing words in a dictionary may relatively stabilize their meaning and facilitate the circulation of meaning, it may render words lifeless; it may petrify or mummify meaning, thereby, reducing a dictionary to one of the items that ought to be placed in a museum. A dictionary secures and promotes conservativeness in meaning. One should be on guard to protect oneself from the dictionary empire, from dictionary bondage.

The word "philosophy" is an English word and, hence, calls for an English dictionary, if one wants to find out what it means. Of course, this is not to deny its social and cultural usage, if only because it had such existence prior to its entry into the dictionary. When one consults this dictionary, one is likely to find out that its roots lie in Greek language. Heidegger tells us:

> We wave uttered the world "philosophy" often enough. If however, we use the word "philosophy" no longer like a worn out title, if, instead, we hear the word "philosophy" coming from its source, then it sound thus: *philosophic*. Now the word, as a Greek word is a path. …The word *philosophia* tells us that philosophy is something which, first of all determines the existence of the Greek world. Not only that—philosophia also determines the innermost basic feature of our Western European history. … The statement that philosophy is in its nature Greek says nothing more than that the West and Europe, and only these, are in the inmost course of their history, originally "philosophical".[25]

Accordingly, it appears that, ultimately, one has to turn to the Greek language to find out the meaning of the word "philosophy." This is not only the case with the word as it exists in the English language. It is equally the case as it exists in Latin and in other European languages. As Heidegger has pointed out, "Western grammar sprang from the reflection of the Greeks on the Greek language."[26]

Historically, it appears that what the word "philosophy" meant in the Greek language has been mediated by Western European languages and by European understanding. This mediation is not innocent. It has taken on a Western European linguistic significance, which may be different from its original Greek meaning. A situation has arisen in which one is no longer sure whether what this Greek word meant to the Greeks is what it means to Western Europeans once it is uprooted from the soil of the Greek experience of language and later inserted into the soil of Western European languages. It is also important to note that a word does not stand alone. Every word is a part of the web of words that make up language. Accordingly, it would be erroneous to believe that what Western Europeans uprooted from the Greek language is a mere word that was planted in the soil of European languages. What they uprooted was a way of life that the word "philosophy" illuminated for the Greeks. The web of language is the web of life and, conversely, the web of life is the web of language. A people's language is so tied to its life, and its life is so tied to its language, that to server this tie is to bring about both the death of its language and its life. When Western Europeans brought their version of philosophy to Africa, this was accomplished through Western European languages, which implied bringing into Africa their Western European way of life. Because of the violent way in which this was done, African languages and life underwent a disastrous devastation. Also, let it be noted that the Greeks did not lead a life of philosophy cut off from the life of philosophy beyond the Greek borders. Contrary to the opposing view that has been embraced and spread by Western Europeans for centuries, the Greeks interacted with non-Greeks, allowing for cultural exchanges. Greek philosophy is not immunized against these exchanges. Professor Christos Evangeliou has done commendable research that provides evidence of a non-Greek (African) influence on Greek philosophy.[27]

The exclusive grounding of the word "philosophy" in the Greek language prioritizes the Greek language. It also prioritizes the Western European languages that derive from the Greek language. Along this line of thinking, for some people, it may appear reasonable to infer that African languages do not offer an indigenous context of the meaning of the word "philosophy." Apparently, to apprehend the meaning of this word, an African has to turn to the meaning embedded in European languages and, ultimately, in the Greek language. This appears obvious especially in academic philosophy, where he or she is initiated into philosophy through the medium of Western European languages. This reduces African philosophers to parasites of Western European philosophers and, ultimately, to parasites of Western European Greek philosophers. What they say about philosophy thereby is nothing more than a footnoting of the Western European footnoting of Greek philosophy. The African African grounding of philosophy turns out to be parasitic on the Western European grounding of philosophy, which itself is parasitic on the Greek grounding of philosophy. Ultimately, African languages have to be parasitic on Western European languages and, ultimately, on the Greek language in order for them to convey the meaning of the word "philosophy." It is precisely this view that was embraced and marketed by the Belgian Christian missionary Placide Tempels. Addressing his fellow Europeans, he said:

> We do not claim of course that the Bantu are capable of formulating a philosophical treatise, complete with an adequate vocabulary. It is our job to proceed to such systematic development. It is we who will be able to tell them, in precise terms, what their inmost concept of being is. They will recognize themselves in our words and will acquiesce saying. You understand us: you know us completely: you "know" in the way we "know".[28]

It is significant that this view of philosophical vocabulary flows out of the mouth of a Christian missionary. It is only the Chosen (Christian Westerners) who are privy to the significance of this vocabulary. It is only they who can fathom the mystery of this vocabulary. Africans have to look up to them to grasp the sense of who they are. Their languages lack the philosophical vocabulary that can convey to them the highest and the innermost sense of who they are. The missionary's denigration and belittling of African vocabulary and, more generally, the denigration and belittling of African languages is a part of the overall colonization of African vocabulary and in general a part of the colonization of African languages. Africans are yet to fully grasp this aspect of colonization, which implies that the decolonization effort is yet to fully register. Hountondji may have compounded the problem in his claim regarding philosophical vocabulary. He says:

> African physicists are not generally ashamed to use the concepts which are proper to their discipline. Likewise, the African philosopher must no shirk the technicalities of philosophical language. We shall never create an authentic African philosophy, genially African (that's what I means mean by the term "authentic), if we skirt round the existing philosophical tradition. It is not by skirting round and still less by ignoring, the international philosophical language that we shall really philosophize, but by absorbing it in order to transcend it.[29]

What he does not appear to be sensitive to is that the technicalities of philosophical languages do not exist in a historical or in a cultural vacuum. The technicalities of philosophical language in Africa are not an exception. The technicalities of philosophical language in Africa must take into account African history and culture. Today, they must address the violence done to African languages by European enslavement and colonization of Africans. The articulations of these technicalities is to take place in a way that resists enslavement and colonization of Africans thorough technicalities of philosophical language. Hountondji is correct in pointing out that African philosophers cannot ignore or skirt around the technicality of philosophical language that has been imposed on them. But they also have to pay attention to the technicality of their own philosophical language. What he refers to as the existing philosophical tradition is Eurocentric. Clearly, he is not referring to an existing African philosophical tradition, if only because, in his eyes—at least according to the claim in his book *African Philosophy Myth and Reality*—the African philosophical tradition is yet to be established. In future, there will be one, but there is none at present. It is a tradition to be created. It also appears that on his philosophical radar, there is no Chinese philosophical tradition or Indian philosophical tradition or any other tradition. The very notion of multiple traditions appears to be ruled out, for, in his eyes, there is only one philosophical tradition, just as it does not make sense to speak of traditions of science since there is only one universal scientific tradition. In his view, philosophical tradition is universal.

To call for an African location of the technicality of philosophical language is not to ignore the Western European location of the technicality of philosophical language. To not ignore it, or not to not skirt around it, however, is to challenge it. Perhaps the initial point is to identify it and to name it. It is Western European and embodies Western European philosophical technical concepts. In the grounding of philosophy in Africa, the grounding cannot be a Western European grounding. It has to be an African African grounding. Today, it has to be a liberating grounding because the historical African condition calls for liberation. Those at the philosophical site must do their homework. They have to liberate this site and make room for the grounding of an indigenous African philosophical grounding. A part of this homework is the decolonization of African languages so that they can be true bearers of the grounding of African African philosophy.

In the African African philosophical grounding of philosophy, one of the major questions facing the African is how to undertake this grounding without hurting himself or herself. In other words, how is he or she to philosophize without self-injury? The African philosopher of today is so wedded to Western European philosophy that were he or she to be cut from it, he or she would suffer from suffocation, and groping for oxygen would be unleashed. The European West continues to be viewed as a mecca for philosophical inspiration. African African philosophers are yet to tap indigenous African inspiration.

The grounding of philosophy is a linguistic event. It is in language that philosophy has its being and expresses itself. The grounding of African philosophy is not an exception. The belief that such grounding can exclusively take place in the Greek language, in Latin, or in modern European languages is philosophically groundless. The vocabulary derived from these languages cannot claim the monopoly of the grounding philosophy. To claim otherwise is to philosophically distort and belittle the philosophical vocabulary and the languages in which this vocabulary is embedded. To ground philosophy, African languages do not need to borrow a vocabulary from any other language. They do not have to be parasitic on any other language. Linguistic parasitism is incompatible with philosophy. The grounding of philosophy in Africa is grounded in an African vocabulary and in African languages. Writing in English, as I do here, should not convey the sense that it is only in English that what I am saying can be said. What philosophy names can be named in any vocabulary—that is, in any language. This possibility keeps solipsism at bay and facilitates communication across languages without undue reductionism. It allows for translation of what is said in one language into other languages. If one is to claim that philosophy is universal and the claim is taken to be indeed true, this claim should not imply that one should set aside the local grounding of universality. Without local grounding, universality is senseless and, at most, ideological. The politics of universality is yet to be fully scrutinized.

Western Europeans may derive comfort in being parasitic on the Greek sense of philosophy—a comfort that is philosophically suspect—but it is another thing for them to recruit Africans and other non-Europeans to this mode of parasitic existence. It is philosophically dangerous to reduce them to parasites of parasites and even more dangerous for Africans and other non-European people to embrace or internalize this parasitism. The grounding of philosophy anywhere and at any time is incompatible with parasitism. It is indeed true that the grounding of philosophy takes place in a dialogical context, but the dialogue must be a true dialogue and not a monologue that is projected as a dialogue. The Judeo-Christian culture out of which most Western European philosophers have emerged has poorly equipped them to enter into a dialogue with Africans or with any other non-European people. Judeo-Christian monotheism has had a lethal effect on philosophical dialogue in the West and with the West. Christians are hard of hearing. The do not understand what genuine dialogue is. They preach to non-Christians. They seek to convert non-Christians. Under the influence of Christianity, Western philosophers engage in a monologue and falsely believe that this monologue is a dialogue. It would take a miracle to dialogue with them.

Although the Belgian missionary is dead and buried, his mission remains alive. After all, it should not be forgotten that he is a Christian and, like fellow Christians, he dares or defies death. "Death, where is thy sting?" is a well-known refrain in Christian thinking, and believers are reminded of it every Easter. Where Christianity in African has triumphed, Africans have been pressured, and are still pressured, to embrace this view. The West has presented itself as the Bethlehem or Jerusalem of philosophy, where any African who aspires to be a philosopher must go on a pilgrimage. That there cannot be an indigenous grounding of philosophy in Africa is a chorus that is heard from the West. Today, this lethal message is to be found not only in philosophy education in Africa; it is also pervasive in all features of African education today. Francis Njamnjoh accurately describe the status of education in Africa. He says:

> The value of education in Africa is best understood in comparison with the soft currencies of the continent. Just as even the most stable of these currencies are pecked and used to taking nosedives in relation to the hard currencies of the West over the years, so have the value of education on the continent. And just as African Presidents prefer to beg and bank in foreign currencies—ignoring even banknotes that their own faces and stamp of omnipotence, so is their preference for the Western intellectual and expert over locally produced

expertise. Sometimes with justifying rhetoric on the need to be competitive internationally, the practice since independence has been to model education in Africa after education institutions in the West, with each country drawing from the institutions in the West with each country drawing from the institutions of the immediate past colonizer and/or the USA. The elite have often in unabashed imitativeness and with little attempt at domestication sought to reproduce, even without the finances to sustain the Oxfords, Cambridges, Harvards, Stanfords, and Sorbonnes of England, and the USA, and France.

Education in Africa has been, and mostly remains, a journey fueled by an exogenous induced and internalized sense of inadequacy in Africans, and endowed with the mission of devaluation or annihilation of African creativity, agency and value systems. Such "cultural estrangement" has served to reinforce in the African self-devaluation and self-hatred and a profound sense of inferiority that in turn compels them to "lighten their darkness" both physically and metaphysically for Western gratification.[30]

Western Europe has sent missionaries of philosophy to Africa, and these missionaries have recruited Africans to serve as missionaries among fellow Africans. This takes place under the guise of professors of philosophy. Today's professors of philosophy in Africa do what the missionaries used to do and what they still do. They are missionaries in disguise. They have become indigenized missionaries and, as such, they are a threat to the affirmation and cultivation of indigenous African African philosophy. The issue of whether philosophy is subject to missionary activity has not yet dawned for these missionaries. Adopting the view that philosophical education is a missionary activity prepares Africans for blind reception of a grounding that is inconsistent and perhaps antithetical to a philosophical grounding. Christianity has transformed Western European culture into a missionary culture. As a part of the culture, philosophy has not been immunized against this transformation.

We are now in a position to see what the African grounding of philosophy calls for. It calls for radical surgery of the African psyche. It is a diagnostic and healing event—an event that is intrinsically traumatic. It is a medical event that has to be undertaken by Africans, since they are the ones who are immediately affected. Ultimately, they are their own doctors. Non-Africans have a role to play too, but before playing it, they have to undergo self-diagnosis and self-surgery. They have to doctor themselves. There are illnesses that only the ill can diagnose and cure. A defect in philosophical life is one of these illnesses. Socrates understood this, and the Westerners who profess to be his heirs are heirs of someone else and clearly not his heirs if they fail to examine themselves. He is widely associated with the maxim "Know Thy Self," but it should not be forgotten that it is not exclusively Socratic or Hellenic. It is a maxim that is at the very heart of philosophy, regardless of its location in time and space. It is what guides, or what ought to guide, African philosophers, as well as every other philosopher.

The African African grounding of philosophy is a grounding that illuminates the African's quest for self-understanding or for self-knowledge—self-knowledge not in a narrow epistemological sense but in a philosophical sense. Today, this quest calls for the African's self-liberation. The grounding of philosophy in the Africa context calls for freeing of philosophical education in Africa. This entails liberation of African philosophy and thus, a philosophy of liberation. Such liberation can sensitize us to the liberation of philosophy in other contexts where it is held hostage. The African grounding of philosophy is inseparable from the self-grounding of the

African. It is a liberating act. Recourse to the notion of liberation may come across as anachronistic today, since it is widely assumed that Africa has been liberated, as evidenced by the existence of the independent African nations. Many who hold this view would be hard pressed to come up with a comprehensive understanding of what Africa has been liberated from. The fashionable view is that Africans are no longer politically oppressed by Europeans, that they are no longer subject to economic exploitation by Europeans, and that, today, they are masters of their own natural resources. Foreign flags are no longer flying over their lands. What is widely forgotten is the African existential ontological violation of the African. It is precisely this violation that African philosophy ought to bring into relief, illuminate, and open up, and ought to illuminate possibilities for remedies. This is a fundamental task in the grounding of African African philosophy

The philosophical education that is prevalent in Africa today constructs negative groundlessness for the African. The African has been, and is being, uprooted from his or her ground—the ground of his or her being. As indicated earlier, the philosophical mode of existence anywhere does not allow for parasitic existence. In this, it differs radically from proselytizing religions such as Christianity. Philosophy is not subject to missionary activity. Given the extent to which Christianity has made an inroad in Western European culture, philosophy in this culture has a formidable task ahead of itself in the attempt to come to terms with its own truth. Western European philosophers have yet to embrace and internalize this task and make it their own. Nietzsche made a historic call to awaken them to this task; unfortunately, the call landed on deaf ears, and it has yet to register in their consciousness.[31] Until Nietzsche is heard by Western European philosophers, there is limited opportunity to have a meaningful dialogue or conversation between African philosophers and Western European philosophers. To hear what Nietzsche says is to practice what he says. Practice provides evidence that what has been said has been heard.

The African African grounding of philosophy calls attention to the Africanness of this grounding. Africanness is a pregnant notion, and what one gets out of this pregnancy depends on the insights and the hermeneutics of the midwife or the obstetrician. Also, it necessarily matters who the impregnator is. If the impregnator is not an African, the issue will be non-African, and it does not matter who the midwife or the obstetrician is. In this phase of African history, one should recognizes the contentious nature of hermeneutics. On one side, there are Western European impregnators, midwives, or obstetricians ready to help give birth to African philosophers and, on the other side, there are African impregnators, midwives, and obstetricians, most of whom appear to be not so sure of themselves. The latter appear to suffer from the anxiety and nervousness that has been created in them by their Western European counterparts and by Western European culture in general. The African African grounding of philosophy is to be undertaken by African Africans and, to do so effectively, they must know what they are grounding. Such knowledge requires African existential analysis. It requires African existential diagnosis to ensure that what is grounded is what ought to be grounded. African philosophers must be guided by African African philosophy if they are to engage in a grounding that is true to African philosophy. To be sure, the grounding must entail an examination of what the Africanness of philosophy is and what the Africanness of the grounding of philosophy is. Hountondji points out a problem that is to be solved regarding this matter. He says:

> The problem is whether the word philosophy when qualified with the word 'African' must retain its habitual meaning or whether the simple addition of an adjective necessarily changes the meaning of the substantive.[32]

He does not specify what he means by "habitual," but it can be assumed that what he refers to as habitual is habitual as has been constructed in the Western European philosophical tradition. He gives no African philosophical reason as to why this tradition should have a monopoly on what is habitual in philosophy or why it should be taken as an uncontested criterion of what is habitual in philosophy. Conceivably, Western philosophical tradition not may only have obscured what ought to be "habitual" in the universal sense but also may have covered up the possibility of the multiple senses of the word "habitual." The fact that the Western philosophical tradition is dominant in the world today should not obscure the need for a philosophical challenge to this domination.

Another point Hountondji makes on what is to be understood as the "Africanness" of philosophy is that:

> The Africanness of our philosophy will not necessarily depend on its themes but will depend above all on the geographical origin of those who produce it and their intellectual coming together.[33]

The "our" that he has in mind refers to fellow Africans. As such, it excludes non-Africans. The membership of "our," or precisely who is to count as a fellow African, remains unclarified unless one extrapolates from what he understands as being distinctive about African philosophy. From the above passage, the membership consists of those who have a geographic origin in Africa. It is also not clear how the expression "geographical origin" is to be understood here. Should it mean someone who was born in Africa, someone whose parents or grandparents were born in Africa, someone who is culturally African? If Hountondji is correct, the African African grounding of philosophy is nothing more than locating philosophy in a geographical territory known as Africa. The grounding takes on a geographical significance. That is, the grounding of philosophy is a geographical designation. Geography has multiples senses.

The word "geography" is a geological expression. It is a particular expression of the logos of the earth. By itself, the earth does not have a logos. Logos is formative of the earth. It is an injection of the human element on the earth. Geology is a work of man, and so is geography. Either is a human formation by man, and for man, that serves human interest. It is one interpretation of man, among other interpretations. Geology as a science, or geography as a science, is nothing more than a particular way forged by human beings in the quest for an understanding of the earth. It is anthropomorphic. This anthropomorphism is universal in the sense that it is open to the agency of all human beings. Geography has its proper place in the humanities. No group of human beings has a monopoly on science. There is an Africa that is a creature of science, and there is an Africa that is a creature of philosophy. The two should not be confused. Hountondji comes very close to confusing the two Africas. The temptation is obvious. Success in science tempts those inadequately grounded in philosophy and in other areas to imitate science. This imitation is doomed, for philosophy can never be a science, and science itself can never be philosophy.

The word "African" in the expression "African philosophy" or in the expression "African grounding of philosophy" is a geographical signifier and requires rigorous philosophical semiotics. Hountondji does not exhibit such rigor. He reduces African philosophy to an empirical geographical setting and is speaking as a geographer of philosophy and not as a philosopher of geography. As a philosopher, he should be on the side of philosophical geography. A philosophical grounding deserves philosophical attention and should not be parasitic on other groundings. Hountondji diverts us from a philosophical sense of Africa and opts for a commonsensical notion of geographical Africa. The proper philosophical grounding of philosophy in Africa must be a philosophical grounding, and such a grounding can make philosophical sense if the normal geographical sense of Africa gives way to the emergence of a philosophical sense of Africa. Contrary to what Hountondji has claimed, Africa is not simply a continent in an empirical sense. Africans do not perceive themselves solely as physical beings and do not perceive Africa solely as a physical space in which they are located. Africans are in Africa in the same way that they are in their bodies. Their bodies are not containers that contain them. They inhabit their bodies. Strictly speaking, they are their bodies. To this extent, they do not own their bodies as if their bodies could be their property. They do not have an external relation to their bodies. Similarly, Africans inhabit Africa. They are coextensive with Africa. Their Africa is a lived Africa. Africa is the world that they inhabit. For the African, Africa is African.

In the sense of a lived phenomenon, we are in the presence of an African continent that bears pre-empirical significance. In the sense of a geographical territory, we are in the presence of multiple hermeneutical senses of geography. We are in the presence of multiple interpretations of the geography of Africa. Each interpretation is a particular formation of Africa. Africa as a thing in itself is formless. Each interpretation is ultimately a construction of Africa. It is a particular way of forming the formless. In the elemental sense, Africa is not essentially Africa. It becomes Africa as a result of our own doing. We Africanize it. Africans Africanize themselves and Africanize where they live. They may also be Africanized by others, just as others may Africanize Africa.

Today, the created or the creating African is subject to amnesia. He or she lies in a state of forgetfulness. The forgetfulness has been generated, in part, by the spirit of scientization of consciousness. The African grounding of philosophy has one of its major tasks in calling attention to this state of affairs. It is an awakening of philosophy, a demummification of philosophy. The African grounding of philosophy must be guided by critical self-reflection. It is not to be taken for granted. It has to interrogate itself as it grounds. It must embody the spirit of interrogation. It must embody the spirit of renaissance—not a European renaissance, but an African renaissance. An African renaissance has to be an African African renaissance—the renaissance of the African African.

Ground may be taken as the foundation on which one rests, as that which supports one and that which sustains one. One may be dislocated from one's grounding and, when this takes place—that is, when one's ground gives way—one's existence is threatened. Because of this possibility, one has to be on guard, and perennially so, for one is never absolutely certain that one's ground will always play its essential role of safeguarding oneself. Essential threat does not come from without. For a human being, it is built in his or her being, and this implies that one has to be on guard against this threat. One has to be on guard against oneself. Those who seek stability in the being of their being seek the impossible. In philosophy, everything is mobile, in motion. Nothing stands still. One should expect the same in the African grounding of philosophy. What is African is in motion. Grounding is in motion, and philosophy is in motion.

There are many obstacles to overcome in the process of the African grounding of philosophy. The obstacles have to be swept aside if the process is to be successful. Unless the obstacles are recognized, they cannot successfully be swept aside. Recognition calls for the appropriate grounding on African philosophy. One has to be already familiar with the home of African philosophy and with philosophy to be on the right philosophical path. Because of its enormous success today, the scientific path has come to be taken as the primary path to truth, and a scientific path can readily be mistaken for a philosophical path. It is worth reminding ourselves that a scientist *qua* scientist is not a philosopher, and a philosopher *qua* philosopher is not a scientist. It is worth emphasizing that a philosopher is a philosopher. When a philosopher and a scientist are confused, one may mistake a philosophical path for a scientific path and vice versa. When this happens, a path that is supposed to lead to the home of African philosophy may take one to the home of African science. Moreover, it is a conventional view that science is universal and is unaffected by the diversity of geographical locations. It can readily be assumed, as Hountondji assumes, that philosophy is equally universal and it should not matter where its home is. In the case of philosophy, the assumption is that the home of African philosophy is the home of philosophy everywhere and that the word "African" should not make any substantive difference. It is undeniable that today, given the imperial imposition that has found its way into philosophy, the universality of philosophy is a contentious phenomenon. The universality of philosophy does not dispense with localization of philosophy. Preserving localization is an antidote to pernicious or bogus universalism.

One must have a sense of African philosophy and a sense of where it is at home, so that one can be in a better position to mount a successful attempt to dispel the mist that brings about obscurity. That is, one must be where one is going for the journey to make African philosophical sense. Dispelling obscurity is not an easy undertaking. Obscurity has an external source and also an internal source. Externally, one must address the colonial fabrication of both Africa and Africans and also address the damage caused by Western cultural chauvinism. Internally, ignorance of the nature of philosophy must be addressed. In any place in the world, those who are indigenous cannot take what philosophy is for granted. If one is ignorant of what philosophy is, one cannot recognize its home or be at its home philosophically. One can lie to oneself about its home, and one may be deceived by others about its home.

Africans cannot assume that what it is to be an African philosopher is self-evident or that what Africa is, is self-evident. They cannot assume that what constitutes the African grounding of philosophy is self-evident.

Hountondji was in error when he asserted that "The Africanness of our philosophy will not necessarily reside in its themes but will depend above all on the geographical origin of those who produce it and their intellectual coming together." He was equally wrong when he asserted that the criterion of African philosophy is "the geographical origin of the authors rather than an alleged specificity of content" and that "Africa is above all a continent and the concept of Africa an empirical, geographical concept and no a metaphysical one." To be fair to him, these views are in error if what he says is taken to be exhaustive of what can be said about the Africanness of philosophy or what can be said about Africa. A geography that is not philosophical can be a serious obstacle in the generation of African philosophy or in the generation of any other philosophy.

Hountondji places undue emphasis on empirical geography and erroneously subordinates philosophy to geography. He overlooks the multiple senses of Africa and the multiple senses of being African. He appears to be held hostage to a physical geographical sense of either concept. The location of philosophy, as is the case with the grounding of philosophy, is primarily a matter of philosophy. Accordingly, one must seek a philosophical location and a philosophical grounding of African philosophy. The Africa that matters to an African philosopher is a philosophical geographical Africa and not an empirical geographical Africa. In identifying and determining the grounding of African philosophy, one must be guided by philosophy and, more specifically, by African philosophy. What is African about philosophy is a matter of African philosophy. Even if it were claimed that the location of philosophy or the grounding of philosophy is universal, the claim would not pre-empt an African determination of the location of philosophy or the African determination of the grounding of philosophy. Let us think about our situation as human beings. Whether one is African or Chinese, one is still a human being, for being human is a universal mode of being. Granted that this is the case, it must also be granted that there is no human being in general or a human being in the abstract. Being human is concretized by the African, by the Chinese, and by anyone else who is a human being.

Assuming that philosophy is a human undertaking, this undertaking should be in a position to illuminate what it is to be a human being. In turn, what it is to be a human being should be in a position to illuminate what a philosophical undertaking it. This reciprocal illumination is precisely where we ought to situate the African grounding of philosophy. It is also where any other branch of philosophy should be situated. This situatedness of philosophy opens up every philosophy to every other branch of philosophy and should necessarily do so; otherwise, it would not be a branch of philosophy.

Philosophical geography or geography of philosophy derives from empirical geography. To the extent that philosophy names the human, the African is thereby named. The grounding of African philosophy is a grounding that is open to all human beings. No human being is a human being in isolation from other human beings, and no one is an African in isolation from other Africans or from fellow human beings. To be African is to be African in the community of Africans, and the community of Africans exists in the community of human beings. To be human is to be human in the community of human beings. It is precisely this mode of being African and being human that is referred to as Ubuntu in philosophical Africa. Ubuntu is where human beings are constituted and illuminated as human beings. As a human activity, the African grounding of philosophy has its place here, and it is where philosophers dwell. It is where philosophy is at home. To philosophize, an African philosopher does not have to move away from here, nor does any other philosopher have to move away from where he or she is to philosophize authentically. To move away from where he or she is, is to move away from himself or from herself. It amounts to self-alienation. It is also from this standpoint that he or she addresses other philosophers. When other philosophers have to address him, this is the place to which they have to direct their addresses. It is also from where he or she has to be addressed by other philosophers. Philosophers address each other from their indigenous locations. Every location is at the same time a location of all locations. It cannot be otherwise, for it is a human location. A human location does not exclude other human locations. If it were to do so, it would cease to be what it is. If Africa is a place, it is a lived place, an inhibited place. An African inhabits Africa as one inhabits his or her body. An African is not in Africa in the way that bees are in a hive, the way that a giraffe is in the savannah, or the way that money is in my wallet. It is not a container that contains Africans, mountains, rivers deserts, and trees. Africa is a lived sign, a living sign that calls for an open-ended deciphering. The placiality of Africa is a lived and a living placiality. The African is nourished and sustained by it. Accordingly, it is both temporal and historical.

Bruce Janz has advocated the view that instead of calling attention to what is distinctive of African philosophy, one should be speaking of the practice of philosophy in Africa, focusing on the notion that African philosophy is nothing more than a designation of Africa as a geographical place where philosophy is practiced.[34] By taking this position, he agrees with Hountondji. Similarly, one can imagine him saying that Western philosophy designates nothing more than a geographical territory where philosophical practice takes place. He appears to take this view to avoid the charge that he is essentializing Africanness of philosophy. What he and other thinkers like Hountondji seem to forget is that there is an unsettled dispute on the geographicity of philosophy. They are yet to come to terms with lived geography—a geography in which philosophy is at home. Geography is more than an empirical place where philosophy is practiced. Philosophy animates where it is practiced. Philosophical geography does not exist in physical geography. What is likely is that physical geography exists on philosophical geography.

Heidegger has expressed a view, held by many Western European historians of philosophy, that philosophy originated in Greece, and this view is still taught in many introductory courses in the Western European world. It has nothing to do with what the Greeks thought about the place of philosophy's origin and has nothing to do with the actual origin of philosophy. I suspect that it may have been constructed by Western Europeans in the course of building their identity.

As a service to philosophy, African philosophy challenges this view, and it has to continue challenging it. But it cannot take this as its only homework. Even if this task did not exist, it would still exist. African philosophy would embark on its central task of illuminating itself and illuminating whatever else that stands in need of illumination. Philosophy is more than a critique. It is not exhausted by argumentation. It is constitutive and illuminative. This must be affirmed strongly to counter the belief that philosophy is nothing more than argumentation. There is what is nonargumentative about philosophy.

The geographical birth place of philosophy is yet to be identified and—perhaps for good reason. As long as it is a philosophical identification that is at stake, it will never be identified. The quest for identification will forever remain what it is: a quest. And because it will forever remain as such, philosophy will never submit to a lineage conception of history giving the impression that it is moving towards a specific end. Philosophy in the present will never be followed by a philosophy in the future or preceded by philosophy in the past. Philosophizing takes place in a perpetual present. It is in such a presence that the African grounding of philosophy takes place. It is a grounding that will never come to an end. The lack of an end is not a deficiency. It is an expression of its fullness. It is its actuality. Moreover, the origin of philosophy can be anywhere and at any time. None of the places where it originates is privileged. All places of the origin are of equal philosophical rank. They inescapably interpenetrate. Philosophy commands that this be the case.

Chapter 3
To Be Received or Not to Be Received

What do you want to know? Tell me. Do you just want to know or you want to understand? Aren't these questions the same? No. They are not the same. If you confuse them, you will neither know nor understand. What is the difference between the two questions? Do you want to know or to understand the difference? Do not confuse knowledge and understanding. If you confuse them will not know or understand the difference. How do I make sure that I do not confuse them? Turn away from me. Look and listen to the Divination Board. It is the seat of knowledge and also the seat of understanding. Pay attention to it. (An exchange between an African elder and a young man)

Modernity has given Africans a brooding feeling that they are refugees in the world—the feeling that they have to provide a justification for their existence. This state of existence is not to be confused with political or economic refugeeism. It is the kind of refugeeism that is tied to their sense of being in the world, to their identity as Africans. It is not simply a psychological state that can satisfactorily be diagnosed and addressed by psychologists, psychoanalysts, or psychotherapists. Democratization and economic development in Africa are not going to eradicate this type of refugeeism. This may postpone addressing the refugeeism that ultimately matters. The phenomenon of racism that bears so heavily on Africans is not perceived or understood in a way that gets to the root of this refugeeism. Even those who say that race matters do not have a radical grasp of what racism is.[35] The brooding feeling that afflicts the African today is largely a product of European modernity. It has not been a major issue in the African world from time immemorial. It calls for a philosophical diagnosis of this modernity to see how it bears on the African and, in this way, bring into the open the possibility of overcoming it. Here is one of the unenviable tasks of African philosophy today: to illuminate the ills that European modernity has inflicted on Africans. This philosophy itself has not been spared from the plight of refugeeism. It is itself an element in the prevailing refugeeism. It must overcome itself to undertake its task. Overcoming itself presupposes an awareness of the need to do so.

Philosophical refugeeism registered to me concretely during the American Philosophical Association (APA) Eastern Division 97th Annual Meeting, held in New York in 2000. At this meeting, there was a reception scheduled for People of Color. I found this event degrading and also found it unconscionable that it should be held under the auspices of the APA. The reception was offensive and, by sponsoring it, the APA condoned this offense. I will readily concede that whoever came up with this idea did not do so with the intent to offend. However, the absence of intent to offend does not render the event inoffensive.

The expression "people of color" is a racist designation of a sector of human beings. That human beings are different is incontestable. But to make race a criterion for this difference is to perpetuate a horrendous offense, especially in the light of modern history. The idea that the human community consists of colored and uncolored human beings is a modern Manichaean idea that is deeply rooted in a racist construction of the human community. It is a secretion of modern European imperial history, which, in turn, has served as one of the major foundations of modern history. To embrace it is to reinforce this history. It is precisely this reinforcement that the APA embraced when it provided a forum for a reception for people of color.

In modern European imperial history, the so-called black people are paradigmatic of people of color. They are the furthest removed from uncolored people. Europeans are projected as paradigmatic of uncolored people. They are the furthest removed from colored people, from African people. The place of the people who lie in between is determined by the degree of their coloration. The degree to which they are removed from the so-called black people or from the so-called white people determines their place in the color spectrum. Thus by sponsoring a reception for people of color, the primary target is the so-called black people. Those who are less colored are the secondary targets. Obviously, since the APA does not officially discriminate, the reception was open to uncolored people. They could come in as guests of the people of color, who were themselves guests of the uncolored people.

In the light of the European presence in the Americas, especially in North America—the home base of the APA—it is interesting to note that the people who are today called people of color (a code word for "black people") were once called colored people, niggers, or Negroes. Now that what they were called has been construed as offensive, apparently, calling them people of color is not construed to be offensive. It appears to be fashionable. But what is the difference between "colored people" and "people of color"? Just in terms of the economy of language, or to make language less burdensome, we can get rid of "of" in the latter expression and simply retain the former. In other words, instead of using the expression "people of color," we can simply use the expression "colored people" in the same way that we can replace the expression "people of America" with the expression "American people." It can be alleged that getting rid of "of" changes the meaning of the expression "people of color" and renders this expression indistinguishable from the expression "colored people," thereby perpetuating the offensive meaning that was in vogue in the past. Apparently, the expression "people of color" is acceptable today because it does not entail retention of the offensive meaning that is entailed by the expression "colored people." However, this belief is groundless and, contrary to what appears to be the case, the acceptance of the expression "people of color" may be an acceptance of the same offensiveness that the expression "colored people" embodied. Moreover, the shift from "colored people" to "people of color" is dangerously illusory. It conceals a perpetuation of what is offensive. It is nothing more than a wolf in sheep's clothing. It should not be forgotten that not every change is substantive. What remains constant in this apparent shift is the simplistic Manichaean construction of the human community that reduces the complexity of the human community into two sectors—one colored and the other uncolored—thereby forcing everyone else to take a place in between. The fixation on skin pigmentation remains unchallenged. This crude and violent biologism is the very centerpiece of racism. Instead of abandoning this biologism, embracing the expression "people of color" gives it a new lease on life.

In the USA, there is an incestuous relationship between black people (people of color) and white people (uncolored people). Both groups of people seek to recruit and force other people into this relationship. The holding of a reception for people of color celebrated this relationship. It should not be surprising if it were to turn out that it was black people or/and white people who were behind this event. Even if it were the case that they are not, they are the ultimate beneficiaries. The APA gave legitimacy to this state of affairs by agreeing to sponsor the event.

Normally, a reception is not where a serious philosophical conversation takes place. It is where one takes a break from serious philosophical reflection. It is where people socialize. It is where friendships are renewed or revitalized, and where individuals take the opportunity to make new friends. In a reception for people of color, there is also an opportunity for people of color to mingle and socialize with one another. For uncolored people, there is an opportunity to do the same and to get to know who is who in the colored community of philosophers. Apparently, serious philosophical reflection goes on in planned sessions. In some cases, this appearance may be nothing more than appearance. Serious philosophical discourse may not be where it is expected to be, and it may be where it is not expected to be. A reception could still provide a forum for serious philosophical reflection without compromising the social dimension. It should not be an occasion to take a vacation from the work of philosophy, as is the case with the reception that the APA sponsored. Although, it would be false to claim that the APA forbade serious philosophical reflection during the reception, it is unrealistic to assume that the reception was consciously designed with the hope that serious philosophical reflection would take place. Indeed the reception was designed with the typical expectation that philosophers would have an informal opportunity to socialize with one another. However, socialization can be a means of luring people to sleep, making people forget the context of their socialization. The socialization in this case was taking place in the context of the world of people of color, a world that is part of a racist world. The APA sponsored a reception to celebrate the forgetfulness of the truth of the so-called people of color.

To refer to people as people of color, or to refer to them as black, is *ipso facto* to insult them. If the insult is not obvious, that may be due to a loss of memory—a loss that is not accidental or a result of natural impairment. It is a result of an institutionalized and concerted effort contrived by those whose stand to gain from depriving others of their memory. If one pays attention to the quintessential people of color (black people) in the USA, one discovers that they did not come to the USA either as people of color, as colored people, or as black people. They referred to themselves on the basis of their African "ethnic" affiliation. Those who enslaved them, however, knew that it would be impossible to successfully transform them into slaves if they were to retain their African ethnic identities. To acquire a slave identity, they were to be born again. They had to be negrified. They became Negroes. They became colored people, and now they have become people of color. It did not matter where they had come from, and it does not matter where they come from. They were fungible, and today they continue to be fungible. They were just Negroes, colored, black, or people of color. In one of his addresses to African Americans, Malcolm X said:

> One of the reasons we are called Negro is so we won't know who we really are. And when you call yourself that, you don't know what you really are. You do not know what you are, you do not know where you came from, and you do not know what is yours. As long as you call yourself a Negro, nothing is yours. No languages, -you cannot lay claim to any language, nor even English; you mess it up. You can't lay claim to any name, any type of name, that will identify you as something you should be. You can't lay claim to any culture as long as you use the word Negro to identify yourself. It attaches you to nothing. It doesn't even identify your color.[36]

One can readily substitute "people of color" or "black" for the word "Negro," and what Malcolm X says could equally apply. On occasion, the change of labels does not affect the substance of what is labeled. Also, on occasion, the change of the label ought to bring about a substantial change in what is labeled. Today, the adoption or the affirmation of the word "African" ought to result in a substantial change in what is labeled African. The condition in which the African finds himself or herself calls for an African renaissance and, hence, a radical rejection of what the European has made of the African.

The holding of the reception for people of color celebrated the self-forgetfulness of the so-called people of color. The sponsoring of this event was part of a long chain of institutionalized racist events that the APA has condoned or abetted. APA has created a Committee on Blacks to take charge of issues in Black philosophy. It has organized or encouraged the organization of sessions on black philosophy is its Eastern, Central, and Pacific Division meetings. In its newsletter, it has continued to support a section on philosophy and the black experience. What, one may ask, is wrong with these actions by the APA? Isn't it the case that these actions have sought to overcome racism in American professional philosophy by recognizing and including black philosophy and black philosophers in the fold of professional philosophy? What is wrong with a philosophical investigation of black issues? These questions may conceal a prejudice that conceals a truthful answer. They can be raised by someone who already assumes that there is nothing wrong in referring to a group of people as black people. Failure to see that there is a problem, however, does not mean that there is no problem.

Suppose the word "Negro" were substituted for the word "black"—surely many members of the APA and a substantial number of individuals in the larger society would find this substitution somewhat offensive. Why is the word "Negro" offensive whereas the word "black" is not? If people who call themselves black in the Anglo-Saxon world were living in the Iberian world, they would be calling themselves Negroes, but because they live in the Anglo-Saxon world, they believe it is offensive to be called Negroes. They believe it is all right to be called black. Similarly, if the people who call themselves Negroes in the Iberian world were living in the Anglo-Saxon world, they would be calling themselves black. But because they live in the Iberian world, they see no problem in calling themselves Negroes. It would not make sense for them to call themselves black. It is for this reason that it does not make sense for those who call themselves black in the Anglo-Saxon world to believe that it is the lack of self-consciousness that leads those living in the Iberian world to refer to themselves as Negroes. The fact is that whether one calls oneself black, a Negro, or a person of color, one remains a victim of skin fixation; one remains a victim of racism. Let us not forget that in Anglo-America, there was a time when the word "Negro" was fashionable. Surely the rejection of this word should lead one to question the suitability of the word "black." Those who find it to be a proper and fashionable term of self-reference may want to take a lesson from history. Perhaps the same reasons that led to the abandonment of the word "Negro" could justify the abandonment of the word "black" or the expression "people of color." If there is hope for overcoming racism, such hope cannot rest on the skin. To have it rest on the skin is to implicate oneself as a purveyor of what one is fighting against. It is to reinforce a racist world.

By embracing the notion of the so-called people of color, the APA perpetuates self-forgetfulness. To end this perpetuation, the APA ought to be a forum for ending self-forgetfulness. It should be a forum where ways can be worked out to retire "black people" and "people of color" as terms of self-reference. These are terms in which there is nothing to intuit, or terms in which what is to be intuited is offensive to people to whom they are applied. For people who have hitherto embraced the word "black" or the expression "people of color" as a term of self-reference, the inescapable task is to undertake a philosophical quest for a philosophically appropriate term of self-reference. Once this task is undertaken with all of the seriousness it deserves, uncolored people will be compelled to come to terms with the problematic nature of their own identity. In this way, the APA can be truly a philosophical association—an association where the truth of self-identity is laid out in the open and subjected to philosophical interrogation.

There are no Negro people. There are no black people. There are no colored people, and there are no people of color. One cannot have a reception for no people. To do so is to celebrate madness—to celebrate paranoia. Failure to see that one is celebrating madness is to labor under false consciousness. If there is any reality to Negro people, to black people, to colored people, or to people of color, this reality is a production of white people. And in producing these peoples, the white people produce themselves as white people. Hence, the reception is a celebration of whiteness. It may appear as if it is a celebration of coloredness, but this coloredness is a secretion of whiteness. Coloredness is whiteness in disguise. To include Africans in this celebration is to entice them to celebrate their absence, their negation as Africans. It is to have Africans celebrate the forgetfulness of being African. Since they were brought here in chains, it has been the historic task of European Americans to make them forget that they are Africans. Although slavery has come to an end, the spirit of self-forgetfulness still prevails. It especially prevails where it should not: in philosophy. One cannot but recall the ancient non-European philosopher Socrates, whose philosophical driving motto was "Know Thyself." In the light of this motto, what has happened to Africans in the Americas (and, to a certain extent, in Africa) is that they have failed to take up the task of knowing themselves and have surrendered to a sense of what and who they are as conceived by Euro-Americans. Euro-Americans have nurtured and have perpetuated this failure. To attend a reception for people of color is to celebrate this failure. It is to nurture the spirit of self-forgetfulness.

The spirit of self-forgetfulness has had an intra-African chilling effect. How one refers to oneself matters philosophically. It would not surprise me that one of the reasons why, for years, it has been difficult to establish a genuine philosophical dialogue between "black" American philosophers and African philosophers has a lot to do with self-perception and, hence, with the terms of self-reference. At APA meetings where sessions on "black" philosophy or on "black" philosophers are organized, they are normally attended by "black" philosophers, "black" philosophy students, and those who are interested in "black" philosophy. When sessions on African philosophy or African philosophers are organized, they are normally attended by African philosophers, African philosophy students, and those who are interested in African philosophy. Although there are many reasons why some people attend some sessions and not others, racism plays a role. The very idea of characterizing a philosophy or a philosopher as "black" introduces a racist dynamic. In APA meetings, there are no sessions on "red" philosophy or on "red" philosophers, and there are no sessions on "yellow" philosophy or on "yellow" philosophers. There are no sessions on "brown" philosophy or on "brown" philosophers. The fact that there are sessions on "black" philosophy and "black" philosophers should trigger concern about the threat that African philosophy faces. When someone who is self-consciously African notices this state of affairs, there is a feeling of uneasiness. This uneasiness is captured in Malcolm X's statement that is quoted above. There is a qualitative difference in being African and being "black." Being African is not being "black," and being "black" is not being African. By supporting "black" philosophy and "black" philosophers, and by providing hospitality for a reception for people of color (black people), the APA indicted itself. It thereby perpetuated racially charged confusion and anxiety. In doing so, it did a disservice to philosophy. The sponsoring of a reception for people of color is such a disservice. The APA has a professional moral and ethical responsibility to ensure that what it sponsors is not in the service of untruth. Even at APA social events, truth is at stake.

The division of philosophers into white and black philosophers, or white philosophers and philosophers of color, is a pernicious division and is a disgrace to philosophy. The point is not to deny differences, for philosophers are clearly different. It is, rather, a matter of radically challenging the attempt to use racist skin pigmentation as a marker of the differences. Differences among philosophers are philosophical. Racist pigmentation differences are creations of European modernity and are intended to reinforce European supremacy over non-Europeans. The hermeneutics of the distribution of melanin in human bodies is troublesome because it is charged with erroneous existential significance. Can one imagine an APA reception for "red," "yellow," or "brown" philosophers? Can one imagine the APA having a session for "red," "brown," or "yellow" philosophy? If this is absurd, why is it not absurd to have a reception for "blacks" or for "people of color"? African philosophy anywhere and everywhere is not black philosophy. It is not philosophy of people of color. It is what it is: African philosophy. Otherwise it is exiled from itself and, when so exiled, it is a disservice to philosophy. Getting the name right is good service not only to African philosophy but also to philosophy wherever and whenever it manifests itself. In philosophy, language matters and, today, philosophy stands in need of the liberation of its language.

Our time calls for a philosophy of the body and for an attendant African philosophy of language. Even in the absence of racism, corporeality still matters. Philosophers are not disembodied beings. They do not inhabit an incorporeal space. Like other human beings, they are embodied. The worship of the intellect/mind/reason that is conventionally associated with philosophy has made many of us blind to the corporal facticity of our being. Christianity has reinforced this blindness. Racism has institutionalized this blindness—a blindness that is harmful not only to Africans but also to Europeans. It is also a blindness that has afflicted Asian people in their perception of Africans and, to the extent that they have been afflicted, their perception of themselves has also been afflicted by Euro-racism. African philosophy illuminates the racist environment in which Africans and other non-Europeans live, and explores the possibilities of eradicating it.

Even in the absence of racism, corporeality still matters. Philosopher are not disembodied beings. They do not inhabit an incorporeal space. Like other human beings they are embodied. The worship of the intellect/mind/reason that is conventionally associated with philosophy has made many of us blind to the corporal facticity of our being. Christianity has reinforced this blindness.Racism has institutionalized this blindness -a blindness that is not only harmful to Africans but also to Europeans. It is also a blindness that has afflicted Asiatic people in their perception of Africans and to the extent that they have been afflicted the perception of themselves has also been afflicted by Euro-racism. Taking race into consideration necessarily implies taking the body into consideration. Today, corporeal hermeneutics has been brought to the heart of philosophizing. African philosophy cannot be undertaken in a corporeal vacuum. African philosophers, like all philosophers, are corporeally bound. Corporeality is central to what they are. Philosophy must not cede the hermeneutics of this corporeality to biophysical science. It has a seminal role to play in this hermeneutics. Africans who pretend to philosophize outside their bodies are delirious. They inhabit a delirious landscape with their non-African counterparts.

My experience with the APA calls attention to recognition of the fact that in a racist world, professional philosophical life is not immunized against racism. For a student of African philosophy and for African professional philosophers, sensitivity to the world of racism can illuminate the pitfalls that inhibit the emergence of a genuine African philosophy. An African philosopher has an intra-African philosophical responsibility to ensure that African philosophy retains its integrity as an African philosophy, and also has a planetary responsibility to ensure this integrity is retained. It is worth reminding ourselves that an African philosopher, like any other philosopher, does not philosophize in a cave. Philosophy dictates that this be the case. What African philosophy is, and what its spatiality and history are, are illuminated and guided by philosophy.

Chapter 4
On the Notion of the African History of Philosophy

Just as a tree without roots is a dead tree, a people without tradition or culture is a dead people. (Malcolm X)

Why do elders sit on a stool? You want to know, or you want to understand? I want to know. Young man, you cannot know the answer to this question. I do not understand why I cannot. Can I then understand why they sit on it? No, you cannot. I see, you are asking the same question as the question whose answer I told you, you cannot know. Set knowledge apart from understanding. How do I do this? You are to sit on the elder's stool. This, you cannot do now because of your age. Only elders sit on it. For you to sit on it now is to desecrate it. It is to offend your ancestors. Stay away until you become an elder and the stool will be yours to sit on it. You will then know and understand and understand the difference between knowledge and understanding. (An African boy talking to an African elder)

Currently, most likely, the student of the African history of philosophy will be presented with a European history of philosophy, making it appear as if the history of philosophy is synonymous with the history of European philosophy. This is in the mode of African history as presented by a distinguished Oxford historian, who said:

> Undergraduates, seduced, as always, by the change of breath of journalist fashion demand that they should be taught the history of Black Africa, Perhaps, in the future there will be some African history to each. But at present there is none, or very little: there is only the history of the Europeans in Africa. The rest is largely darkness, like the history of pre-European, pre-Columbian America. And darkness is not a subject for history.[37]

The black Africa he has in mind is not African Africa, and the African history he has in mind is not African African history. Both are products of European imagination. The darkness he sees in Africa is European darkness. It has nothing to do with African darkness other than that it is a darkness that he and fellow Europeans have imposed on Africans. In European eyes, it would follow that there is no African history of philosophy if only because Africa is without philosophy. Europeans should not assume that their eyes are African eyes or that Africans need their help to see. What they need is a philosophical eye doctor, and if it happens that the doctor they turn to is European, he or she is not likely to offer a proper diagnosis. They could benefit from an African philosophical doctor trained in African African philosophy.

What is named "philosophy"? Why not ask, what ought to be named "philosophy"? Distinguishing "is" from "ought to be" matters, but how it matters is not self-evident. The two questions may call for different answers. The first question may invite answers that are formalistic or lexical, or answers that are conventional or traditional—answers that are not necessarily philosophical. The second question calls for a more deliberative answer. It compels one to pause and reflect on the answer that one gives, and opens the possibility that the answer is out of hand. The ever present possibility of this possibility makes it harder to distinguish "is" from "ought to be." But this is a risk that one should take if one is to remain in the domain of philosophy. It is in the presence of this ever present possibility that the notion of the origin of African philosophy arises.

We begin by making the assumption that philosophy has a history. We also note that the assumption does not self-evidently illuminate what it is for philosophy to have a history. That is, despite the histories of philosophy that have been written, it is not philosophically clear in what sense philosophy is said to have a history. If philosophy has a history, it should be assumed that, like other philosophies, African philosophy has a history. It would be an anomaly that philosophy in other traditions has a history, and that it is only in the African tradition that it does not—unless, of course, it is assumed that there is no tradition of philosophy in Africa. If this assumption is made, it should not be forgotten that it is what it is—namely, an assumption.

What a history is a history of must be known or must be intelligible; otherwise, it would not be possible to have an intelligible notion of the history. Thus it is not possible to make sense out of the history of philosophy without an understanding of what philosophy is. Accordingly, if we are to undertake a discourse on the history of African philosophy, it is crucial that we know not only what philosophy is but also what African philosophy is. It is also the case that the history of African philosophy itself may throw light on what African philosophy is, for, as we make an effort to understand this history, we will undoubtedly be guided by the manner in which philosophy is understood in this history.

The knowledge of African philosophy ought to be a reflection of one's understanding of philosophy in general. African philosophy is, after all, a branch of philosophy, and just as a branch is a branch of something, without the knowledge of what the branch is the branch of, it is not possible to have an adequate understanding of the branch. In this regard, the histories of philosophy are not isolated from each other. In addition to their particularities, they also express a common theme that makes each intelligible, and that makes an intertraditional philosophical dialogue possible. That is, those who investigate the history of philosophy in one tradition can engage in a philosophical dialogue with those who investigate the history of philosophy in other traditions. To be sure, the ground for such an engagement remains to be worked out, given the diversity of traditions of philosophy and the conflicts that exist among some traditions. As to what this ground is, philosophical inquiry has an essential role to play in coming up with an answer. It is philosophy investigating its own nature.

The fact that a cross-tradition philosophical dialogue is largely nonexistent, or is not as extensive as it should be, does not imply that the status quo will endure. The variety of the histories of philosophy does not, and cannot, preclude the unity of these histories, for in unity lies what nourishes and sustains each of them insofar as each is truly philosophical. The fact that such a unity is rarely recognized, or the fact that such a unity is contested, does not render it inessential to these histories.

If an intelligible conception of the history of African philosophy depends on identification of African philosophy, one must begin with such identification. The identification has not proved to be an easy task. Indeed it is one of the most serious tasks taken up by African philosophers in the twentieth century. Perhaps, there is no serious African philosopher today who has been able to avoid the imperative of determining what African philosophy is. The concern with such determination is central to African philosophizing today. Yet it would be amiss not to note that, in the general realm of philosophy, the task of determining the existence or the nonexistence of African philosophy is an anomaly. It is anomalous because it is a task that has gained pre-eminence primarily in regard to African tradition.

Although some Latin American philosophers are confronting the task of determining the existence or the nonexistence of Latin American philosophy, most, if not all, professional Latin American philosophers are descendants of Europeans and continue to embrace European philosophy as the forerunner of their philosophy. Leopoldo Zea, a leading Latin American philosopher from Mexico, has stated that the existence of Latin American philosophy depends on the existence of Latin American culture, then asserts that Latin American culture has its parent in European culture.[38] What Zea understands as Latin Americans are largely descendants of European settlers in Latin America. In contrast to his view that Latin Americans are descendants of Europeans, Africans are not descendants of European settlers in Africa and, evidently, in a fundamental sense, the African cultural tradition sense is not a product of European culture—at least, not in the way that Latin American culture is. Of course, this is not to deny that in colonial Africa, European culture was imposed on Africans or that, even today, European culture continues to influence the formation of African culture. Latin American philosophers may claim that Latin American philosophy is a new phase in the evolution of European philosophy. Africans cannot similarly claim that their philosophy is a new phase in the evolution history of European philosophy. What they can validly claim is that, today, African philosophy is, in part, influenced by European philosophy.

The task of determining the existence of the nonexistence of African philosophy falls to Africans with an unparalleled gravity. This task does not arise in regard to German, French, British, Indian, or Chinese philosophy. Today, the existence of such philosophies is taken for granted. Why, one may ask, is the existence of African philosophy not equally taken for granted? To answer this question by pointing out that the reason why the existence of the abovementioned philosophies is taken for granted is that there exists a long tradition of identifiable philosophers and philosophical texts in these traditions, and that the reason why the existence of philosophy in the African tradition cannot be assumed is that this tradition possesses no such tradition, is to result in a position that is philosophically suspect. The position is philosophically suspect in that identification of the existence or nonexistence of philosophy in this or that tradition presupposes an understanding of what philosophy is. This presupposition cannot be taken for granted, especially when what philosophy is remains an issue for philosophy.

Insofar as it is taken philosophically, being philosophical cannot satisfactorily be determined solely by pointing to a long-standing tradition in which someone or some text has been regarded as philosophical. There are no easy answers to philosophical questions because philosophy is inherently difficult. The determination of the existence or the nonexistence of philosophy in this or that cultural tradition cannot be abandoned to conventional understanding. Conventional understanding is not necessarily philosophically meritorious. Unless such understanding is truly philosophical, what it claims may be in opposition to philosophical understanding. But it is important to bear in mind constantly that what philosophical understanding itself is, is one of the most elemental issues that philosophy faces. Mere characterization of an understanding as philosophical does not necessarily make it so.

The assumption that philosophy exists in other traditions but not in the African tradition is not African. It is made by non-Africans—specifically by those paternalistic Europeans who profess to speak on behalf of philosophy and on behalf of Africans. It is a Eurocentric assumption that reflects the perception that European peoples have of themselves and that they have of Africans. The assumption is made without an input from Africans. The absence of this input flows from the premise that it is philosophically senseless to ask those that one has already defined as being without philosophy whether they have one. The adoption of this assumption and of what flows from it is not simply a matter of ignorance. It is a part of the flowering of Eurocentric racism on the conceptual level specifically, and more generally, of

Eurocentric cultural chauvinism. That such chauvinism has a place in the conception of philosophy in the West will not readily be admitted in the West, especially given the puristic or objectivistic manner in which philosophy is therein conceived and projected. It is difficult to imagine how a conception of philosophy in such a cultural environment could be immune to prejudice about the nature and the history of philosophy. It is widely assumed today that reason is the central element in philosophy and that reason is free of cultural biases. This assumption should be taken as an assumption. Those who embrace it have a philosophical obligation to defend it. It should be noted here that a philosophical defense does not take place in a cultural vacuum. It embodies the defender's culture. Given the diversity of human culture, one should speak here about culture defenses. Should there be a clash of these defenses, it should be the business of philosophy to examine and determine whether there is or there is not a way to minimize or get rid of it, or to embrace the possibility that it should be provisionally embraced.

It is essential to racism that the racist be uninterested in having a dialogue with his victim. The racist has an authoritarian attitude toward his victim. He is a dictator who holds his victim in subjection. It is beneath him to consult the subject, and he does not welcome a dialogue with the subject. If the European assumes the nonexistence of African philosophy, the assumption is most likely rooted in European racism. The European racist philosopher does not welcome a dialogue on the philosophical merits of this assumption. There exists a general disposition among the bulk of the Western philosophers not to discuss what constitutes philosophy with non-Westerners. The bulk of Western philosophers appear to be more inclined to pursue a philosophical dialogue with fellow Europeans or, in some cases, to proselytize their version of what constitutes philosophy to non-Westerners. The proselytizing has gone the farthest in Africa, where it is assumed that, unlike Asia, there is a pervasive philosophical barrenness that calls for outsiders to come and plant and water the seeds of philosophy. The proselytizing aspect of Western philosophy may have taken shape from the influence that Christianity has had on the conception of philosophy in the West. Western philosophy has yet to fully recover from medieval and scholastic co-option of philosophy by Christian theologians. The absence of full recovery has and continues to have a devastating effect on Western philosophy—a devastation whose effect has been felt, and continues to be felt, by African philosophers to the extent that they continue to be victims of Western missionaries of philosophy. To this extent, there is little that is Hellenic in the current conception of philosophy in the West. Hellenic philosophy was a pagan philosophy and perhaps to the extent that Westerners have regarded Africans as pagan, depicting African as pagan should not necessarily lead one to conclude that Africans do not philosophize. It is also equally the case that nonpagans do not necessarily philosophize.

From a Hellenic perspective, philosophy is not a proselytizing activity, whereas Christianity is. Indeed the tension that originally existed between philosophy and Christianity has now become blurred to the point at which philosophy is no longer distinguishable from Christianity. It is not that Christianity has become philosophical. Rather, what is the case is that philosophy has become Christianized and, to the extent that it has become Christianized, it has lost its status as philosophy. Just as

Christians claim that they have the monopoly on truth and believe that those who truly seek truth must become Christians, it appears to be a pervasive view among Western philosophers that it is they who have the monopoly on the truth of philosophy, as well as a monopoly on the history of this truth. They believe that those who truly seek this truth must do so under the guidance of Western philosophers. It is in this context that Western philosophers confront Africans. The bulk of Western philosophers expect Africans to become converts to the way that the truth of philosophy is understood by Western philosophers, as well as becoming converts to the way that the history of philosophy is understood in the West.

Perhaps, it is only by reaffirming their "paganism" against the Western "civilizing" mission that Africans can truly philosophize. Such a reaffirmation may put Africans on the same footing with other people for whom philosophizing is not a missionary activity. It may even open up a more original relationship between Africans and the Greeks, a relationship that has been obscured by Westerners—the self-proclaimed heirs of Greek philosophy. Furthermore, it may open a more original relationship with Asian philosophers, insofar as they too have not fallen under the sway of a missionarized Western European philosophy. To be sure, it is more difficult to send the missionaries of philosophy to Asia, especially to China and India, if only because these two Asian communities are increasingly being recognized by Westerners as having some notable philosophy. There is growing literature on the Daoist and Confucian philosophies in China, and there is also growing literature on the Hindu and Buddhist philosophies in India. For the most part, African has nothing to offer to Westerners in philosophical literature. This situation is analogous to what is portrayed in the religious sphere. Asia can offer Daoism, Confucianism, Hinduism, and Buddhism, but other than what is generally and disparagingly projected as animism, or what Western cultural anthropologists offer to the Western audience, Africa is portrayed as land without religion.

One who writes the history of African philosophy, or indeed, one who sets out to identify African philosophy, cannot do so without coming to terms with the racism that Europe has unleashed on Africans. Rather than being a digression, taking note of this racism is one of the cardinal factors to be taken into account in any genuine meditation on African philosophy and its history. As branches of philosophy proliferate almost endlessly, and as philosophers get attached to this or that branch of philosophy, it is easy to overlook this factor. If we bear in mind that no branch is fully intelligible if the whole tree is not taken into account, and if we also bear in mind that in African philosophy, what is at stake is the Africanness of the African, one can overlook the race factor only at the cost of overlooking the interconnectedness of the forces that bear on the African. Racism attempts to secure and encourages self-overlooking both in the racist and in its victim. An African philosopher must be vigilant in carrying out the work of philosophy, lest he or she become thereby an accomplice in the construction and perpetuation of his or her own self-forgetfulness, lest he or she perpetuate European racism. Racism may appear irrelevant to certain branches of philosophy, but if, as previously indicated, we keep in view that every branch of philosophy is what it is and is nourished by the tree of philosophy, there is no branch that can be fully conscious of itself if it forgets what makes it be what it is.

Today, the world of philosophy, like any other human world, is thoroughly racialized, and to pretend otherwise is to do a disservice to philosophy. As we focus attention on the African history of philosophy, our attention will be better focused if we bear this mind. Although one is to guard oneself from paranoia in philosophical investigation, one must bear in mind that, at times, racism has a chameleon-like face. It is not easy to detect. The racist does not always announce himself or herself as a racist. It is not enough to detect racism in this or that European philosopher. To be enslaved in such detection can obscure a less detectable racism that exists in a diffused form in the European philosophical tradition. Likewise, it cannot be assumed that the victim of racism is fully aware of the extent to which he or she is victimized by racism. Because a racist situation is not self-evidently racist, combating racism is a difficult undertaking. Those who are interested in combating racism in philosophy must be open to the encounter with racism where it is least expected. In the realm of philosophy, there is also room for racism. This state of affairs may be trivial or insignificant to those who philosophize in the Western, Chinese, or Indian traditions, but it cannot be so for those who philosophize within the African tradition. The African tradition, perhaps more than any other tradition, has been subjected to systematic European racism and, under this subjection, the African tradition has been deprived of a philosophical status. Such deprivation has been largely the work of Europeans—the primary perpetrators of racism in Africa. Insofar are they are truly African, African philosophers are bound to have a strained relationship with their European counterparts and, at times, the relationship is bound to be antagonistic.

Racism has created an ongoing tension between the African and the European traditions of thinking and culture, and the relationship between philosophers in the two traditions cannot be immune to this tension. If the tension does not appear to be present, this may be largely due to the fact that most European philosophers pay no attention to the race factor in the construction of philosophy and in framing its history. They rarely bother to engage African philosophers on philosophical matters that involve the race factor. When African philosophers bring up the race factor in philosophical discourse, they are likely to be dismissed by their European counterparts as engaging in an ideological rhetoric that does not merit a philosophical response. What European philosophers appear to suppress in this case is the fact that what merits a philosophical response is disputable. Avoiding a dispute on what is philosophically meritorious is an abdication of philosophy.

An African African history of philosophy, insofar as it is philosophical, is the history of the African. It is the manner in which the African historicizes himself. It is the autobiography of the African. But it is also a part of the autobiography of humanity. It illuminates one of the ways in which humanity historicizes itself. The historicization of the African is a part of the historicization of humanity. To think and write about African philosophy and its history is to invite all of those who are interested in philosophy to participate in a dialogue on African philosophy and on its history, regardless of their respective cultural traditions. Alternatively, it is to join those who are already carrying out the task of defining philosophy and thereby charting its historical course. That Africans are speaking about African philosophy and its history is essential to the definition of philosophy and to the manner in which philosophy historicizes itself. No one who is truly interested in philosophy and its history can ignore this African undertaking. When the thinking on the nature and history of philosophy is at stake, no sector of the human community can be relegated to the margins. Each sector plays an essential role. Moreover, the contribution of each sector is subject to a critical response from other sectors.

A philosopher who sets out to write a history of African philosophy explicitly or implicitly is guided by a particular understanding of philosophy. Conversely, a philosopher's understanding of philosophy calls for a particular history of philosophy. Odera Oruka, a Kenyan philosopher, has placed African philosophy into four categories: ethnophilosophy, nationalistic–ideological philosophy, philosophical sagacity, and professional philosophy.[39] Ethnophilosophy—a term made popular by the Benin philosopher Paulin Hountondji, is a paternalistic invention by Europeans ethnologists and social anthropologists, which is primarily intended to persuade European audiences that Africans are not philosophically barren. They have an infantile philosophy that European friends of philosophy can nurture into maturity. The seminal work in this type of philosophy is *Bantu Philosophy*[40] by Father Placide Tempels, a Belgian missionary. Under this type of philosophy, Africa is reduced into a mosaic of tribes, each of which has its respective philosophy—a philosophy that apparently has its unique history. As examples, there are Dogon philosophy and its history, Yoruba philosophy and its history, Bambara philosophy and its history, and Dinka philosophy and its history. Some of the African philosophers falling under this type of philosophy include Alexis Kagame of Rwanda and John Mbiti, a Kenyan Christian theologian.

Nationalistic–ideological philosophy is a creation of African nationalists and ideologues in which philosophy is seen as a weapon in the struggle against European colonialism, neocolonialism, and imperialism. Philosophy is seen as a political or ideological weapon to be used by Africans to liberate themselves from European oppression and exploitation. A perspective on philosophy that is inherently apolitical is viewed as counterrevolutionary and, for the most part, serves or obscures neocolonial and imperialist forces. Among those who fall into this type of philosophy are Kwame Nkrumah, Julius Nyerere, Senghor, Amilcar Cabral, Sekou Toure, and Frantz Fanon.

The third type, philosophical sagacity, consists of an effort by university-trained philosophers to extract philosophical gems from traditional African culture. Oruka is the leading spokesperson of this type of philosophy. The contention in this philosophy is that in traditional African societies, there were African sages distinguished by their critical ability and skills—attributes that are essential to philosophy. Hence, it is erroneous to claim that tradition African societies were devoid of philosophy. In addition to Oruka, Marcel Griaule (who is not African) falls under this category.

Professional African philosophy is a creation of professors of philosophy who have been trained in either European or American universities or in African universities by European- or American-trained philosophers. They tend to equate philosophy with academic philosophy and are very critical of the claim that there is philosophy in traditional African societies. Although they are not necessarily anti-ideological, they reject the idea of dumping philosophy and ideology together and tend to draw a sharp distinction between philosophy and ideology. One may call them philosophical purists, since it appears to be their objective to purify philosophy from everything "unphilosophical." They take the position that philosophy has universal features and should be conducted in the same way as science. Such a position is obscured by ideology, and philosophy becomes indistinguishable from politics. Philosophers who adopt this position include Paulin Hountondji, Kwasi Wiredu, and Peter Bondunrin. They are quite at home in Western European philosophical orthodoxy.

Each of the above categories of philosophy calls for its respective history of philosophy. The history of ethnophilosophy originated with European explorers, missionaries, and colonizers, and is perpetuated by anthropologists of all kinds and by those who have singled out the so-called African tribes for their respective studies. The history of philosophical sagacity originated at the time when African sages came into being. Since we have no evidence that they were conscious of their place in the history of African philosophy, it is those who are in possession of such consciousness to locate them in history. Oruka, the major advocate for philosophical sagacity, has not stated the origin of such a philosophy, and it appears today that the sages are dying out of old age or that the would-be sages have entered into the life of professional philosophy in colleges and universities. Thus, it is not easy to distinguish the history of philosophical sagacity from the history of professional philosophy.

The history of nationalistic–ideological philosophy has its origin in the origin of the African struggle against the European invasion of Africa and, if this history has not come to an end, it is because Africa continues to be dominated by foreign interests. Apparently, when such domination is over, the history of African philosophy will come to an end too, just as in Marxist historiography, history will come to an end when the class struggle is over.

The history of professional African philosophy has its origin in the origin of the professional philosophical training of Africans by European or American professional philosophers. Although Africans continue to receive such training, Africans have joined the training of missionary cadres as a part of the Africanization of teaching philosophy. The graduates of this training have embarked on the task of training fellow Africans who will perhaps themselves join the teaching of philosophy and keep professional philosophy alive. The history of professional philosophy will go on until professional philosophy becomes extinct.

As is evident, in general, these histories have a very short span. They are quite remarkable for their brevity in comparison with the history of philosophy in non-African traditions. In the Western European philosophical tradition, for example, the fifth century BC is construed to be the starting point of philosophy. The history of philosophy in China and India antedates the birth of Christ. In comparison with these traditions, it appears that Africa has been philosophically asleep and, apparently, not until recently have Africans been able to awake from this slumber. Despite the apparent disagreement among the advocates of the various conceptions of the history of African philosophy referred to above, it appears that all are united in the belief that African philosophy is a recent phenomenon, and so is its history. They share the view that African philosophy is essentially contemporary African philosophy. However, the term "contemporary philosophy" as used in the context of African philosophy is not analogous to the term "contemporary philosophy" as used in Western European philosophy.

In Western European philosophy, the term "contemporary philosophy" is used to refer to a phase of the history of Western European philosophy that is preceded by modern philosophy, modern philosophy is itself understood to have been preceded by medieval philosophy, and medieval philosophy is preceded by ancient philosophy. Contemporary Western European philosophy itself may have run its course, for there is a generation of Western European philosophers, joined by their descendants in other parts of the world, who believe that we are living at the dawn of postmodern philosophy.

If the term "contemporary philosophy" is applied to African philosophy, it may appear natural to ask whether contemporary African philosophy in this context is preceded by African modern philosophy, and whether, in turn, African modern philosophy is preceded by medieval African philosophy, and medieval African philosophy is preceded by ancient African philosophy. In other words, the question is whether the term "contemporary philosophy" as applied to African philosophy has the same meaning that it has when applied to Western philosophy. In addition, it may be asked whether in the age of postmodern Western European philosophy, equally there should also be a postmodern African philosophy. If the history of African philosophy is understood along the same lines as the history of Western European philosophy, then it should be possible to inquire into the substance of postmodern African philosophy and modern African philosophy, as well as the substance of ancient African philosophy. In the light of these concerns, it ought to be evident that what is to constitute an African African history of philosophy is an issue that cannot be avoided by those who take African philosophy and its history seriously.

The brevity of the history of African philosophy that offers itself to us once we equate African philosophy with contemporary African philosophy should not necessarily be a source of shame or embarrassment for Africans, or an indication of a shortcoming on the part of African historiographers of African philosophy. It may be the case that we are experiencing the dawn of philosophy in Africa, and if this is indeed the case, there is no cause for alarm. Such an alarm, for example, does not characterize the Greeks who, according to Western historians, stand at the dawn of the history of the so-called Western European philosophy. Before one is an adult, one must be born, and one must undergo the experiences of childhood and adolescence. What should trouble us is the possibility of an erroneous timing of one's birth. An erroneous timing can give rise to a false history, and this is the type of history that we, as lovers of truth, have to stay away from. Many European and American historians of Western philosophy may take for granted the conventional view of the timing of the origin of Western philosophy and thereby take leave of philosophy, but those who are interested in the history of African philosophy need not follow course by uncritically accepting a conventional view that African philosophy is essentially a contemporary product.

To claim that African philosophy has its birth in the contemporary period implies the ability to identify and recognize African philosophy. The ability to recognize and identify is possible only in the case of a being that has the ability to misidentify, as well as the ability to misrecognize. How can we be sure that do not mistake identification for misidentification or mistake recognition for misrecognition? We must allow ourselves to be guided by African philosophy. But how can we be sure that we are guided by an African African philosophy rather than by a non-African version of African philosophy? This is not an idle question, for what is at stake is the very nature of philosophy. How is one to distinguish the African version of philosophy from other versions? Is there a common version in all versions? What is philosophy, and how is it exemplified in the various versions or in various traditions?

As previously stated, the truth of philosophy does not yield itself to us that easily. If the determination of this truth is taken up by the African, there is a good possibility that he or she has already been conditioned to see philosophy in the context of the truth of philosophy as it is understood in the Western European tradition. From the standpoint of Western Europeans, it is Western European professors of philosophy who have initiated the majority of professional African philosophers into the truth of philosophy. How are the initiates to tell whether what they have been initiated into is indeed the truth rather than the untruth of philosophy? This is a terribly complicated issue for African philosophers.

It is worth noting that the advent of the European professors of philosophy in Africa was at the same time the advent of the European Christian missionaries, European explorers, European traders, and European colonizers. Allegedly, it was a civilizing event in which Europe was the civilizer and Africa was the civilized. This may have been good news for Europeans, but it was bad news for Africans. The evidence in support of the latter perception is the fact that Africans had to wage war, and still wage war, against being civilized. European missionaries sought the religious and spiritual conquest of Africans as a prerequisite for civilizing Africans. European professors of philosophy sought the "philosophical" conquest of Africans as a prerequisite for the civilizing of Africans. European Christian missionaries sought to vanquish the heart of the African, and European professors of philosophy sought to vanquish the mind of the African. Just as Africans had to, and still have to, resist the religious conquest, they had to, and still have to, resist "philosophical" conquest. There has been, and there continues to be, a struggle—at least between some African philosophers and the orthodox Western philosophical tradition—for the truth of philosophy. To many of us, this is not evident, for the view of philosophy that reigns in the world today—the Western European view—obscures the existence of the struggle and encourages an accommodationist attitude and passivity.

The initiation of Africans into the truth of philosophy can no longer be taken for granted, especially when the invaders of Africa constitute and institute themselves as the sole masters of the initiation into the truth of philosophy. Would-be African philosophers should contemplate the possibility that they may be impregnated by European philosophers, thereby conceiving and giving birth to a European philosophical baby, a baby that they may have mistaken for an African baby. A European baby is European, and an African baby ought to be African. One's baby should be in the image of oneself. For the African, the danger of a mistaken philosophical identity is real. An unexamined identity may not be worth holding onto and may indeed lead to a life that is unbecoming of a human being. Self-examination is essential not only for establishing philosophical parameters of one's identity but also for affirming one's humanity. If one concedes to having others establish the philosophical parameters of one's identity, one's identity will most likely end up being a construct of others. Being a construct is inconsistent not only with being philosophical but also with being human. What is at stake in the struggle for an African philosophy and for an African history of philosophy by the African is the philosophical being of the African. It is also a struggle for the human being of the African insofar as what philosophy is, is essential to what it is to be a human being. The struggle constitutes an attempt to ward off the danger that faces the African in the attempt to generate and secure these modes of being.

One of the theaters where the danger to African philosophy manifests itself is in language. First, the African is taught that the word "philosophy"—a word that has been domesticated into European languages—is a Greek word, and insofar as it appears in the phrase "African philosophy," it links Africans to the Greek and European languages. It is not a word found in African languages. This may suggest that Africans become philosophical by appropriating the word "philosophy" into their languages. First, they appropriate the world in its European context, and then more originally as it is in the Greek context. This suggestion is what Europeans would like Africans to assimilate and make their own. However, it is a suggestion that is philosophically problematic.

The fact that the word "philosophy" does not appear in African languages does not entail the absence of what the word entails. The word "human" does not appear in the vocabulary of African languages, but this does not mean that Africans are not human or cannot express in their languages what it is to be human. To be sure, at one time, Europeans thought that Africans were subhuman, and a good many Europeans today continue to think this way, especially in their treatment of Africans. This thought was, and is, more or less a reflection of a dangerous European nonsense or insensitivity regarding the scope of human dignity.

Neither the Europeans nor the Greeks have a monopoly on the understanding of what the word "philosophy" names. To be sure, the history of Western philosophical anthropology has tended to reinforce this view in Western Europeans, and their descendants have sought to convert the rest of the world to it. However, contrary to this view, what the word "philosophy" names is open to all human beings in the most elementary way. It is up to each people to enquire and articulate what is so named. In determining what is named, we should not allow ourselves to be stampeded or blinded by the arrogance of European thinkers. We should not sanctify what they have hitherto insisted to be what the word names and demonize what others have contributed to the determination of what is named by the word "philosophy." We should prevent the mystification of what the Greek named by this word. European languages have been influenced by the Greek language, but they did not influence the Greek language. The Greek language appeared before the rise of the European languages and has been formative of them. Although when Greece flourished, there was no Europe, this fact has not prevented Europe from creating Greece in her own image. It would be difficult for ancient Greeks to recognize themselves in the manner in which they have been portrayed by Europeans. The Greeks did not think of themselves as Europeans and did not think of their philosophy as European philosophy. Athens was a Greek polis. It was not a European city. Europeans have hijacked and perverted what the Greeks named "philosophy," and it should not be taken for granted that Greek philosophy in European philosophy speaks Greek. Under European hegemonism, it speaks European languages. The Greek language was not a European language. The Greeks never thought of themselves as the first in human history to usher what the word "philosophy" names. The belief that they were the first is a concoction of European philosophers in their effort to build their identity as European philosophers. Africans do a disservice to themselves if they allow themselves to be pre-empted of their autochthonous philosophical identity and have it used as raw material in the construction of European identity.

The history of philosophy is a formative force. Through it, a people forge their identity. A meditation on the history of philosophy is a meditation on one's being, a meditation on the historicity of one's being. The history of Western European philosophy is the history of the Western European man. It is not the history of all men and, specifically, it is not the history of the Africans. The European man has attempted to render the African man parasitic to his history, and since it is unbecoming for a human being to be a parasite of another human being, the African man can be fully human if, and only if, he recognizes and charts his own historical course. This is what is at stake in the quest for an African history of philosophy: the quest for the manner in which the African has philosophically historicized his being. Modern European history has made the confrontation between the African and the European man inevitable in this quest. Modern European history has sought to portray the African as a resource in the construction of human history or at least has sought to confine the African to the margins of human history. In order to affirm his humanity and the history that is proper to it, the African has had to resist, and must continue to resist, this historical European imperative.

Before the advent of the European man in Africa, Africans initiated themselves into the truth of their being. It is consistent with the truth of being human that human beings initiate themselves into the truth of their being. The truth of philosophy is integral to the truth of being human, and as human beings, Africans cannot let themselves be initiated into the truth of philosophy by non-Africans without abdicating their own responsibility and duty to themselves and to philosophy. In philosophy, there inheres the truth of what is human, and this truth is not subject to being passed on from one human being to another, or from one people to another. In other words, philosophical life is not the sort of life that can originate from one human community and be passed onto other human communities. It is not an invention of a particular community that in the course of time spreads to other communities. Just as no individual can determine for another individual what philosophy is, no community can determine for another community what philosophy is. Each human being, as is the case with each human community, contains the seeds of philosophical life. In this regard, the site of the history of African philosophy is to be found in the African and not in the Western European or in anyone else—hence, the error of trying to project the history of African philosophy as if it were in the mold of the history of the Western European philosophy.

If the history of African philosophy is construed along the same lines as the history of Western European philosophy, is this coincidental, or is it a historical design to institute and perpetuate Western European cultural hegemonism? Is African history of philosophy an emulation of Western European philosophy by the historians of African philosophy? Why must the history of African philosophy be construed in the same manner as the history of Western European philosophy? If it is not to be so construed, how is it to be construed? Is it intrinsic to the nature of philosophy to historicize itself in a linear manner—the manner that appears favored by Western European historians? These questions point to the need for clarification of the nature of philosophy and the manner in which it historicizes itself. The fact that these questions appear to have been answered in the West does not pre-empt the answers that Africans can give to them. To ask these questions is an essential feature of what it means for the African to philosophize. It is also to call into question the answers that may have been offered elsewhere. What has been said about the nature of philosophy in the West and has been said about the history of philosophy in the West need not be definitive of what philosophy is universally.

In the Western European history of philosophy, philosophy has a specific birthplace (namely, Greece) and time of birth (the fifth century BC). From Greece, it spread to Europe, then to the other parts of the world. Where is the birthplace and the time of birth of African philosophy? If it has spread, where is its province? The determination of the birthplace and the time of birth of philosophy presupposes a determination of what philosophy is. Otherwise it is not possible to identity intelligently when and where philosophy came into being. It is indeed tempting to claim that African philosophy is a product of colonial experience and that it is only in postcolonial Africa that it has assumed a distinctive form. On the basis of this claim, the history of African philosophy is a product of the extension of West European philosophy.

Insofar as what comes to be has a birthplace, African philosophy too has a birthplace. If it is genuinely African, Africa is her birthplace. One may ask, where in Africa? Since, as previously indicated, what is at stake in African philosophy is the African, the question seeks the birthplace of the African. Wherever in Africa the African has come into being, there is the birthplace of African philosophy. The origin of African philosophy is the origin of the African. The site of the African is the site of African philosophy. If Greece is the mecca of Western European philosophy, Africa is the mecca of African philosophy. Herein lies one of the essential differences between Western European philosophers and African philosophers. To go to their mecca, Western European philosophers must trek to Greece. Clearly, one should wonder why Europeans have had to trek to Greece in the quest for European philosophical identity and for a basis upon which to legitimize and render intelligible the European history of philosophy. African philosophers do not have to trek out of Africa. Africa, their birthplace, is their mecca. Their pilgrimage is a homecoming, a homecoming that entails finding themselves where they already are. It is one in which they appropriate themselves in the very manner in which they are. It is precisely such a finding of oneself at home in one's home that Western European racial and cultural hegemonism has sought to subvert in the African.

Western European philosophers have largely attempted to turn the African away from his philosophical home and have sought to construct a new home for him in Greece, via Europe. In a similar manner, Western European religionists and theologians have attempted to turn the African away from Africa—the home of his religions and gods. Africa is depicted as being no longer the African's holy land. Rather, it is Bethlehem and Jerusalem, via Europe. The Nile, the Congo, the Zambezi, the Niger are no longer African sacred rivers. Now, it is the River Jordan that is sacred. Mount Kilimanjaro, Mount Kenya, the Ruwenzori are no longer sacred African mountains. It is now Mount Sinai. Because the Western European has accepted his religious and theological homelessness in Europe, he has turned away from Europe and has embraced Bethlehem and Jerusalem as his home. Thereafter, he has attempted to persuade the African that he too is religiously and theologically homeless in Africa, and that it is only in Bethlehem and Jerusalem that he can find a home. In other words, having concluded that he is philosophically, theologically, and religiously homeless in Europe, the Western European has sought to, and still seeks to, persuade the African that he too is homeless in Africa and that his true home is where the European has found his home. European homelessness has become contagious. African philosophy seeks to ward off this contagion.

Africa is the birthplace of African philosophy, and the securing of this birthplace is an essential task for African philosophers. Since what is at stake in African philosophy is the African himself/herself, in the securing of Africa as the birthplace of African philosophy, the African will thereby be securing his or her own birthplace. To say that Africa is the African's birthplace is to recognize Africa as being more than simply a geographical or physical expression. It is to come to terms with Africa as the embodiment of the human, as the embodiment from which philosophy is generated. African philosophy is the flesh of the African. If we bear this in mind, it may be possible to avoid looking for the birthplace of African philosophy in a mere physical space—a space that is external to the African. It will pre-empt the search for the birthplace of African philosophy in this or that part of Africa. In this regard, we again part company with those Western European historians of philosophy who seek to identify this or that objective space as the birthplace of philosophy. Africa is the location of the African's philosophy text. From it, the history of African philosophy is generated and sustained. The text is the African life; it is not a book. To read the history of African philosophy is to read the life of the African. The African writes his philosophy in his life.

Just as a birthplace is essential to what comes into being, time is equally essential. The search for a birthplace of African philosophy is triggered by the question, "Where in Africa did African philosophy originate?" History is important in the context of determining when African philosophy came into being. This determination is essential for the conception of the history of African philosophy. To raise the question regarding the origin of African philosophy is to raise the question regarding the origin of the African. Thus when it is asked, "When did African philosophy come into being?" it is also being asked, "When did the African come into being?" These questions are so intertwined that it is meaningless to conceive of the existence of the African prior to the emergence of African philosophy. Here, the idea that African philosophy appears at a certain stage in the evolution of the African is ruled out. African philosophy is not an invention of the African. It can be deemed to be an invention of the African only if the African himself is deemed to be an invention of African philosophy. There is a mutuality of determination that does not permit the prior existence of either of the codeterminants. Since one cannot witness or account for one's origin, the African cannot be in a position to account for his origin. Similarly, insofar as the African's philosophy is linked to his/her being, he/she is not in a position to account for its origin. For the African, the origin of African philosophy is steeped in the same mystery that shrouds his/her own origin. In this age, in which what is deemed to be beyond knowledge is either an object of possible conquest or irrelevant to human progress, the origin of African philosophy is clearly out of place. For it to accommodate itself to our age, in which the prevailing version of philosophy is a version that is dominated by the West, is for it to succumb to epistemologism. Epistemologism not only is incapable of comprehending the origin of African philosophy but also has resorted to depicting it as antiphilosophical or as prephilosophical. It dismisses the origin of African philosophy as so much rubbish that needs to be discarded.

Not only does mystery lie at the origin of African philosophy, but it continues to dwell in it. Since its origin, African philosophy has continued to exhibit its mysterious background. Its history is a history of this mystery. In this regard, the typical manner of presenting the history of Western European philosophy is irrelevant to the manner in which African philosophy has historicized itself. The history of African philosophy cannot be divided into the ancient, modern, and contemporary phases in the manner of the Western European conception of the history of philosophy. These phases are not only constructs of Western European cultural tradition but also indicators of the manner in which Western Europeans understand philosophy. It is a reflection of the manner in which Western Europeans understand history in general. The ancient, the modern, and the contemporary are concepts that are alien to the African understanding of history in general and, specifically, to the African understanding of the history of philosophy. These concepts allow for a linear conception of history and permit Western Europeans to introduce the notions of progress and development. The absence of these concepts in the African understanding of history does not reflect a static view of history. A charge that the African harbors such a view can arise only from the standpoint of one who harbors an evolutionary view of history. If one is not a hostage to an evolutionary view of history, the possibility of other views of history arise. The belief that a linear or an evolutionary view of history is the only true view of history is perhaps a religious or quasi-religious dogma, which is a product of modern European metaphysics and is symptomatic of a conceptual tyranny that Europe has unleashed in every region of the world.

What we have in Africa is a conception of history as a dynamic process in which what is mysterious is constantly present. What has been is what is, and is what will be. To view this state of affairs as a reflection of what is static is to misconstrue the import of what is being said. Insofar as it is mysterious, what is, is unfathomable in terms of its possibilities. As a reflection of what is, African philosophy is not progressive, regressive, or static. It is a dynamic process, which constantly generates, affirms, and articulates possibilities. What is deemed past is nothing more than a present possibility to be affirmed and articulated. The past is appropriated in the womb of what is mysterious, and offers itself as a standing possibility. What is past can be a part of African history only to the extent that it is appropriated in the present. The past is the present and the future, the present is the past and the future, and the future is the present and the past. Each is what it is by being pregnant with the others. There is a continuous creative recreation. The mysterious origin of philosophy is not simply a thing of the past. It is still the manner in which philosophy originates, and also the manner in which philosophy will originate. Once it is originated, it retains the mysterious aspect of its origin. In a sense, then, it never originates if originating entails abandoning that from which it has originated. Being on a philosophical path is being on a path whose origin is unknown and unknowable, and whose end is equally unknown and unknowable. This may be very distressing to those who are hostages in the modern realm of knowledge. If the historian of African philosophy is to be faithful to philosophy, it is essential that he/she avoid being entrapped in this realm. The resolve to stay away from entrapment can be strengthened by constant proper nourishment from the African cultural tradition and by constant vigilance against the assaults that emanate from the West or from any other part of the world.

One of the greatest dangers the African philosopher faces is not internal, and it is not from Asia. It is primarily from the West. At present, he must constantly wrestle African philosophy and its history from the mold in which the Western European wants to cast it. Internally, he must, likewise, ward off any attempt by fellow Africans to aid the Western European "philosophical" missionary effort in Africa. This effort has been institutionalized in African academic institutions. These institutions are now the formal bases where the struggle for African philosophy is taking place. An African philosophy student studies there at his or her own risk. Professors of philosophy at these institutions are not neutral workers. They are a part of the struggle for philosophy, although it cannot be assumed that all are aware of the historical implications of what they are professing. The academic institution where they profess philosophy is a historico-socio-cultural product whose mission stands in need of African philosophical scrutiny.

Traditionally, it appears to be the position of European historians that philosophy is, in its essence, a Western European phenomenon and non-Europeans are philosophical to the extent that they have been grafted, or are being grafted, into the Western European philosophical tradition. Indeed, wherever the history of philosophy is taught in African colleges and universities, the texts that are used tend to reinforce the view that Greece is the cradle of philosophy, and from Greece, philosophy has spread to other parts of the world. Even when philosophy in the West is not overtly taught in the context of Western history of philosophy—for example, when it is taught thematically—the background is always the history of philosophy as construed by Western European historians of philosophy. The Africanness of what largely passes as African philosophy is problematic in that the assumptions that are made about philosophy and its history are essentially Western European. By accepting these assumptions, African philosophy essentially becomes an extension of Western European philosophy. It is therefore not a surprise that as soon as a fad in Western philosophy arises, it appears in African academic philosophy.

The prominence of scientific and technological thinking in the West and the equation of such thinking with philosophical thinking seduce the budding "African" philosopher into thinking that African philosophical thinking can prosper only if it patterns itself after Western philosophical thinking. Wiredu, an African philosopher, informs fellow African philosophers that:

> In practice the contemporary African philosopher will find out that it is the philosophies of the West that will occupy him most, for it is in that part of the world that modern developments in human knowledge that have gone the farthest and, where, consequently, philosophy is in closest touch with the conditions of the modernization which he urgently desires for his continent.[41]

Undeniably, Wiredu has made an important contribution to the conversation on African philosophy. In the above quote, however, there are remarkable omissions. First, contrary to what appear to be the case, the notion of "human knowledge" is multifaceted. It is not clear what aspect or aspects of human knowledge in the West have gone farthest. Since Wiredu is a philosopher and his remarks are directed to African philosophers, one would assume that he is referring to philosophical knowledge. If this assumption is correct, he omits to point out the sense in which philosophical knowledge in the West has gone farthest. African philosophers *qua* philosophers are more likely to pay attention to Western philosophical knowledge, and it would have served them better had Wiredu indicated what aspect or aspects of Western philosophy they should pay more attention to.

Secondly, although it is undeniable that not all African philosophical woes are due to the presence of Westerners in Africa, it is equally undeniable that Westerners have contributed significantly to them. Nowhere does Wiredu address Walter Rodney's charge that Europe contributed significantly to the underdevelopment of Africa.[42] It is unquestionable that the colonization and enslavement of Africans, and the looting of resources in Africa, have contributed not only to the underdevelopment of Africa but also to the development of the West. In the European colonial/slavery regime, African philosophical life was severely repressed or distorted. In the eyes of the colonizers and enslavers, there was no African philosophical life to repress or to distort. African life was projected as savage life and, among savages, there was no philosophical life. Philosophical life was a part of the life of civilized people. More generally, African life was steeped in superstition and, as such, among Africans, knowledge was rare. The European regime of knowledge, in part, solidified at the expense of African knowledge. Moreover, it was a one-sided conception of knowledge. This state of affairs needs to be taken into consideration in the evaluation of the sort of knowledge that Wiredu credits to the West.

If philosophical thinking has paved the way for the modernization of the West, and if this modernization has taken place at the expense of Africa, it is important to investigate the extent to which Western philosophical thinking may have undermined modernization in Africa. Wiredu does not undertake such an investigation and, by not doing so, he spares Western philosophers from the responsibility they may have to assume for what has happened to Africa at the hands of fellow Westerners. He appears to assume that philosophical thinking is a positive force in the process of modernization. He fails to illuminate what he understands by the "closeness" of philosophical thinking to the conditions of modernization. If by "closeness," he implies the closeness of philosophical thinking to scientific and technological thinking, the danger here is that philosophical thinking may be so close to scientific and technological thinking that one may easily mistake one for the other. Such a mistaken identity may foreclose a philosophical critique of scientific and technological thinking.

Although modern and contemporary positivism has made a remarkable effort to reduce philosophical thinking to scientific thinking, it would amount to category confusion to identify either scientific or technological thinking with philosophical thinking. The confusion tends to breed and nourish a type of thinking that equates the history of philosophy with the history of science or the history of technology. Wiredu's version of philosophical thinking, as appears to be the case with Hountondji's version, seems to fall prey to this confusion and, consequently, feeds the Euro-American prejudice against "traditional" African thinking—a thinking that is easily dismissed as pre- or nonscientific. Perhaps it is in the light of a philosophical thinking that has been equated with scientific and technological thinking that African thinking appears to be a stumbling block to modernization.

The scientization of philosophical thinking does a disservice to both scientific and philosophical thinking. It obscures the essential distinction between the two. This obscurity is a liability not only to the conception of philosophy in Africa but also to the conception of the African history of philosophy. The African history of philosophy is likely to be erroneously identified with the history of scientific thinking in Africa. Even more ominous is the possibility that the practice of African philosophy will be seen as either inconsequential to African modernization or a distraction from the serious business of modernizing the continent.

It is very tempting to disregard or marginalize philosophical thinking because it does not appear to deliver the tangible goods that are delivered by scientific and technological thinking. To succumb to this temptation is to fall prey to the tyranny of one-dimensional thinking—thinking that has grave consequences for the manner in which human beings perceive themselves and the way in which they perceive the world around them. It is to fall prey to the tyranny of "materialism" whereby all that is, including man, is viewed as mere material resource for exploitation, where everything is viewed as a standing reserve for scientific and technical manipulation. Indeed it is undeniable that this view is prominent in the West. If the development of such a view is perceived by Africans as their historical objective, it may serve them better to emulate the West. Should Africans choose this path, they should be aware of the danger of emulation. Such emulation can easily secure the domination of Africans by the West and, where domination prevails, the historical destiny of a people is thereby compromised. Being dominated by others is inconsistent with the free self-historicization of human beings. Free self-historicization is what is consistent with what it is to be human.

In regard to philosophy, today, the historical objective of Africans cannot be assumed to be identical to the historical objective of Western Europeans. The assumption of such an identity is likely to be false or to be a reflection of a contrived identity in which Africans have been pressured to appropriate and accept the Western European objective. If there is a true or genuine common historical objective, such an objective has been obscured by the parading of a private objective as if it were a common objective. Service to a common objective can be pursued only if this parading can be exposed and set aside. In an age where cultural chauvinism, racism, and nationalism still have sway over the manner in which human beings think and live, it is very difficult to render such a service. If there is a history of philosophy that is common to all people, such a history remains buried in the destruction that has been brought about by partisan forces. Every account of a particular history of philosophy that is inconsistent with the common dignity of all peoples will be inconsistent with itself. Particular histories of philosophy are to be evaluated, in part, in the light of this common dignity. A genuine African philosophy of history is not exempt from this criterion. An African history of philosophy is truly philosophical if it is capable of affirming itself in a manner that is consistent with the affirmation of other histories that are truly philosophical. The determination of what is truly philosophical is not self-evident. It is what must be worked out in every tradition. In other words, what the histories of philosophy have in common is yet to be worked out philosophically. Philosophizing appears to have taken place within the confines of various cultural traditions, which have generated their own histories of philosophy. A truly intercultural world is yet to fully emerge and, once it emerges, an opportunity for cross-cultural dialogue on philosophy and its history will fully emerge.

The issue of the history of African philosophy is an essential issue in African philosophy. Insofar as African philosophy is a branch of philosophy, the history of African philosophy is a branch of the history of philosophy. Thus the regionality of the history of African philosophy should not obscure the manner in which this history is essentially linked with the whole history of philosophy. Insofar as one is concerned with philosophy and its history, one cannot be a total stranger to the question regarding the nature and the history of African philosophy. Insofar as they are philosophical, all human beings can contribute to the clarification of this question and to the finding of an answer, if there is one. It is not, and it cannot be, an exclusive concern of Africans. That it appears at this time to be exclusively a concern of African philosophers is an indication that what is at stake is not fully understood.

An African history of philosophy is not intelligible unless an African philosophy of history is rendered intelligible. That is, the intelligibility of the former depends on the intelligibility of the latter and, conversely, the intelligibility of the latter depends on the intelligibility of the former. This interdependence may give rise to the charge of circularity, but circularity may not necessarily be philosophically fatal. In a geometrical context, a circle is not an absurd or meaningless phenomenon. Circularity in this context is not repugnant to us. Although philosophy is not geometry, philosophical thought is capable of grasping geometrical thought. This capability is intrinsic to philosophical thought. Consequently, it is not repugnant for philosophical thought to conceive of the codetermination of the history of philosophy and the philosophy of history. Those who have spoken of or written about the history of African philosophy without indicating how this history has been shaped by the African philosophy of history have not provided us with a definitive view.

Just as the history of African philosophy is the history of the African, the African philosophy of history is the philosophy of the African. In both, what is at stake is the historicization of the African. Both are Afri-centric. Both codetermine what it is to be an African by exhibiting the African in history. Just as Europeans attempted to marginalize the African in the European history of philosophy or to accommodate him in it, they have attempted to treat him as if he is at the margins of the European philosophy of history or as if he is to be accommodated in the European philosophy of history. In modern European thought, history is essentially linear. Europeans place themselves in the most advanced phase of history and regard other people, especially Africans, as being in the least advanced phase. This belief is largely muted today, but the continued racist treatment of Africans demonstrate that the belief continues to have traction. The pervasive silence on racism on the part of European historians of philosophy does not imply that their view on the philosophy of its history has been immunized against it. Alain Badiou is correct in pointing out that, "It is important that philosophy determine itself in such a way that it is philosophy itself that judges its history, and not history that judges it."[43] In the case of Africa, it is African philosophy that is to determine the African history of philosophy. It is not to be determined by Western philosophy, by the history of Western philosophy, or by Western Europeans in general.

It is indeed the case that when Africans students are exposed to the history of philosophy, the history they get exposed to is the history of philosophy viewed from a European perspective. It is rare that this perspective is qualified as European. It is also presented in this way to Europeans students and to other students who have European or European-trained teachers of philosophy. This perspective is often presented as universal, beside which there is no other. In a lecture on the history of philosophy, Georg Hegel observed that:

> What the history of philosophy shows us is a succession of noble minds, a gallery of heroes of thought who by the power of Reason, have penetrated into the being of things, of nature and of spirit, into the Being of God, and have won for us by their labours the highest treasure, the treasure of reasoned knowledge.[44]

It can readily be imagined that when an African student of the history of philosophy is exposed to this view, he cannot fail to note that, as portrayed in European imagination, there is no African mind that is a part of the succession of the noble minds. He or she does not see an African in the European gallery of heroes of thought who, by the power of reason, has penetrated into the beings that Hegel speaks about. Reasonable knowledge is nowhere to be found in his society or culture. He or she is not alone in recognizing this void. His or her European counterparts recognize it too, and so do others who have embraced the Eurocentric view of the history of philosophy. Instead of challenging this view, an African student of philosophy is under tremendous pressure to embrace this view or dream about an African development of a history of philosophy that would give rise to the kind noble minds and heroes that he or she sees in the European gallery. He or she could be tempted to aspire to be rational in the way the European is rational, and make a contribution to the building of African rational knowledge. The possibility that such knowledge can deprive philosophy of its vitality does not readily arise. The possibility that philosophy has no heroes and that the nobility of the mind does not constitutes what is essential about philosophy, likewise, rarely emerges. The existence of heroes and/or the existence of noble minds is likely to lead to the worship of such heroes or such minds. Philosophy is not in the business of worshiping. Worshiping is primarily a feature of religious life, not philosophical life. It appears that Hegel was radically mistaken about the nature of philosophy and, hence, about the nature of the history of philosophy. His view of the history of philosophy appears to be deeply rooted in the Christian religion. If he was suspicious of the maturity of the Greek philosophers, it was primarily because these philosophers were pagans; it was because they were not Christians. For Hegel, it appears that rational knowledge is but a rationalization of the Christian way of living.

For an African—or indeed anyone who has a genuine interest in the history of African philosophy—such an interest must be philosophical. The determination of what makes an interest philosophical is a matter of philosophy. In making such a determination, an African cannot be an outsider or rely for help on others. He must play the essential role in such an undertaking. It has to be an African philosophical determination. This does not imply that he or she is to do this in isolation. He has to do this communally with others for, despite the differences, philosophy also has a communal basis. In cultivating the communal, it may be a sign of health to be somewhat paranoid, for when one encounters thinkers such as Hegel, one is likely to lose a sense of healthy communality. Instead of aiming at the construction of an African gallery of African philosophical heroes or a gallery of African noble minds, African philosophers should be aiming at the construction of an African life that is equally shared by all Africans and that has a place for every other human being. Every African—not just those who pass off as professional philosophers—has to play an essential role in the construction of such a life. It must be a communal effort—an Ubuntu effort.

Like every other human community, African people are a storytelling people. Storytelling is one of the ways in which a community preserves the memory of its identity, and it is a means of perpetuating this identity. The African history of philosophy is such a story for Africans. It testifies to what an African community. It is a major contribution to African identity and also contributes to African care for an African self. An African philosopher who ignores it ignores herself or himself. It also communicates to non-Africans what it is to be African.

Chapter 5
The African Body as an Ethico-aesthetic Site

You write on paper to express yourself and to communicate with others. Our ancestors wrote on their bodies to accomplish the same. Seek what is more intimate to you and do the same. Your body is more intimate to you. It is what you are and how you are seen by others. It is also how others are and how you see them. (An African elder's advice to a young man)

5 The African Body as an Ethico-aesthetic Site

Every human body tells a story, not always a story that is already there, but also a story in the making. In either case, the body authors its own story. The African body is not an exception. It is where the story of the sense of being African is constituted and where it is expressed. Prior to the constitution and expression, it is nothing. It is this nothing that makes constitution and expression possible. Even after constitution and expression has taken place, nothing remains as an ever abiding presence, always open to reconstitution and to other constitutions and expressions. This is illustrated in the manner in which the African's body presents itself to the African.

A young man in a marketplace is selling his goats. His entire set of front lower and upper teeth has endings that are filed needle-sharp. He smiles at a prospective visitor, hoping that not only his goats but also the beauty of his teeth will be recognized and appreciated. A young woman, with a face that is full of vitality, is distinctively pregnant, baby due in a matter of days. Her exposed belly manifests innumerable small patterned protrusions. Her neck can barely be seen, because of a heavy set of beads of myriad colors. Her head is clean shaven, and her cheeks are painted. Around her waist, there is a multicolored beaded belt. A middle-aged woman, bracelets on both ankles and arms, has a stack of multicolored beads around her neck and a coiffure that appears to exaggerate the true size of her head. A middle-aged man has patterned scars below his eyes. He has a monkey-skin hat with long eagle feathers mounted on top, a painted face, and silver bracelets on both ankles. An elderly woman, barefooted, firewood on her head, pierced ears, jewelry inserted in the earlobe perforations, is on her way back to her home to prepare an evening meal for her family. Her earlobes have stretched from the weight of the jewelry and appear to be resting on her shoulders. She is bare chested, with tattooed breasts that have been sucked dry over the years and are so long that they appear to overlap her exposed belly. An elderly man, resting on a stool outside his hut, is stroking his beard and smoking a decorated corn pipe. He has pierced ears, and his earlobes are stretched from wearing heavy jewelry over the years. The scarification on his cheeks is no longer distinguishable, because of his old age. The scarification appears to have aged with the body, and inevitably so, because it is itself an inalienable feature of this particular body.

What a living visual spectacle Africa has to offer! A living art exhibition. A living art gallery. A living museum of African art. African art in motion. The human body in Africa is transformed into a living sculpture, the body intentionally chiseled out, the body intentionally scarified, the body intentionally perforated, the body intentionally contoured and molded as if it were clay. A human body whose flesh is assaulted and branded as if it were an inanimate object or the body of a beast. When the body is not subjected to this deliberate assault and battery, it is transformed into a canvas, into a surface where one can generate a live painting, a painting in motion, a painting that needs no museum, that needs no gallery or exhibition hall because it is itself the gallery, the museum, the body that exhibits itself to itself in multiple formations. The human body in Africa is transformed into a mural—at once, the painter and the painted. A body that is, at the same time, the sculptor and the sculpture; a sculptured painting that walks eats, sleeps, laughs, feels, sees, touches, smells, hears, dances and, at times, copulates, impregnates, and is impregnated. Here, one faces a phenomenon that is more than a spectacular object. It is not a mere cultural artifact or a conventional object of art, and nor is it simply a matter of ethnography, or so-called tribal art. A mere cultural object or a conventional art object lacks the power to see, to hear, to touch and, in general, to sense. The body that presents itself as a spectacle embodies and expresses these powers. As a spectacle, it needs to be grasped spectacularly, and to grasp it, one must be spectacular. If the spectacular body presents itself to the eye, the eye must be spectacular, and because the eye is the eye of the body, it cannot be spectacular unless the body is spectacular. The seer and the seen are rendered spectacular. This is not a mere mesmerization by the so-called tribal phenomenon. It is a seduction of the body by the body, which reveals the enigma of human embodiment. Maurice Merleau-Ponty has already called our attention to such a body in his description of the painter. In his beautiful essay titled "Eye and Mind," he tells us:

> The eye is an instrument that moves itself, a means that invents its own ends; it is that which has been moved by some impact, which it then restores to the visible through the offices on agile hand.[45]

For the painter, the hand is the prolongation of the eye and, conversely, the eye is the prolongation of the hand. In this prolongation, every organ of the body is implicated, for the body—the lived body, as phenomenologists have reminded us—is not an assemblage of parts. It is a unitary being. In the spectacle that is the African body, it is such a body that comes into relief. And it comes into relief in a manner that evokes its likeness in our bodies.

We want to understand this body, a body that subjects itself to a metamorphosis, that body in which the African is an African. We take up the aesthetics of this body as a gateway to the understanding of what it is to be an African, as a gateway to the understanding of the African world and, ultimately, a gateway to the understanding of the human world and a gateway to the understanding of the world in general. We want to understand this aesthetic that abandons itself to the sensuous without reservation and does so in a way that exhibits what is beautiful as the site for the manifestation of human reality. We want to understand this body and its aesthetics, a body and aesthetics that have traditionally been subjected to ethico-aesthetic disapproval by Europeans, with the ultimate aim of disapproving such disapproval.

The appearance of the African body in its aesthetic sense generates a site where phenomena are aesthetically constituted and rendered subject to aesthetic consideration. As a site for aesthetics, the African body does not attest to what is unique about itself. Rather, it summons us to consider the human body as what is primordially the site of the aesthetic world. All phenomena that fall under the regime of aesthetics derive their aestheticity from the body. Just as they are constituted and elaborated as aesthetic, they too constitute and elaborate the body as aesthetic. The body constitutes and presents to us not only aesthetic phenomena; it also constitutes and presents to us the phenomenal world as aesthetic. It does so in such a way that, on account of our bodies, we are shown to be inherent in it. Our bodies inhabit the aesthetic world.

Although, among modern Europeans, the conventional view is that beauty is the focus of aesthetics, what aesthetics is yet to be fully worked out and understood in a manner that does not privilege European understanding. For the most part, Europeans have indulged in a discourse on aesthetics solely among themselves. They have presented beauty from a Eurocentric perspective. What is attempted here challenges this indulgence. Our interest is in that aesthetic that is multicontextual—an aesthetic that does not privilege one sector of the human community at the expense of other sectors. To the extent that aesthetics have something to do with beauty, our interest is in that beauty that is appropriately affirmed in a particular cultural sector of the human community without negating how it is appropriately affirmed in other cultural sectors of the human community. Thus by taking up the sensuous, nothing is said definitively thereby about aesthetics. One must still explore the ever changing cultural context of the culturally sensuous. Contrary to the profession of the positivists (at least the classical ones), the sensuous is not culture free. Aesthetics lead us to the sensuous. But this leading takes place in a cultural context. It is for this reason that nothing is fully understood about the African body in its aesthetic context if one does not take African culture into account.

As an expression of the incarnate, aesthetics have many senses. There is a conventional interpretation of Plato in which the body is the prison of the true, the prison of the truly beautiful—the beautiful that is accessible only to the soul, the soul itself being a prisoner in the body. In the conventional reading of Plato, if the body is beautiful, it is because it participates in an incorporeal form of beauty. The Christians, for whom true beauty is ultimately generated by God—a spiritual being—true beauty is spiritual, and it is only by taking on the spiritual that the body can be said to be beautiful. Here, one cannot fail to sense some kinship between Platonism and Christianity. Friedrich Nietzsche correctly observed that Christianity is Platonism for the people.[46] Platonism and Christianity have collaborated in the denigration of the body, in the denigration of the sensuous . There has been a holy matrimony between Platonists and Christians, and this matrimony has yielded an offspring, an aesthetics whose regime has threatened what is essential about the body and, derivatively, what is essential about African aesthetics. It is precisely from the perspective of this matrimony that the African body has been perceived as heathen or as savage by Europeans. A human body in which the human fully expresses itself without reserve, a body that is not a container of anything superior to itself and that is open to collaboration with other bodies in denying the truth of what is transcorporeal cannot but appear as heathen or as savage to those whose perception and understanding has been taken over by Platonism and Christianity.

For the African, the body that is the site of beauty is not a prison for what is truly beautiful. It is anti-Platonic and anti-Christian. The body is not beautiful by participating in what is spiritual. It is not a receptacle of what is beautiful. It is truly beautiful. The African's body is not only the site for a body-centered beauty. It constitutes and exhibits what being human is and also what is, in general. A human being, as is the case with what is in general, is a corporeal being. Aesthetics originates from the human body and moves aesthetically to other phenomena, only to return to itself as a way of constituting and appreciating their aestheticity. The return is enigmatic in that it is not a return of the human body from what is foreign to it. It is a return of the body from itself. A body that alienates itself and dis-alienates itself is what a human body is. If it can do this to itself, it reveals itself as what it is by not being what it is. It is a positivity of being that remains as such until its death. The African body is the theater of being African. It is where the drama of being African takes place.

The human body is not a stranger to nonhuman bodies. In its incarnate nature, human reality is more than itself. It is extrahuman. The human body is the body of bodies. In opening itself to us as what we are, it opens us to all that is. The aesthetics of the African body point to the singularity of human reality in its African instantiation, but also points to the body as the site for the manifestation of any instantiation of human reality. What is singular does not stand in opposition to what is not singular. What is singular instantiates what is not singular. Aesthetics calls attention not only to what is beautiful but also, and primarily, to the type of being that we are. In inviting us to dwell in the sensuous, aesthetics invites us to dwell in ourselves sensuously. We are not aesthetic beings because we cultivate aesthetics; it is because we are aesthetic beings that we cultivate aesthetics. Every segment of the human community announces its humanness through its respective aesthetics. Human beings are not the only sensuous beings. The entire world is sensuous. Thus aesthetics are not humanism. It is not human beings that are at the center of aesthetics. It is the sensuous world—a world that includes both the human and the nonhuman. We barely touch on the essence of aesthetics when we limit ourselves to the standards of taste, to the principles of what makes phenomena beautiful or to the manner in which beautiful phenomena are generated. Standards or principles of what constitutes phenomena as beautiful draw our attention not only to what they are or to what beautiful phenomena are, but also to us, to us for whom the standards are standards, for whom principles are principles, and for whom beautiful phenomena are beautiful. But there is more at stake here.

If we understand that both our being and the being of the world are at stake in aesthetics, then we should also be led by aesthetics to see that any discussion of the principles or the cannons of taste that does not yield the truth of being and the truth of existence is incomplete. From an African perspective, the perennial dispute that one finds in the Western world on whether beauty is or is not in the eye of the beholder misses the central feature of aesthetics. For the African, what is at stake is the being of the viewer, the being of the world; it is life that is at stake. Even if one is to assume that beauty is in the eye of the beholder, the assumption would make full sense only if one fully understood who and what the beholder is. Perhaps, it is nothing more than a prejudice of a particular culture to maintain that the viewer is a viewer only apart from, and in opposition to, the viewed. Likewise, if one were to assume that there is an objective sense of beauty, what being objective is still remains to be clarified. Objectiveness—a disguised subjectivism—may be nothing more than an expression of a particular culture at a specific period in its history. In opting for either of these assumptions, there is a danger of obscuring what should be experienced and understood about beauty.

As an alternative to the discourse that has conventionally been taken up in the West, it is tempting to see the aesthetics of the African body as focusing exclusively on the African. If we succumb to this temptation, we will not only fail to understand the African and his aesthetics. We will also misunderstand others and their aesthetics. There is an internal sensuous bond that holds all human beings together in a unified manner. An aesthetic that fails to bring into relief this bond is incomplete and can easily obscure what is truly human. Regardless of how esoteric or how foreign the body of the African may be to non-Africans, it still retains the human linkage to other human bodies. The body of an African and the body of a non-African constitute one body, one human body. Insofar as it is a human body, the body of the African is an extension of every other human body, just as every other human body is an extension of the African body. The exoticizing of the African body, which reached its zenith at the height of the colonization of Africans by Europeans, removes the African body from the African and from common humanity. Anthropologists of all kinds have made a contribution to this effort. The photographers of the National Geographic magazine have been among the leading purveyors of this exoticism.

The fact that one's body is not painted or scarified does not imply that one's body has nothing in common with the painted or scarified body of the African. Nor should it be assumed that if an African has an unpainted or unscarified body, he or she is not African. The painted or scarified body is a contingent body. There is nothing inherently African about it. It is not an eternal form of an African body or of any other human being. If there is an essence to the African body or to any human body, this essence is nothing. Out of nothing, an African is made into an African either by himself or by others. Nothing is unavoidably in the background of whatever is made of the African and reverts into it.

In our contemporary world of racism, it may sound farfetched to entertain the community of human beings in the community of human bodies. It is the nature of racism to engage us in a practice that shutters the unity of human bodies and to generate antagonism among the resulting detritus. Like the proverbial phoenix, the body of the African arises out of this detritus and, in so doing, calls all other bodies to similarly arise and forge a corporeal unity in which each becomes fully what it is. This arising—this anti-racism—is an aesthetic event. In retaining the singularity of African aesthetics, the African body also retains the aesthetics of non-African bodies. African aesthetics are not object focused; they are not a self-enclosed phenomenon from which all other aesthetics are closed out. Precisely because they are aesthetics, they are open to all other aesthetics. It is in this openness and as this openness that aesthetics exhibit their essence. Racism fills this openness with toxicity, which threatens the vitality of the body. It threatens life, all life.

The sculptured, scarified, and painted body of the African is not an object to be looked at. It is a looking body. It is not the body of an inferior human being. It is not the body of a savage. When it is so construed, it is a ghost, a lifeless body—a human being without a body. One who constructs it in this manner constructs oneself similarly. One renders oneself a ghost, a bodiless soul. One performs a miracle of abandoning one's body. The sculptured and painted African body is a living body, and it is only another living body that can make sense out of it. This making sense is possible because of the blending of living bodies. A living body is not exterior to any other living body. Living bodies constitute one living body. Out of this oneness, understanding of the body is generated. Aesthetics play an important role in this generation. Aesthetics are more than what delights. They constitute us and our world. They bring into relief the truth of our being, and they also bring into relief the truth of the world—two truths that make the appearance of each other possible.

In the effort to understand the aesthetics of the African's body, we are not to imagine something that lies beneath the body sculpture or the body painting. It is unnecessary and misleading to enter a Hegelian path as a means of understanding the aesthetics of the African body. That is, one does not have to inquire into the life of the spirit to see how it aesthetically unfolds in the body of the African. The aesthetics of the African body are native to the body of the African. They are the African's body. To understand its self-manifestation as a sculpture or as a painting, it is not necessary that one go beyond it. Whatever one understands of it is inscribed on its flesh. Moreover, if we bear in mind that the aesthetics of the African body are a manifestation of the logos of the African, we should not be tempted to go into the interior of the African body to get to the essence of what it is to be an African. What is African does not lie concealed in an African body. The African's body is not a container of the African. It is not a possession or a property of the African. The African is his or her body. He or she is to be found in this or that sculptured or painted body. European colonizers, it appears, understood this fact. That is why, to transform the African into a colonial subject, they sought to transform the body of the African. The heathen and savage African body had to be replaced by a civilized body. The sculptured, the painted, and the scarified body had to give way to the unsculptured, unpainted, and unscarified body. To give rise to a new African, a new body had to be generated; the old aesthetics had to give way to new aesthetics—the aesthetics of the precolonial African had to give way to the aesthetics of the colonized Africa, aesthetics imposed on the African by the European. A similar transformation was extended to the New World by Europeans.

In the New World (a creation of Europeans), Africans were not to paint themselves, sculpt, or scarify themselves. They were to cease the practices they carried out "on" their bodies. Enslaved bodies do not belong to slaves. Slaves are cut off from their bodies. They are not their bodies. Their bodies belong to the slave master. A new African body (a Negro or a black body) was to be substituted for the old African body. In the making of a slave out of the African, the African body was destroyed and, in destroying the African body, African aesthetics were destroyed. In their place, the slave body and the slave aesthetics came into being. The African body in the New World was subjected to a brutal and violent attack. It was savaged. It was paralleled by a similar attack in colonial Africa. As long as he or she remained his or her indigenous body, the African could not be enslaved or colonized. Being colonized, like being enslaved, is a corporeal event, an event that generates its own brand of aesthetics—perverted aesthetics. The recovery of Africans aesthetics calls for a restoration or a renaissance of the African body. Understanding of African aesthetics necessitates a dialectical phase—an affirmation of what has been negated, a negation of a negation. This dialectic is worked in the body by the body. The struggle against the aesthetics of the colonized and the enslaved body, against the racialized body, must be waged and won in and on the body. True freedom is the freedom of the body. One cannot be free unless one is corporeally free, for one is what one is by being corporeal. Today, the aesthetics of the African body must be emancipatory aesthetics. If this is not taken into account, aesthetics become a dangerous diversion.

Subjecting the moving, sculptured, and painted African body to a racist regime has distanced the African's body from the African, and it has also distanced the African body from the European body. It is a distancing that has also distanced the European's body from the European, thereby distancing both from the human body. The European has made this distancing into a gospel that is preached throughout the world. The tragedy is that some Africans have embraced this gospel and have joined the missionary crusade to spread it among fellow Africans, thereby reinforcing the alienation of human beings from themselves. Today this alienation is sugarcoated and has generated a distorted aestheticism. It is this aestheticism that reigns in the world body.

In aesthetics, understanding is corporeal, and so is misunderstanding. To understand the corporeal in its aesthetic context is not to add the intellect to the corporeal. It is to yield and be claimed by the corporeal so that the corporeal can stand in relief and come face to face with itself. If it were not the case that Cartesianism has taken hold of many of us, there would be need to stress this point. The African is saved from Cartesianism for, in his eyes, corporeality is not alien to what a human being is. For the African, it is what a human being is. Both understanding and misunderstanding of aesthetics are intracorporeal processes. Corporeal processes can only be understood corporeally. What is corporeal has its own language in which its meaning is inscribed. This meaning is accessible only corporeally. For example, what is audible is understood audibly, what is visible is understood visibly, and what is tactile can be understood in tactility. The corporeal understands itself without the mediation or intervention of the incorporeal. The ability to understand itself in this manner removes it from that abstract corporeal that is the correlate of the mental or the intellectual.

The acknowledgment that understanding and misunderstanding are intracorporeal processes deprives these processes of a pedestal upon which they are placed in some cultures. In the West, for example, it is assumed that there is a faculty independent of the body that understands or misunderstands phenomena—the mind. What is independent of the body cannot understand the body. It inherently remains alienated from the body. The view that the body is to be understood from without is an expression of a particular culture, and it cannot be attributed to all cultures. The body itself—it must not be forgotten—is a cultural construct. This is the case even when the body is understood from the standpoint of science. Science itself is a cultural construct and, consequently, everything that is understood from the point of view of science is inescapably understood from a cultural point of view. Failure to grasp the body in its appropriate cultural context may lead one to impose one's cultural sense of corporeality on others. In this regard, the body of the African has

5 The African Body as an Ethico-aesthetic Site

immeasurably suffered at the hands of Europeans. Europeans have used their own cultural conception of the body as the criterion for judging the conception of the African's body. It is therefore not a surprise that they find the body of the African lacking in what they aesthetically esteem in the European world. The body understands itself without mediation. Generally, in the past, it was held by the bulk of Europeans that all human beings are created in the image of Europeans. It is the internal logic of this belief that all non-European people fall short of being truly human. This belief has a religious undertone. It is a common notion among a substantial number of European believers that human beings are created in the image of God. Since they are white, they appear to reason that God must be white too. That is, God must have a white body. Moreover, since, from their point of view, God is a man, it follows that God is a white man. If it is borne in mind that these believers are monotheists, nonwhite versions of God are heretical, and so are the versions of the nonwhite embodiments of God. For a white person, to paint himself and, hence, become a painting—or to sculpture himself and, hence, become a sculpture—would amount to the subversion of his being, since he is, insofar as he is truly himself, disembodied. For the white person, to be is not to be seen. When the body is sculptured and painted, it focuses attention on itself. It offers itself as a visible phenomenon. It drags the essence of what it is to be human into the body and identifies what is to be human with the body. The religion and orthodox philosophy of the European has not prepared him to accept this. His conception of what he is and the theology that defines what he is do not permit self-expression in terms of painting or sculpture, since these modes of self-expression presuppose a self that is essentially corporeal. The admonition from his God tells him not make a graven image of God. And, evidently, since he is created in the image of God, making a graven image of himself is to betray self-misunderstanding.

The African, in the theology of white people, is the very antithesis of God, an antithesis that is revealed in the heavy concentration of melanin in the African's body. In religious pictorialism, the African has been depicted as Satan—the antithesis of God, for the most part because of the heavy concentration of melanin in his body. It is a part of the theology of white men that man is created in the image of God. But, apparently, it is also a part of their belief that it is only men without melanin who are so created. The discourse on melanin cannot be divorced from racism. We have become increasingly consious of this because of the pressure exerted by racism. To sculpt the body, to paint the body, or to scarify the body is to bring attention to the body and to divert human beings from what they truly are. The white man stresses the spirituality, the invisibility of God. If man is created in the image of God, then he is spiritual; he is invisible. Besides, civilized men and women do not sculpt or paint their bodies; it is the heathens, the primitives, the savages, who do. This conception of God and the conception of man that it yields is alien to the African. In African theology, God is incarnate. If God were not incarnate, he would have no contact with human beings and, conversely, human beings would have no contact with God unless, of course, one assumes that human beings are incorporeal. In African religions, there is no commandment forbidding human beings from making graven images of God. God must assume a bodily form if he is to concern himself with the affairs of human beings. Even the Christian God understood this; he became man/male, perhaps an imperfect man, since he is portrayed by the New Testament writers as a man who is aloof when it comes to bodily pleasures. He was a saintly monk—a naysayer to the body.

If human beings are to concern themselves with divine matters, they can do so only in a bodily manner, for as human beings, they are deprived of any other means of having access to God. The corporeality of human reality is taken for granted in Africa. As indicated previously, it is in the body that the truth of human reality is made manifest. To not see ourselves, to not touch ourselves—in short, to be unable to access ourselves through the senses—is to be unable to access ourselves. Contrary to the protestation of Cartesianists, we sense, therefore we exist; we sense, therefore we are. We are embodied, therefore we are. And because we sense, we are sensuous. Sensing is inalienable from what we are. White men have been lead to believe that there is something sacred about their bodies. The absence of melanin is a symbol of this sacredness. It makes them invisible. It is this perception and interpretation of their bodies that they have sought to impose on all other men. In this theology, men with melanin, especially Africans, are depicted as infinitely removed from God. If, in this theology, God is a perfect expression of beauty, what we have is a theory of aesthetics that equates what is beautiful with what is white. White people construct themsleves as white people and whiteness becomes the locus of their sense of beauty.

White people have had no qualms in construing their own bodies as quintessentially beautiful, as the perfect manifestation of the embodiment of the form of beauty. The white body is, in the reasoning of white people, paradigmatic of beauty. It is the aesthetic standard they have used a measure of beauty of the bodies of other men. Even if the body is construed as the prison of the soul, it is the most beautiful prison. It is a prison that negates itself as a prison. A human being is at home in it, does not seek to escape from it, and cannot escape from it. In the light of this standard—the beautiful white body—the body of the African cannot but appear as ugly. Indeed from the perspective of white people, the body of the African is quintessentially ugly, a perfect embodiment of ugliness. It is the absoluteness of this criterion of beauty that Africans find offensive. It is a racist criterion that has been unleashed by white people in their quest for hegemonism in the aesthetic world. It is a part of the ideological struggle against nonwhite people. Today, it is in the context of this struggle that one is to situate the discourse on the aesthetics of the body of the African. The body is at the center of the basic conflict between Africans and white people, and the aesthetics of the African body is integral to this conflict. What the white people find horrifying and ugly about the African body is not the anatomy or the physiognomy of the African body, or the apparent abuse to which Africans subject their bodies. It is primarily due to the conception and the interpretation they attach to the physiognomy and the heavy concentration of melanin in the body of the African, an interpretation that is predicated on the interpretation they attach to their own bodies. Because what is at issue is interpretation, or differently stated, since what we have is a conflict in interpretation, it is in vain that we resort to genetics or to biology generally to account for bodily differences. The resolution, if there is one, can be found only in the consciousness that we have of our bodies. Neither the presence nor the absence of melanin can explain any of the attitudes we have toward our bodies. The meaning that we attach to the presence of absence is not inherent in our genes. It is a construct generated by the cultures in which we dwell. Our bodies inhabit the cultures in which we live. Our cultures are not patinas on our bodies or outer clothing on our bodies. Our bodies are thoroughly cultural. It is only from the perspective of the biocultural that we can fully understand our embodiment. The markings on the African body are cultural signifiers. They are not, and are not perceived by Africans as, deformations of the body. The African does not see himself as a receptacle of melanin. As a lived body, his body is melanin free. When he paints his or her own body, it is not a black thing that he or she is painting. It is not a thing that is being painted. It is the self that is being painted. It is self-painting itself.

What is projected as perverse and absurd by a white person is rendered possible by the African. The African can be a painting or a sculpture because both his anthropology and his theology make this possible. His body expresses his essence, as well as his theology. His gods manifest themselves to him in a bodily manner. He has no qualms in giving them food or drink, particularly the food and the drink that he himself uses. He speaks to them, and they speak to him. Speech is possible because the speaker and those spoken to are corporeal. If gods did not have bodies, to speak to them or to expect them to speak to human beings would be absurd. To speak of a speaking disembodied being is to utter nonsense. We must also bear in mind that the body is neither a human persona nor a divine persona. A human body is not an outer garment that clothes what is human. It is absolutely and exhaustively the human. It has no interiority where anything could dwell. Accordingly, it cannot be the temple of the lord or the sacred vessel of the lord. There is no room in the human body for anything, not even for a spirit. The body is the human and the human is the body. It is from this standpoint of the human body that one is to approach the logos of the African body.

The intertwining of understanding and misunderstanding has its locus in the body. It is the way in which the body makes itself manifest. In so saying, there is no intention to rob the mind of what is exclusively germane to it. Understanding and misunderstanding are not the exclusive domains of the mind. Such exclusivity robs the body of its essential mode of being and attributes to the mind an erroneous mode of being. It is not hereby suggested that there is a division of labor whereby mind and body have their respective spheres of understanding and misunderstanding. There is only one sphere, the human sphere—a unitary sphere that is irreducible to either mind, body, or the total of the two of them. A human body is therefore not separate from the mind or a conduit to the mind. To be sure, this view may be embedded in this or that culture. It is another thing to say that this is a view that is shared universally by all human cultures. What we have in the African is an alternative view of human body expression, a view in which the body is an understanding body. The African body that understands and that, at the same time, misunderstands is not the proverbial body that is posited in opposition to the mind. It is an elemental body. It is a body that exists in its own right, a body that does not require the mind to be what it is. It is a body that claims the whole of what it is to be a human. The human body carries the entire weight of what it is to be a human being. It is this body that manifests the intertwining of understanding and misunderstanding. The human body, a bearer of an ambiguous mode of being, is subject to diverse and conflicting perceptions and understanding, while it is itself responsible for generating diverse and conflicting perceptions and understanding.

In some cultural traditions, the aesthetic relation is such that the body is construed as intentional. The body is directed to aesthetic objects that are other than itself. In fine arts, these objects are created by the body and, consequently, in aesthetic contemplation, the body comes face to face with its own creation as something that has an autonomous existence. The body is mediated by what it creates, and what it creates acquires a right to exist on its own but not in opposition to it. The body creates itself in what it creates. What it creates is not an object that stands in opposition to it. Because the body has kinship with the material it uses for creation, and because it mediates the creation of an aesthetic object, the body retains a degree of intimacy with the material that enters into the constitution of the aesthetic object, as well as the aesthetic object. Perhaps, it is more correct to say that the aesthetic body makes a mockery of the subject–object distinction. The aesthetic object is an abstraction. Merleau-Ponty noted this intimacy. He says:

> Visible and mobile my body is a thing among other things; it is caught up in the fabric of the world, and its cohesion is that of a thing. But because it moves itself and sees it holds things in a circle around itself. Things are an annex or prolongation of itself; they are encrusted in its flesh, they are a part of its full definition, the world is made of the same stuff as the body. This way of turning things around (*ces renversements*), these autonomies are different ways of saying that vision happens among, or is caught in things—in that place where something visible undertakes to see, becomes visible for itself by virtue of the sight of things, in that place where there persists like the mother water in the crystal, the undividedness (*l'indivision*) of the sensing and the sensed.[47]

In Africa, intimacy is more radicalized. We find out that in the African aesthetics of the body, the body does not stand at a distance from itself. The body itself is the material from which it fashions the aesthetic object, and it is itself the aesthetic object. The body is directed to itself as an aesthetic object while, in so doing, it nullifies itself as an object. The body is conscious of itself as a sculpture, as a painting, and the attempt to understanding a sculpture or a painting is fundamentally an attempt to understand the body. This is the body that we want to understand, and we want it to understand it in the very manner in which it presents itself to us. In sensing, the body senses itself, for it belongs to the sensible. Hence, the body seeks to understand itself when it seeks to understand the sensible. It is a body that stands in violation of the subject–object duality—a body that is subject and object, at the same time, while not being one or the other.

It is worth noting that in the West, the painter paints on a canvas or on something that is other than his body. He uses his body as an instrument of painting, but the body itself is not what is to be painted. Even when the body is painted, it is always painted on something else. The African, on the other hand, not only paints on what is other than his body but also paints his body. The African body paints itself on itself. The African paints himself on himself. Similarly, when a Westerner sculpts, he sculpts what is other than his body, other than himself. He uses the body as a tool of sculpting, but this tool does not use itself on itself to sculpt itself. The Westerner does not sculpt his own body. The African sculpts not only what is other than himself. He sculpts himself by sculpting his own body. His body is a self-sculpting body. For the Westerner, painting and sculpting are ways of self-estrangement. For the African, painting and sculpting are ways of being at home in Africanness, ways of projecting the African's ways of being at home in his Africanness. The projector and what is projected are one and the same. That one can work on one's body and subject one's body to what in other cultures is subjected to what is other than one's body is what we learn from Africans. Africans present to us a self-creating body of the African, that body that paints and sculpts and scarifies itself.

Perhaps, under the influence of modern Western understanding of art, what African artists produce today represents Africans who are alienated from themselves. Being estranged from themselves is what is portrayed in their works. Their works are works of self-estrangement—works that are a flight from their bodies. They appear on paper to embrace the view that getting too corporeally intimate with their work is a sign of "permittivity," a sign of "savagery." They want to produce "civilized" works—works that can be consumed by "civilized" people. They want to be "civilized" and join the company of the "civilized." To be sure, they refer to their works as works of self-expression. The self that is expressed, however, is a disembodied self. They have abandoned the African body as a site for the expression of the African self.

What manner of aesthetics are generated by such a body? Aesthetics that appear to affirm themselves at the expense of the body? Aesthetics that appear to thrive on disfiguration of the body? What manner of body is generated by these aesthetics? How can a human being find joy in the disfiguration of the body? Joy in self-nullification? Self-identity in self-disfiguration? An intentional self-infliction of pain as an aesthetic creative act? How could human beings create and preserve beauty at the expense of the body? Perverted aesthetics? Anti-body bodiliness?

The historic man of Europe has spoken about this matter. In the light of his speech, what we have in Africa are the aesthetics of a developing region of the world, a region where the aesthetics are yet to catch up with the aesthetics in developed regions of the world, where the aesthetics are underdeveloped or in the early stages of development, where the aesthetics are in their infancy. But this is a recent statement in the discourse on aesthetics by the man of Europe. Formerly, it was his view that the body spectacle that is the locus of African aesthetics was nothing but savagery at its zenith. The African body spectacle manifests not art, not aesthetics but the depraved mentality of the savage mind, the mind of man who is not yet man. The African body, it appears to the white man of Europe, is the bearer of this pre- or anti-man. But for whom does the white man speak?

Hitherto, the man from Europe has conferred on himself the right and the authority to speak on behalf of all human beings. He has imposed, or has sought to impose, on the entire world the regime of his version of what art and aesthetics are. He cannot be speaking for the African, for the African has not conferred on him the right or the authority to speak on his behalf. The European man speaks for himself, and he speaks to himself. His speech is a monologue, but a monologue that mistakes itself for a dialogue. In the speech of the white man, the African is silent, provocatively silent. The silence of the African in the speech of the European man is perpetually pregnant with speech. In the speech of the African, the white man is deaf, his ears sedimented with a patina of deafness. When, for centuries, one has learned not to listen to others, one becomes deaf and if, in these circumstances, one hears, one hears only oneself—perhaps a sign of man who has gone mad. When, for centuries, one has learned not to be heard, one ceases to be heard, though this does not prevent one from believing that one is heard. One only hears being unheard without recognizing what one hears as such. One hears the echo of oneself even though one believes that one hears the voice of others. Hearing is not simply a physiological process. A physio-naturalistic account of hearing is an incomplete account of hearing. For a human being to hear is to hear culturally. Human beings have cultural ears, and it is in the context of culture that they hear. Human audiology is cultural and, given the diversity of human culture, human audiology is, accordingly, culturally diversified. Speech, as that which is destined for hearing, is itself is inherently cultural. Thus when it is claimed that the European man is a victim of his monologue and that when he hears, he hears only himself, we are to understand that this monologue is a cultural phenomenon. The European man has generated and sustains a self-enclosed culture that effectively cuts him off from a meaningful dialogue with those who are not white. He is imprisoned in his culture. This imprisonment is a landmark in the history of his civilization. It is one of his major achievements.

The European man's aesthetics are incorporated into his speech. That is, he has incorporated his speech. This incorporation is exclusionary. It engages the speech of the African—and, accordingly, the aesthetics of the African—negatively. The autochthonous speech of the African is excluded and, with this exclusion, the aesthetics of the African are excluded. The exclusion, moreover, is not a mere setting aside. It is a setting aside that is a degradation, a disparagement of the African and of whatever is African. It is a degradation and a disparagement of the African body and of what it signifies. The white man has his art, his aesthetics, and the African has his aesthetics, his art. Between the two aesthetics, the two arts, there exists a deep fissure, which reverberates in the discourses on either side. The fissure is a constant reminder of the difficulty and perhaps the present futility of a common discourse on art and aesthetics between the African and the white man. The possibility for the discourse appears to be obscured by the fact that African art and African aesthetics exist exclusively for the African, and the white man's art and aesthetics exist exclusively for the white man.

The European man's view of African art and its attendant aesthetics is not the African's view, and nor is the view that he has of his own art and aesthetics. Likewise, the African's view of his art and its attendant aesthetics is not the white man's view, and nor is his view of the white man's art and its attendant aesthetics the white man's view. If the difference in the views appears exaggerated, it is, perhaps primarily because the white man's universe of discourse on art and aesthetics does not allow for moderation. The European man suffers from an exaggerated self-worth, from self-valorization. He has so disguised himself with his version of beauty that it

5 The African Body as an Ethico-aesthetic Site

is difficult to decipher what he really is. His art is driven by an insatiable craving for self-beautification at the expense of non-whites. If he stands in this need for self-beautification, he must have seen a fundamental lack of beauty in his being that he needs to eradicate. He attempts to meet this need by affirming the superiority of the beauty of his being over the beauty of all other human beings. It is difficult to exercise moderation in combating this superiority. The real test is how to combat it without falling prey to what one is combating, an ever present danger for the African combatant. Although the other is different from me, and I am different from the other, the other is not a negation of what I am, and I am not the negation of the other. Racism compels us to deny this mode of being, this mode of interpreting difference. It compels us to deny non-conflicting difference.

The rest of the human beings have grown weary, or are growing weary, of aesthetics that are rigged in favor of the white man. They can no longer bear the unbearable monologue and the weight of the conceit or the stupidity of the white man's regime of aesthetics. The rest of the world is weary of body snatchers, weary of those who disembody others and impose their own conception of body as a replacement, weary of those who cannibalize the bodies of others to fatten their own bodies, weary of human vampires. The body of the European man is like a tick. It nourishes itself, fattens itself by bloodsucking the bodies of those who are not white. Its beauty is relational. It is largely beautiful only to the extent that it uglifies the body of those who are not white. Its aesthetics are parasitic. In part, its aesthetics are derived from the negation of the aesthetics of the non-European bodies. The negation of the aesthetics of the others is, at the same time, the negation of the body of the other. In the racist universe that has been constructed by the European man, the beauty of the white man's body is affirmed at the expense of the beauty of the bodies of others.

To disembody is not simply to take away the body of the other; it is not to relieve the other of his or her body. It is to deprive the other of his or her being. It is to liquidate the other as the other. To be disembodied is to be deprived of one's being. The replacement of the body is the replacement of being. One is one's body, and once one's body is taken away, one is taken away. In the extreme case, one assists one's disembodiment, in one's estrangement from oneself. What is human abhors a body vacuum. It is not possible to live without a body. Thus disembodiment is attended by re-embodiment. The body of the African is taken away from the African, only to be replaced by another body. The replacing body is an imitation of the body of the body snatcher. In the case of the African, the replacing body is an imitation of the white man's body.

Since what the African does with his or her body is intentional, this doing presupposes an elemental body, a unformed body, a *tabula rasa*—that body that is what it is by being nothing. This expression of self-consciousness is not foreign in the West. Speaking of man ("the for-itself"), Jean-Paul Sartre reminds us:

> The for-itself is the being which is to itself its own lack of being. The being which the for-itself lacks is the in-itself. The for-itself arises as the nihilation of the in-itself and this nihilation is defined as the project toward the in-itself. Between the nihilated in-itself and the projected in-itself, the for-itself is nothingness.[48]

It is out of the nothingness that we are that the African sculptures and paints his or her body. The aesthetic body that comes into relief come from it, and to understand it is to take us to its origin. It does not eternally freeze the African into the aesthetic form that it takes, although it is to this freezing that the racist West has sought to subject the African. That an African does not sharpen his teeth, that he or she does not scarify his or her body, or that he or she does not paint his or her body should not be taken as an indication that the African has ceased to be African. Being African is the possibility of being African. There are many ways of being African, or let us put it this way: being African is synonymous with becoming African. One is never African. The body that is the African is thoroughly historical; that is, it is thoroughly temporal. It is in the context of this becoming, body becoming, that all human beings encounter one another and consummate being human. It is precisely nothingness in motion that preserves us in the kinship that we have with one another. It is this nothingness that is embodied in the African and in every other human being. I am your body, and you are my body. It does not matter whether one is African or non-African, female or male. But in a world where racism and sexism are rampant, it matters. The point is not to pretend that there are no differences among us. To exist is to be differentiated. The point is to rid ourselves of those constructed differences that are dehumanizing and see ourselves in the mobile reinforcing differences. Moreover, whatever differentiates us is problematic. It constantly undermines itself. There is no difference that is static. Because of the problematic nature of what is understood, understanding itself is problematic. Understanding is mobile, and it is only as such that it understands. What is understood is understood in its mobility. It is in this context that the body distinguishes itself. It constantly loses its own insubstantial identity by taking up predications and, simultaneously, it surfaces in its substantiality, not as anything to which these predications apply, but as that which exhausts what it is by perennially availing itself of formations, reformations, and counterformations.

Frantz Fanon has pointed out that colonialism has forced the African to ask himself or herself, "Who am I in reality?"[49] The question has a corporeal anchorage, and nowhere is this question more real than it is in racism. Racism prevents the African from fleeing his or her false corporeality. The question forces the Africa to come face to face with himself or herself as an embodied being and, at the same time, forces him or her to come face to face with the futility of fleeing this embodiment. To affirm himself or herself calls for a radical erasure of the negativity to which his or her body has been subjected. In calling attention to the inevitable question that the African must raise, colonialism has also given rise to an inevitable question that the colonizer must raise: "Who am I in reality?" As is the case with the African, this question has a corporeal anchorage in the colonizer. The colonizer must come face to face with his or her own embodiment. In this embodiment, the colonizer has overvalued and distorted the value of his or her own body. He or she has robbed it of its human value—the value it shares with the African and all other human beings. This self-inflicted robbery—a robbery that, in part, thrives at the expense of the African's body—is precisely the robbery that is inevitably disclosed by the struggle to affirm the human dignity of the African body. The struggle the African wages

5 The African Body as an Ethico-aesthetic Site

against racism is a struggle for the affirmation of the dignity of the human body. It is a struggle that Europeans must wage if they are to affirm the dignity of their own bodies, if they are to affirm the dignity incarnate in their bodies. Moreover, no human being is an outsider to this struggle. We are all in it, for it is the struggle for our dignity. Our dignity is corporeally indivisible.

Ahead of us, lies the human body—a body that is to be constituted by all human beings—a body that stands for the unity of all human bodies in their diversity. This is the body that we have been all along and it is the body that we are. Racism has been a major obstacle in the emergence of such a body. A genuine African philosophy illuminates the emergence of this body and does so in conjunction with other genuine philosophical illuminations. Racism blocks the understanding that human body has a tomorrow and the day after tomorrow. This is the drama of the African body—a drama in which all human beings are actors.

Chapter 6
Seeing: An African Way

—Le Noble Savage by Wangechi Mutu

Rise up but do not forget where you are rising from. Where you rise from to determines and continues to determine who and what you are and will forever continue to do so. The shrub is a part of who and what you are. It surrounds you and you surround it. It is you. You are in it and it is in you. You are of it. Its roots are your roots. Its branches are the branches of your being. Its soil is the soil of your being. Learn how to see it and yu a will learn not only how to see yourself but also how to see everything else Even what is not seen is the other side of what is seen. Both sides penetrate each other. (You and the shrub)

Why qualify the way of seeing? Are we doing justice to seeing when it is qualified? Doesn't the qualification of the way of seeing undermine the universal way of seeing and thus deprive it of its essential nature? Evidently, the qualification of seeing suggests that there are multiples ways of seeing, and an African way of seeing is but one among other possible ways. This suggestion should be taken for what it is—namely, a suggestion. As such, it could be erroneous if it turns out that seeing is seeing without qualification. So, how is it with seeing? More specifically, what is African about seeing?

A long time ago, in an African village, there was a conversation between an African and a European tourist. After introducing himself, the tourist asked the African, "How are you?" The African responded, "Not so well." The tourist then asked, "Have you seen a doctor?" The African responded, "No, I have not seen one, and I do not intend to see one. There is a European doctor in our village who runs a dispensary, and I do not want to go there." "Why?" the tourist asked. The African said, "I do not believe in the diagnosis he makes or the cure he provides." The tourist responded, "What difference does it make if he is able to make you feel better?" The African responded, "He cannot make me feel better, and he will not make me feel better. He may even make feel worse." The tourist asked, "Why don't you go ahead and consult an African doctor?" The African said, "There is one in my village but, because he has been trained in European medicine, he is not likely to conduct a proper diagnosis or provide me with proper medicine." "And how do you know that?" asked the tourist. The African answered, "I just know." "What do you mean when you say 'I just know'?" asked the tourist. The African responded, "A man must doctor himself to know what ails him and know how to cure himself." The tourist said, "I take it then that you know not only why you are not feeling well but also how to cure yourself, how to make yourself feel better." "Precisely," said the African. "In matters of diagnosis and therapy, self-knowledge is required. One cannot diagnose an African patient without being an African." "And who is an African?" the tourist asked. "This I cannot tell you," said the African, "for it takes one to know one. But what I can tell you generally is that one is an African because of where one lives and how one lives. You yourself are what you are by where you live and how you live. Earlier, if you recall, I informed you that I am not well. I do not know whether you understood what I meant, or whether you can understand what I mean. Not being well is more than not being well for an isolated individual. When my children are not well, I am not well. When their mother is not well, I am not well and they are not well. When my relatives and friends are not well, I am not well. When neighbors are not well, I am not well. When my chickens, my goats, my sheep, my camels, or my cattle are not well, I am not well. When it does not rain and I cannot plant my food crops, or when they wither and dry up for lack of rain, I am not well. When the well and the river dry up, I am not well. When the environment in which I live is not well, I am not well. For me, to feel better, my environment must feel better. If I need to take medicine to make me feel better, it is environmental medicine that I need. You do not see the environment the way I see it. You think like a European. I have yet to meet a European doctor who understands this kind of medicine. An African who has not abandoned his or her African roots understands this

6 Seeing: An African Way

and sees what I see. He is the kind of a doctor that I need. A European sees such a doctor as medically ignorant, as superstitious, or as a witchdoctor. He does not live in my environment. He is not a part of my environment. He does not see the way I see myself and, obviously, I do not see him the way he sees himself. Medical education has everything to do with environmental education, everything to do with how one sees oneself in relation to one's environment. Medical science is an environmental science. Let us see whether we can see each other. What is evident is that between us, seeing is a problem that calls for a solution. I appreciate your visit but, honestly, I do not know how to welcome you in our village. If you are to be properly welcomed, it is the environment that has to welcome you."

I heard this story from an elder in my village when I was a small boy. This story has been formative of my philosophical consciousness, and it is what inspires what I want say about the African seeing of seeing. Seeing is deeply rooted in one's cultural tradition. This is true of one's seeing whether it is or it is not philosophical. Moreover, it must be understood that one's cultural tradition is a living tradition. Its boundaries are perennially open, and so is the seeing that is expressed in and by it. Seeing is open seeing. What lives, lives in that it is open.

It is tempting to determine what seeing is by listening to what we are told by the biology of the eye, or by the physiology of the eye—in short, by turning to biophysical science. However, a scientific account of seeing or a scientific account of the eye may be but one account among other accounts. To be sure, scientists may raise their eyebrows if a suggestion is made that science does not have a monopoly on the account of seeing or that it does not have sole custody of the disclosure of what the seeing of seeing is. They are likely to garner support throughout the world since, today, scientism has become a planetary religion for many of us. Many of us have adopted a dogmatic attitude toward science. We turn to it in the way some believers turn to Judaism, Christianity, Islam, Buddhism, Hinduism, or any other religion. There is little room for atheism or for skepticism in this religion, despite the claim that scientific accounts of truth are more or less probable and that science does not claim to possess absolute truth. One may reject the absoluteness of a particular scientific truth but, apparently, the truth of the scientific truth itself is unassailable. Any nonscientific account is likely to be dismissed by devotees of scientism as a product of ignorance or as superstition. The frenzy generated by science has led us astray and has driven us from what seeing itself calls for, and from the authority of seeing generated by seeing itself, under which we ought to take our bearing if we are to see seeing in its elemental sense.

The way of seeing seeing in Africa has fallen prey to the aggrandizement of seeing that scientism promotes globally and also to the aggrandizement that has also been generated by some non-African ways of seeing. Seeing seeing in an African way is intended to provide resistance to this aggrandizement and to open a broader possibility of seeing seeing. This broader possibility does not seek to get rid of the seeing that is promoted by science. Seeing seeing in an African way is not an antiscientific way of seeing. It recognizes and affirms the way of seeing promoted by science as long as the way is not seen as the only way of seeing. What the African seeing of seeing does is contribute to the liberation of seeing from the overreach of the scientific way of seeing and from the overreach of any other way of seeing. The above painting by Wangechi Mutu illuminates this seeing. It is an instance of an African way of seeing seeing.[40] It is, at the same time, a seeing that has a universal reach. More powerful than the way of seeing that is promoted by science or by any other narrow instance of seeing, it illuminates the site of the seeing of seeing itself and invites us to be active seers in the seeing of seeing. All instances of seeing draw their inspiration from the seeing of seeing and, ultimately, it is this seeing that each of them serves. They can truly be what they are if they are, and remain, open to one another. Accordingly, there is what is singularly African in Mutu's painting, and there is also what is universal about it. It is the seeing of seeing that directs her hand as she paints. Her paintbrush enables us to see seeing. It paints seeing and calls attention to what painting is. Mutu, as is the case with any other essential painter, teaches us how to see. Painting is a way of seeing the world.

Painting is a way of seeing—a seeing that, at the same time, sees the seer in seeing—a seeing that is creatively recursive. In its elemental sense, painting is a seeing. It teaches us not only how to see but also how to see ourselves in seeing. It is unfortunate that, for many of us, painting produces paintings. It is normally anticipated that it will produce objects destined for a gallery, a museum, a private collection, or the commercial world, in which they exist as objects for commerce. On occasion, they are referred to as art objects. Apparently, painting exhausts itself in the process of producing these art objects. Viewed this way, the elemental nature of painting is concealed. The elemental nature of painting lies in illuminating itself and, in this way, it illuminates illuminations. It is a seeing. To paint is to invoke seeing. A painter is summoned by seeing, and what he or she produces is a response to this summons and is guided by seeing. Mutu shares with us her response to this summons. We respond to her painting in the light of what inspires her. What inspires her is the same as what ought to inspire us in the presence of her painting. We see her in her painting and, at the same time, we see ourselves in her painting. In painting herself, she paints us. She is painted in her painting, and we are painted in it. What paints her is what paints us.

As is the case with every other way of seeing, an African way is what it is by being seen as it sees. How it is seen is contextual even if it is also the case that contextuality is not self-enclosed. Every context has a past and a future. It is a present that is pregnant with these temporal, spatial, and historical ecstasies. In part, how the African way of seeing is seen today is a product of the modern European way of seeing African seeing. The landscape of African seeing has been colonized. That is, it is a seeing that was produced during the enslavement and colonization of Africans by Europeans. What these oppressive processes have produced is a way of seeing Africans and a way of seeing African seeing. The African who has been produced is the antithesis of the native African, and the African way of seeing that has been produced is a seeing that is antithetical to the native African way of seeing. Moreover, the seeing that Europeans have associated with the African is a seeing that is antithetical to the seeing that Europeans have associated with themselves. Georg Hegel, a German philosopher, wrote a historic exposure of this contrast. On behalf of fellow Europeans and, presumptively, on behalf of humanity, he notes:

6 Seeing: An African Way

> The Negro, as already observed, exhibits the natural man in his completely wild and untamed state. We must lay aside all thought of reverence and morality—all that we call feeling—if we would rightly comprehend him; there is nothing harmonious with humanity to be found in this type of character.[41]

He further says:

> In Africa proper, man has not progressed beyond the merely sensuous existence, and has found it absolutely impossible to develop further. Physically, he exhibits great muscular strength, which enables him to perform arduous labours: and his temperament is characterized by good-naturedness which is coupled, however, with completely unfeeling cruelty.[42]

He also claims that:

> After the creation of the natural universe, man appears on the scene as the antithesis of nature; he is the being who raises himself up into a second world. The general consciousness of man includes two distinct provinces, that of nature and that of spirit. The province of the spirit is created by man himself; and whatever ideas we may form of the kingdom of God, it must always remain as a spiritual kingdom which is realized by man and in which man is expected to translate into actuality.[43]

The obvious point Hegel makes here is that the African is exhaustively a sensuous being and is inseparable from the sensuous nature. It is the way to see the African and, apparently, it is the way that the African ought to see himself if he had human eyes to see himself. It is apparent to Hegel that the African way of seeing is not a human way. Where there is no human, there is no human seeing. It is only human beings who can see the way human beings see.

In the light of Hegelian seeing, Mutu's painting may serve as an illustration of the condition of the African. Hegelian seeing would see an African who is yet to emerge from nature—an African in the jungle as a part of the jungle, as an uncivilized wild being. According to Hegel, what comes closer to human seeing in Africa is the seeing that he associates with Egyptians. He says:

> Egypt confronts our soul at the outset with the image of the sphinx like how dragons, centaurs, and giants generally call to mind the East; distorted shapes are as such the rule in the Orient. The symbol of sphinx, however, is this twofold figure, half animal and half human, and indeed female. It symbolizes the human spirit that tears itself away from the animal domain, that frees itself form the animal and casts its gaze about but has not yet completely grasped itself, is not yet free does not yet stand on its own two feet.[44]

Hegel's interpretation of the sphinx illustrates the way he sees and understands what a human being is. For him, the head represents what a human being is. Its emergence from nature sets man free from nature so that he can be himself. The freedom of the head to turn around and see what is to be seen distinguishes a human being as a human being. What is below the head does not truly matter in the determination of the essence of a human being. The feet of man that enable him to stand, as is the case with the rest of the body, do not bear an essential relation to what a human being is. The head may appear sensuous or physical, but this appearance is misleading, since the head of a human being is ultimately spiritual. A mere physical thing cannot be free. According to Hegel, the head is to be taken as the mind, since it is only the mind that can truly be free. To be human is to turn away from the body, from what is physical, from animality, and from nature. The ontological problem with the Egyptian is that he is yet to fully cut the fetters that bind him to what is physical, what is animal, and what is natural. However, his status is far superior to the ontological status of the African proper since, in the African, the head is yet to emerge. The African's head is stuck in the physical, in the animal, and in nature. It is not even recognizable as a human head, since the humanity of the African is yet to emerge.

For Hegel, Egypt is not to be seen as a part of Africa proper, and Egyptians are not to be seen as real Africans. The northern part of African is not a part of true Africa. As he sees it, Africa proper lies south of Egypt, which late European modernity refers to as Africa south of the Sahara. This is the true homeland of Africans or the true home of Negroes—a term he uses to refer to Africans. These Negroes show no sign of humanity. Here, there is no half-animal, half-human figure to be seen such as is seen in Egypt or elsewhere. What is human has yet to show itself among Negroes. Negroes are seen and projected as prehuman or as extrahuman. Outside Egypt, the rest of Africa is a jungle inhabited by Negroes and, as jungle inhabitants, they share their jungle identity with other jungle inhabitants, such as animals. They are inhabitants of the proverbial Dark Continent. They reside in the Heart of Darkness—the way the continent was seen and projected by Joseph Conrad and by other European architects of how Africa was to be seen.[45] This way of seeing Africa and her indigenous inhabitants was broadcasted throughout the world. Today, for the most part, the way Africa is seen and the way Africans are seen in most of the world is through the mediation of European seeing. Likewise, an African way of seeing is largely mediated by the European way of seeing. To see it is to see it the way that Europeans see it. This European way of seeing the African way of seeing has been spread throughout the world. Europeans took the imperialist and racist seeing of African seeing to Asia and to the "New World," and sought to institutionalize a negative way of seeing African seeing. Africans have an unenviable task of negating this negativity to make it possible for the indigenous peoples in these territories to see African seeing from the standpoint of African seeing. These indigenous peoples also have an unenviable task of ensuring that their own seeing is freed from a distorted seeing of African seeing.

As Hegel notes, Egyptians were not the only people who had a figure that was half human and half animal. In his way of seeing, such a figure, however, is not to be found anywhere among Negroes. Since, for him, the existence of such a figure symbolizes a people who have torn themselves away from the animal domain, Africans have yet to tear themselves away from the animal domain. Hegel does not give us hope that this will indeed happen. Negroes appear stuck in the animal domain. Because Negroes are stuck in it, they have no consciousness of themselves as human beings. Their seeing is not human seeing. It is indistinguishable from animal seeing. Moreover, since they cannot recognize themselves as human, they cannot recognize the humanness of others. It also appears to follow that, since they are not conscious of themselves as human, they lack moral consciousness and cannot expect to be treated morally, and they cannot be expected to treat those who are human in a moral way. They are to be treated the way that animals are to be treated.

And one cannot expect them to treat each other morally. In short, they are savages, mere brutes. They have to be seen this way. Morality is rooted in human seeing. If one does not see the other as moral, one will be amoral in the treatment of the other. In Hegelian reasoning, it appears clear that, among Negroes, there are no ethics and there is no moral philosophy. As nonhumans or prehumans, it is absurd to associate them with philosophy. Since ethics and morality are matters of reason, and Africans are devoid of reason, ethics and morality have no place in their lives. Africans are confined to the domain of animals—a domain that is without ethics or morality. As Hegel tells us:

> The Negroes indulge, therefore, in that *contempt* for humanity which in its bearing on Justice and Morality is the fundamental characteristic of the race—The undervaluing of humanity among them reaches an incredible degree of intensity. Tyranny is regarded as no wrong and cannibalism is looked upon as quite customary and proper.[46]

In Hegel's way of seeing, it is not until beings tear themselves away from the animal domain that they can truly become human. Such tearing endows human beings with their true identity—an identity that principally consists of freedom. That is, in his eyes, to be human and to be free are one and the same. Hegel claims that:

> The Germanic nations were the first to come to the consciousness through Christianity, that the human being as human is free; that the freedom of the spirit constitutes humanity's truly inherent nature. This consciousness first arose in religion, in the innermost region of the spirit; but to incorporate tis principle into secular existence was a further task whose solution and application would require a long and arduous labor on the part of culture.[47]

Possession of freedom and consciousness of this freedom enable human beings to tear themselves away from the animal domain and enable them to truly assert themselves as human beings. The way Hegel sees it, the Germanic nations achieve this historic mode of being through the mediation of Christianity. That is, Christianity was instrumental to the humanization of the Germanic nations and provided evidence that they had attained full humanness. Being Christian provided evidence that they had truly become human. Apparently, in his eyes, among all nations, the German nations were the first in human history to truly become conscious of, and to embody, a human identity and the first to inaugurate true human history. Others nations were prehistorical or ahistorical. Since the movement from the animal domain to the human domain was facilitated by Christianity, Negroes could not make the transition to the human domain, because they were heathens or infidels. This mode of being prevented them from being human and from seeing the way that human beings see. If there was any hope for them to make the transition, it was through conversion to Christianity. This was the primary purpose of the European Missionary Project in Africa. The goal was not solely or primarily to convert Africans to Christianity. It was to humanize them. It was to get the animal out of the African and replace it with the human. It was to get the jungle out of the African, or to get savagery out of him, and open space for the emergence of the human. It was an attempt to revolutionize seeing so that Africans could participate in human seeing. It would enable Africans to see themselves as human and to see the humanness of other human beings.

If being Christian marks the transition from the domain of the animal to the domain of man, would it not make sense to see pre-Christian Europe as a heathen land inhabited by heathens and savages? Where in the annals of European history does one read about the existence of such a Europe or the existence of such Europeans? Moreover, assuming that there is such information, why must Africans see pre-Christian Africa the way Europeans see pre-Christian Europe, and if pre-Christian Europeans saw themselves as heathens or as savages, why should pre-Christian Africans or other pre-Christian peoples see themselves as heathens or as savages? Before the advent of Christianity, where is the evidence that Africans or other non-Europeans peoples saw themselves as prehuman? These questions compel one to pay more attention to what being human calls for and to what human seeing of the human calls for. They are more than vacuous interrogatives. If Hegel and fellow Europeans believe that man has evolved from the animal domain, it should not be assumed that non-Europeans share this belief. Even among Europeans, one cannot rule out the existence of atheists. Friedrich Nietzsche readily comes to mind.[48] European humanism is one among other humanisms. It should not be seen as paradigmatic of humanism. What is paradigmatic is constituted and illuminated in all human beings. There is a humanism that is implicit in all humanisms to make them human.

Central to the Christian faith is the belief that man is created in the image of God—the image of the Christian God, who for Christians is the only true God. This God is disembodied. He does not have a body. He is incorporeal. If His being is the being in whose image man is created, true man is disembodied. True man is without the body. Moreover, since, in this doctrine of creation, the animal is not created in the image of God, animal and man are distinct from each other, and a man who is fully conscious of his humanity is conscious of himself as severed from, and other than, the animal. He has to see himself this way and has to see the animal the way it ought to be seen: as an animal. The God of the Christians and the human that this God has created are beyond what an African can comprehend, according to Hegel. In part, this belief is a product of Hegel's imagination, and it should not be assumed that other human beings share this belief. Imagination is a way of seeing and, contrary to what Hegel may believe, imagination is multiple, and so are ways of seeing.

In Hegel's notion of the hierarchy of being, a human being stands apart and higher than an animal. The animal is on the lower domain of being. Possession of reason defines the level of being that defines being human. Hegel shares this belief with fellow Europeans. Because animals do not share this mode of being, they are not rational. One sees the triumph of the claim that man is a rational animal. Possession of reason provides evidence that man has severed ties with the animal. Zealousness in being rational has led many in the West to relegate the animal part of being human to the background. In the West, there has been a historical amnesia regarding this part of man. The animal part has been left behind. To the extent that it cannot be permanently left behind, it has been subject to repression. Modern European history is a history of the repression of the animal part of man. Christianity has played a major role in securing and furthering this repression and amnesia, and pressures Africans and other non-Westerners to follow suit.

As was clearly recognized by Sigmund Freud, Western civilization in general has held the animal part of being human hostage. It is indeed true that Europeans are not the inventors of the view that man is a rational animal. It is a view that is traceable to the Greeks and more specifically to Aristotle. If one pays closer attention to the fact that the Greeks were not Europeans, one cannot assume that Europeans understand this view the way it was understood by the Greeks. As Shusaku Endo, a Japanese thinker, observed in reaction to the Christian missionary activity in Japan:

> A tree that flourishes in one kind of soil may wither if the soil is changed. As for the tree of Christianity, in a foreign country its leaves may grow thick and the buds may be rich, while in Japan the leaves wither and no bud appears. Father, have you never thought of the difference in the soil, the difference in the water?[49]

The West has a Christian appropriation of rationality, and the soil in which, and on which, this appropriation has taken pace is radically different from the Greek soil. It is a Western Christian soil. The Christianized Western notion of rationality has played a major role in the tearing away of the human from the animal. In the West, rationality has been embraced fanatically, and so has the attempt to flee animality. This fanaticism has taken on a universal scope and is at the heart of Western culture. It is an unparalleled global force that seeks to destroy any obstacle that stands in its way. Speaking on behalf of his Western culture, Giorgio Agamben pointed out:

> In our culture, the decisive political conflict is that between animality and the humanity of man. That is to say, in its origin, Western politics is also biopolitics.[50]

The political conflict he speaks about is the conflict in being a human, for politics is ultimately about the practice of being human. In Western culture, politics is about the conflict in being human—a conflict that does not necessarily apply to African culture or to other non-Western cultures. Moreover, this conflict is more than a conflict between the human and the animal. It is a conflict between the human and nature. It must not be forgotten that the animal domain is a part of the domain of nature. In Hegelian thinking, one cannot be truly human if one is not torn off, or if one does not tear oneself off, from nature. For Hegel, Africans have not met this criterion. They remain bound to nature. They are brutes. It is not such a long time ago when Africans were placed in zoos in Europe and in America to be displayed among other exotic animals.

To be torn off from nature is to be torn off from animality—to be torn off from a mode of being that is not conscious of itself. The conflict that Agamben speaks of is more than a conflict between the humanity of man and animality. Ultimately, in Western European culture, it is a conflict between the humanity of man and nature. To be itself, Western European humanity has put itself at war with nature. Apparently, Western European humanity is not at home in nature. Nature is seen as an intruder in the being of man. Moreover, what is indubitable is that in modern history, Europeans have not been satisfied in keeping this way of seeing to themselves. They have exported and imposed it on non-Europeans. Under the inspiration of Christianity, they have attempted to compel non-Europeans to be at home in a state of alienation from animality and from nature. This conception informs the Western way of seeing. The modern Western way of seeing has taken on an imperial mission. Apparently, seeing is often not immunized against the imperial mission. It can be exported and imposed on others. This imperial mission has been at the heart of the planetary Western European civilizing mission. Africans have borne the brunt of this mission.

To carry out a missionary project of civilizing a people, one must see those one is civilizing as uncivilized. Moreover, if being civilized is seen as a criterion for being human, the uncivilized must be seen as nonhuman or as prehuman. In the Hegelian way of seeing, as is the case with the general modern way of European seeing, the African fails to meet the criterion of being civilized, and hence the criterion for being human. It is precisely for this reason that the African is seen as a Negro. As a Negro, the African is the very antithesis of being human. He is a savage, a brute. The divinely inspired and arduous task is to transform this savage, this brute, into a human being. Those who have been transformed or in the process of being transformed are the *evolués*. They leave behind their savage brutish kin. This nineteenth century—and a good part of twentieth century—language is yet to fully lose its vitality. In part, today, the notions of "development" and "modernization" may be code words that conceal continuation of the previous characterization of Africans.

Clearly, Hegel is operating within and under an evolutionary framework of history. It is within this framework that he sees himself and fellow Europeans. It is within it that he and fellow Europeans see Africans. It also appears clear that, in his view, this is the only framework within which one must see himself or see others. In his way of seeing, this framework is rational, and seeing within it is the rational way of seeing. It is the framework of the human and the framework of genuine human seeing. The African way of seeing stands in opposition to this framework and to the seeing that is dictated by it. Africans have a nonevolutionary history of being human and they are not alone in having it. They do not see being human in an evolutionary sense. The Greeks, from whom Europeans trace the birth of the rational mode of their being, were not evolutionists. *Logos* was not a product of evolution. They did not see man or see human seeing in the way it has come to be seen by Europeans. They did not see the domain of the human as being apart from the domain of the animal. This is how one is to make sense of Aristotle's claim that man is a rational animal.

In the light of African seeing, Africa was not and is not a land of Negroes. Moreover, Africans have not seen themselves and do not see themselves as Negroes. In their eyes, Africa is seen as Africa, and they see themselves as Africans. African seeing is not synonymous with Negro seeing or with black seeing. It is precisely what it is: African seeing. The Negro Africa and Negro Africans are products of the European fiction industry. They are major products of European imagination. They are not products of the African fiction industry or products of African imagination. What we have here is a contradiction between two industries and a contradiction in their products—a contradiction in two ways of seeing. Each not only is different from the other but negates the other.

In the African framework of seeing and in the African way of seeing, being human does not call for severance from the domain of the animal or from the domain of nature. The domain of being human is inseparable from these domains. This inseparability is the home of human being. It is the home of human seeing. Whereas Hegel sees the human domain as torn away from the animal domain and from the domain of nature, African seeing sees the human domain as a part of the animal domain and as a part of the domain of nature. A human being does not evolve from the animal domain or from the domain of nature. To say that being human is inseparable from the domain of animals or from the domain of nature does not imply that an African or a human being is wild, barbaric, or savage. One should not see nature as a wild domain inhabited by the wild, the barbaric, and the savage—a domain from which a human being has to tear himself herself away to be himself or herself.

There is what is ecological about being human, about being an animal, and about nature. That is, the domain of humanity, the domain of the animal, and the domain of nature are ecological. One sees here a nexus of ecologies. Such a seeing is African, but not exclusively so. Non-Africans are a part of this ecology. Asians, the indigenous peoples of the Americas, and the people of the islands are a part of this ecology. Even Europeans are a part of this ecology, despite what they may think about themselves or how they may think about Africans. In addition to the ecological nexus of human seeing, the nexus includes animals, plants, insects, reptiles, and nonliving things. The notion that anthropology does not exhaust what being human is and that a human being is what he or she is by being more that what he or she is has been seen as preposterous by Europeans. It is the ecological embedment and immersion of the African in everything that is that has led Europeans to see and think about Africans as superstitious beings, as irrational beings, or as savages. It is what has made them paranoid about Africans. They could not see or understand how this cosmic and ecological seeing could count as human being, or how this seeing could be regarded as human.

To think of nature as wild—or to think of any human being as wild, barbaric, or savage—is to impose a meaning where such meaning did not exist prior to the imposition. Africans did not see themselves or the animals they encountered as wild. The world in which they lived was not wild. Neither they nor animals lived in a wild domain. Nature was not seen as a wild environment that harbored wild people or wild animals. Prior to the imposition of these categories by Europeans, African never saw themselves as such. The notion of the wild was a product of European imagination in the effort to make sense of themselves and to make sense of the world in which they lived. It was not a product of African imagination.

Hegel's Egyptology is radically mistaken. His seeing and interpretation of the sphinx as a symbol indicating the transition of the human being from the animal domain to a true human domain mistakes Egyptian seeing and interpretation for his own seeing and interpretation. Egyptian seeing was essentially an African seeing that affirmed the inseparability of the human and animal domains. His misconstrued the historicity of the African. An imputation of the evolutionary framework to the sphinx is radically mistaken. The sphinx is not a symbol of the human emerging from the animal. It is not a symbol of the human emerging from the animal. It is an affirmation of the inseparability of the human and the animal.

Seeing African seeing calls for de-Hegelianization of African seeing. It calls for de-Westernization of African seeing. It calls for de-Christianization of African seeing. It has to forego any mediations by these ways of seeing. In setting aside these mediations, one is to set aside the Islamic way of seeing. Islam has contributed its own share to the obfuscation of African seeing. The orthodox view held by Muslims is that Africans are infidels. They are Kaffirs. They are a people without a true religion and without a sense of the true God. Both Christianity and Islam have a theocentric humanism that excludes African humanism. This exclusion sees Africans as nonhuman, since without God, no one is human. Africans cannot participate in human seeing. Both uproot the domain of the human from the domain of the animal and from the domain of nature. They share a way of seeing that is theocentric. Let it not be forgotten that Christianity and Islam have the same parent. In spite of their differences, they have a common ancestor. They both belong to the Adamic heritage and seek to impose this heritage on all human beings, or seek to incorporate all other peoples into this heritage and force all other peoples to see themselves in the way that Christians and Muslims see themselves. Just as the Christianity that was imposed on Africans was mediated by Europeans, the version of Islam imposed on Africans was mediated by Arabs. African humanism suffers under these two humanisms and suffers from the seeing that they impose on Africans. Africans are not descendants of Adam. Adam is a product of Judaic/Christian/Islamic mythology. This is not African mythology. Africans do not see themselves in the light of this mythology. To be itself, the African way of seeing must be liberated from this imposed way of seeing. This is inescapable African homework. Ultimately, it is a part of human homework. By engaging in this liberatory homework, they make a contribution to human seeing.

The liberating work that Africans have to undertake calls for a revolutionizing of the relations that Africans have with other people, especially with Europeans and Arabs. This will not be an easy undertaking, for the oppression and repression to which Africans have been subjected have been globalized. Non-Europeans and non-Arabs see Africans and the African way of seeing through European and Muslim/Arabic lenses. It is human to see though one's lenses and not through the lenses of others, especially when these other lenses have a default in the way they are crafted. Rendering the African way of seeing as parasitic to the way in which others see dehumanizes Africans.

Africa has a unique relation with the West. This relation has contributed to the generation of the modern African and European identities. The study of either identity cannot be complete without taking into account the study of the other. Accordingly, Africans have much to gain in the study of themselves if they pay attention to the study of the generation of the modern European identity, and Europeans have much to learn about themselves by paying attention to the generation of the modern constitution of the African identity. The two generations are codependent. Non-Africans and non-Europeans who seek to understand either of the two identities in their modern sense will fall short of understanding either if they ignore their destructive codependence. It is precisely for this reason that the seeing of African seeing is distorted by the European seeing of seeing. Accordingly, one should not make the mistake of thinking that when European seeing is injected while speaking about African seeing, there is a digression. What may appear as a digression is essentially an ingression. Not to be forgotten is also the fact that the conflictual nature of the relation between African seeing and European seeing is not elemental. Conceivably, in the premodern world of seeing, the African and European modes of seeing were nonconflictual. There is nothing that is necessarily or perennially conflictual between African seeing and European seeing. That is, there does not have to be a conflict between African seeing and European seeing. It is undeniable that seeing is multiple, but difference in seeing is not necessarily conflictual. Jean-Paul Sartre is not entirely correct when he asserts that conflict is the meaning of the relations with others.[51] It is not necessarily true that hell is other people.

Nothing said above should be taken to imply that outside the relation between Africa and Europe, Africa is not and Europe is not. Even if this relationship did not exist, still there would be Africa and still there would be Europe. Before the rise of modernity, Africa was and Europe was. Put differently, Africa is not entirely a creature of Europeans, and Europe is not entirely a creature of Africans. Africa is not entirely a creature of European colonialism or European imperialism. Part of the homework for Africans is to see what premodern Africa was or is and, correspondingly, part of the homework for Europeans is to see what premodern Europe was or is. This homework is interrelated and has to be interrelated, for all of it is human homework. No human being is a total stranger to any other human being. A human being is his or her homework.

The homework to be undertaken by Africans cannot be undertaken without paying attention to the seeing that is indigenous to non-European or to non-Arab peoples. The European and the Arabic architects of the modern African way of African seeing have institutionally shielded Africans from seeing the seeings of non-European and non-Arabic peoples. They have blocked the possibility of African contact with other ways of seeing. Christianity and Islam have been major forces in the course of this shielding. Reason has also been used to reinforce this process, especially under the cover of philosophy. More generally, European culture and Arabic culture have been mobilized to fuel this process. Culture, it must not be forgotten, generates and enforces a particular away of seeing. Without cultural liberation, African seeing cannot emerge and secure a lasting place in the landscape of seeing.

Seeing, whether African or non-African, is subject to provisional boundarying. Provisionality calls attention to the historicity of seeing. Accordingly, although every seeing has a boundary, the boundary does not absolutely bind. It is pregnant with other boundaries. It gives birth to them. These other boundaries are themselves pregnant with other boundaries—boundaries that are themselves pregnant with other boundaries. This process is without a foreseeable end. That is, the process does not have a conceivable end. Both the origin and the end of this process are enigmatic in that they themselves are infinitely what they are. There is no absolute origin, and there is no absolute end. The seeing to which they are subject takes on their characteristic. It is just as open as they are. It cannot be circumscribed. African seeing, as is the case with the seeings that are inherent in it, is not immunized against this process. There is an African seeing to come, and there are African seeings to come. Moreover, insofar as African seeing defines what an African is, the African is not fully African. There is an African to come. This African to come is still African. He or she is not yet.

When one looks at a clear sky, there is limit to what one can see. The limit, however, is what it is by giving way, by yielding to another limit, to another seeing. One does not see the end of the sky. There is always more of the sky to see. Even on a cloudy day, it is evident that there is what is above the clouds. There is more of the sky to see. The sky is what it is by being inherently open. It comes across and is seen as open ended. It is tempting to restrict this characteristic of seeing to sky seeing. This temptation, however, should be resisted if seeing is to be seen in the very way that it is.

What is true of celestial seeing is equally true of terrestrial seeing, because there is always more of the terrestrial to be seen. In giving itself to us, it does not do so exhaustively. Without breaking its unity, it provisionally presents itself to us, promising more to be seen. The so-called objects that are seen by us—trees, rocks, birds, mountains, animals, houses, utensils, for example—take on this mode of being. None of them is ever seen exhaustively, because each is itself inexhaustible in its being. Each is what it is by being more than how it presents itself to us. This more is pregnant in what presents itself. This is equally true of the self that sees. It is never exhaustively what it is. It is more than what is presented, and this more is inherent in it. It is a part of its being. It does not come into it as if it were from the outside. Indeed, there is no outside from which it could present itself. The seer and the seen share a common bond of being—a bond of openness.

As pointed out above, it should be clear now that what is seen as African seeing is without firm boundaries. It is a seeing that is essentially open. It never allows itself to be seen or understood exhaustively. It is what it is by being more that itself. It is perennially pregnant. When it reaches a point of taking a definite form, it devours itself without absolutely doing so. Like the phoenix, the proverbial bird, it arises from its ashes. It is devoured by time just to be again a child of time. The devouring is internal to seeing. It is the flesh of seeing. It is the house of seeing—where seeing is seeing. One also inhabits one's seeing, and if seeing is temporal without boundaries, so is oneself. We are seen by what we see. African seeing is not self-enclosed. It is a part of seeing; it is a part of the dynamic of seeing. It is bound by the law of seeing. Falling into the temptation of looking at so-called African genes or the pigmentation of the African's body (Africans as black or as Negroes—the racist thesis), or the temptation of looking at geographical Africa as what defines African seeing, distorts and misconstrues what it is. The clue to the meaning of "African" in the expression "the African way of seeing" lies in seeing. One sees it and understands it from the standpoint of seeing, a standpoint that is perennially elusive—elusivity in which one and everything is caught up.

Seeing gives birth and nurtures thinking. Thinking is truly what it is if it does not forget its bearer and nurturer. Not forgetting implies the obligation to care constantly for its bearer and its nurturer, for seeing. The reciprocity of care between seeing and thinking—this back and forth movement—is not a repetition of the same. Thinking impregnates seeing and, in turn, seeing impregnates thinking. Thinking also helps seeing give birth to seeing, and seeing helps thinking give birth to thinking. Each is the midwife of the other. Beginning and ending devour each other without annihilating each other. Here one can learn about time, and one can also learn about history—at least learn about an African version of time and an African version of time and history in an African context. The temporality and the historicity that are operative here is not linear. Time and history are combinations of linear and nonlinear. There is recursivity whereby memory is preserved in its openness and whereby openness to differences and newness avail themselves. The so-called African bush is one of the hiding places for what is African about seeing. It is a mysterious place that preserves and nurtures both the expected and the unexpected. The African is at home in the so-called bush. He or she has a bushy self—not the Western European but the African bush. There is no metatheory of the bush. The bush is subject to multiple constitutions and multiple hermeneutics.

Contemporary African seeings are pregnant with African seeings to come. Thinking about them is informed by them, while they themselves are informed by it on condition that the thinking that is appropriate here is proper to them. There is a dialectical relationship between thinking and these seeings. What is present here is a pregnant relationship—a pregnancy that is destined to come into fruition by giving birth. Pregnancy in each constitutes pregnancy in this relationship. Nature is nature by perennially being pregnant. Thinking and seeings are children of nature and have the genes of their parent.

Chapter 7
Chiwara: The African Antelope Speaks

Chiwara: the mother and the teacher of agriculture. Source of nutrition and nurturer of all that alive, both human and non-human.

At the conclusion of his reflections on "The Origin of the Work of Art," Martin Heidegger says, "the reflections are concerned with the riddle of art, the riddle that art itself is. They are far from claiming to solve the riddle. The task is to see the riddle."[62] I propose that we open ourselves to what Heidegger claims in preparation for what Chiwara presents to us, and in preparation for how we are presented by Chiwara. What is at stake here is the riddle of seeing—seeing that both speaks and listens. The seeing that is operative in the work of art is animated by the riddle. Let us not try to solve the riddle. The attempt can only lead to the withdrawal of Chiwara. I suspect that much of what Heidegger has in mind has something to do with the Greek sense of the oracle. This is not a farfetched suspicion. Those who are familiar with his thinking know that, for him, what truly matters has already been noted more fundamentally by the Greeks. A part of Heidegger's problem is that the Greeks he had in mind are his Greeks, not Greek Greeks, and clearly not African Greeks. Had he a correct view of the Greek Greeks, he would have known that the waters that wash the Greek shores or the Greek islands are the same waters that wash the African coasts. These waters do not wash German coasts. The Greek oracularity has much in common with African oracularity. Accordingly, let us take the African antelope speaking as an oracle—an oracle to be interpreted in a way that does not cause speaking to cease. Chinua Achebe, a well-known African writer, reminds us that in Africa, proverbs are the palm wine with which words are eaten.[63] In Africa, what is proverbial is oracular in an African way, but a way that is inherently open to other ways.

Before I proceed further, some disclaimers are in order. I am not going to say what normally would be expected of this topic. I will not talk about an exotic or rare antelope that is a freak of nature, that has been trained by a zoologist to speak along the same lines as a trained parrot, or that is a product of zoo engineering. I do not have in mind an electromechanical antelope or a computerized antelope that speaks the way we do. I am not a ventriloquist. Because we are not used to seeing or hearing antelopes speak, it would not surprise me if the question "What does he have in mind?" is readily and naturally directed at me. A truthful answer to this question is that I have nothing in mind. I do not seek to draw attention to my mind, for there is nothing in it. I am mindless. Attention is being drawn to Chiwara, for it is the one that does the speaking. It speaks without contrivance on my part, without the contrivance of anyone else, and without the contrivance of anything else. To hear or to listen to it is to be drawn into it, just as to see it is to be drawn into it. Moreover, if it is to speak to us, we have to pay attention to it. This paying attention is not turning away from ourselves. It is a reawakening of our kinship with it. It awakens our belonging to it and its belonging to us. This word "belonging" should not be understood as holding and making it one's own. Such holding has a concealing effect. The word "belonging" should be understood ecstatically. The riddle that the work of art is, is ecstatic. It is ecstasy that works itself out in Chiwara—the African speaking antelope. We have to recover hearing of what is normally not heard. This calls for the recovery of our membership in the audible world—a world that has been subverted by the dominance of an anthropocentric audibleness. Under such dominance, we ourselves are not fully audible to ourselves. We become alienated from ourselves when the audibility of what is not human is denied.

I have benefited from art historians, from artists, from ethnographers, and from ethnologists for bringing Chiwara to my attention. Even more, gratitude should be extended to the Bamana people, who are the creators of Chiwara, and who are themselves perhaps creations of Chiwara. Without them, there would be no Chiwara studies. My topic would be without anchorage. But what is this creation that I and

7 Chiwara: The African Antelope Speaks

others want to call to our attention? What did the Bamana create—a creation that created them? What is brought to our attention in what is brought to our attention? Much has been heard and is still being heard from art historians, from artists, and from social scientists. I am not to be counted among these benefactors, and I have no expertise in what they do. Moreover, I do not want to mislead anyone. I am not an expert on Chiwara. As a matter of fact, I am not an expert on anything—not even in doing what I am doing now. I could say that I am an expert in philosophy—a field in which I have my training, but to my knowledge there are no experts in this field. As soon as a philosopher professes to be an expert in philosophy, he or she ceases to be a philosopher. Since expertise has no place in philosophy; one can readily understand why many people succumb to the temptation of believing that everyone is a philosopher. What those who embrace this belief usually forget is that, in claiming that one is a philosopher, one runs the risk of putting oneself up as an expert in philosophy, thereby disqualifying oneself as such.

In the absence of expertise, to understand Chiwara, I suggest that we pay attention to what it draws out of us. For this to happen, we need to submit to it. This is a difficult undertaking, since we are to divorce ourselves from the proclivity for violence when it comes to understanding phenomena. We have a tendency to impose ourselves on what we want to understand. We often demand that what we want to understand surrender itself to us. In our demand, we want to devour what we want to understand. But it is precisely such a devouring that leads to the withdrawal of what we want to understand. In the demand, what we want to understand conceals itself from us. As the faithful in Islam profess, to understand Allah, one has to totally submit to Him. Perhaps this is paradigmatic of any phenomenon that we want to understand. Submission is a way of understanding. It is a way of seeing. And it is precisely what is needed if we are to make sense of the Chiwara that speaks. Chiwara cannot speak to us about its speaking unless we submit to it. Our speaking about it emerges in its speaking. Self-overcoming is essential for the understanding of what is elemental. It is precisely such understanding that is at stake in the understanding of the Chiwara that speaks.

In matters pertaining to speaking, we normally pay attention to fellow human beings and not to animals, and especially not to things. But how do we pay attention to what strikes us as absurd—a speaking antelope, especially an antelope presented to us as a piece of sculpture, which Chiwara allegedly is? Does this paying attention not contradict itself in the sense that to pay attention is to pay attention to nothing? How does one listen to what apparently does not speak? How does one listen to nothing? These questions bounce back onto us in such a way that to question the speaking of Chiwara is to question the speaking we engage in. Although it is not immediately self-evident, in the being of the speaking Chiwara, our being too is at stake. How it is, is not self-evident. In any case, what speaking is, is at stake. It is also to question our hearing, to question our listening. The questioning awakens the unusual, the extraordinary, and the paradoxical—perhaps what Heidegger refers to as a riddle.

I have often heard it said that every cloud has a silver lining. This saying reminds me of a statement by one of the most vilified public figures in the twentieth century—Mao Tsetung. He says, "Our practice proves that what is perceived cannot at once be comprehended and that only what is comprehended can be more deeply perceived."[64] Let us also add that it is only what is deeply comprehended that is deeply perceived. What we comprehend is not immediately deeply comprehended. A living dialectic lies at the heart of perception, as it does at the heart of comprehension. Let us use this dialectic to guide us in our attempt to make sense of Chiwara's speaking and the way we see it. To be so guided is to have a rupture in our everyday world, in the everyday sense of perception, in the everyday sense of comprehension. Chiwara has horns that can do the piercing, provided that we can withstand the pain. Chiwara is horny. That does not mean that it has horns. Being horny is what it entirely is and, in this regard, it is what pierces our everyday world. It is the lightning bolt in the world of Maya, Zeus's thunderous lightning bolt, Shango's thunder. We should also not expect to comprehend anything, for everything is ultimately incomprehensible. We too are incomprehensible, not because we are things but because the incomprehensible claims our being in its being.

In the presence of Chiwara, what we are immediately aware of is the fact that we see it. But what is seen, however, is not immediately understood, just as what seeing is, is not immediately understood. There is depth to seeing. To truly see is to see deeply, and to perceive deeply is to understand deeply. When and where the dialectic that is inherent in seeing, in perceiving, and in understanding comes into relief is when and where Chiwara—the speaking African antelope—is likely to emerge and show itself. In this context, there is no amazement in hearing it said that Chiwara speaks. It is also in this context that Chiwara ceases to exist as a wooden sculptured antelope. Clearly, we are in the presence of what is extraordinary, in the presence of what is paradoxical. We are in the presence of a riddle. This transformation is, at the same time, a transformation of self. Where Chiwara has ceased to exist as an object of perception, there is no self that perceives it. Or, let us say, one perceives without perceiving. The self too becomes paradoxical or a riddle, and it is only as such that it can experience the paradoxical, the riddle. That which sees vanishes. What remains is seeing without a seer and without the seen. Chiwara is not merely an object of sight, what one can look at. It is seen blindly and is looked at by not looking. Differently stated, if it is an object of sight, it is an object that dissolves as an object when it is looked at. And as it dissolves, it takes with it what looks—the self that looks. It takes away with it the eyes that look.

What is paradoxical arises and abides in what is not paradoxical. Chiwara is obviously visible. The apparent wooden Chiwara antelope sculpture is visible. It registers as such to our eyes. Equally obvious is that we too are visible. We register as such to our eyes. But it is not only Chiwara and we that share the visible. All that is visible is inseparable from everything that is visible whenever anything that is visible presents itself. Thus whatever is visible corroborates in the constitution of, and in the disclosure of, the visible. Maurice Merleau-Ponty insightfully observed that:

> The visible about us seems to rest in itself. It is as though our vision were formed in the heart of the visible, or as though there were between it and us an intimacy as close as between the sea and the sand. And yet it is not possible that we blend into it nor that it passes into us, for then the vision would vanish at the moment of formation, by disappearance of

the seer or of the visible. What there is them are not things first identical with themselves, which would then offer themselves to the seer, nor the is there a seer who is first empty and who, afterward, would open himself to them—but something to which we could not be closer than the palpating it with our look, things we could not dream of seeing "all naked" because the gaze itself envelopes them, clothes them with its own flesh.[65]

Consequently, let it be noted that Chiwara is more than an object of sight—an object that stands in opposition to us. And we are not subjects that stand in opposition to it. Our relation to it is not oppositional. Here, language gets tricky. We refer to Chiwara as "it" and, of course, we would never refer to any one of us as "it." This language of pronounal reference is subverted in the presence, and by the presence, of Chiwara. The clothing or enveloping of Chiwara with our own flesh brings about the vanishing of the space that separates it from us and that separates us from it. The flesh of our being and the flesh of things blend. It is indeed true, as Merleau-Ponty points out, that even if we were to blend into the visible, or if it were to pass into us, vision would vanish. But the vanishing of the vision is at the heart of vision. Vision vanishes so that there can be vision. That is, vision is possible only in the vanishing of vision. The two are not in opposition to each other. Each is the condition for the existence and appearance of the other. But let us note that the intimacy Merleau-Ponty speaks about is more that than proximity. There is indeed a blending of the seer and the seen, of the perceiver and the perceived. To help us get a deeper perception of the visible and the blending that is native to it, let us pay closer attention to Chiwara.

Chiwara, scholars tell us, is a wooden antelope mask won by the Bamana people of Mali, West Africa, in celebration of agricultural activities, in dances, and in initiation rituals. The antelope, it is said, taught human beings the art of agriculture. It is also believed that the antelope gave seeds to human beings. In its honor and to express gratitude, the Bamana re-enact the birth of agriculture by taking on the persona of the antelope. The re-enactment of the nativity is an artistic act. What is essential about the work of art works itself out in this act. Agricultural work is a work of art. To be sure, this does not make sense today, since agricultural work is presented as mere physical work. It has become thoroughly scientized. In this context, thinking of an agriculturalist as an artist is far removed from our consciousness. The loss of memory that is at work here is precisely what the Bamana seek to call to our attention in their sculpturing and in their re-enactment of the birth of agriculture. They don the antelope headgear and make antelope-like movements. Normally, the mask that is worn is dressed in raffia and has other add-ons that enhance the beauty and the vitality of the ceremony. However, once it is placed on the head, it ceases to be a hollow piece of carved wood placed on the head of a human being. The head does not fill a void, since there is no void to be filled. The mask is charged with creative human energy and, in turn, it charges a human being with creative energy. It is not the same energy that appears in a mechanical exchange. It is a creative energy that gives birth to the visible and to visibility. Chiwara is no longer a dead object that is placed on the head of a human being. It becomes animated and, as it becomes so, it animates the animator. The animator becomes the animated, and the animated becomes the animator. The animation takes the form of a trotting antelope that the human movement re-enacts, while the antelope itself re-enacts human trotting. At this moment, what one sees in the form of a sculptured antelope is mobile sculpture. It is this mobile sculpture that one sees, and one cannot see it unless one too is in motion. It is in mobility that sculpture is sculptured. The Chiwara that one sees in museums, in galleries, in books, in magazines, and on the screen is immobile. It is a Chiwara that has already expired. It is not the living Chiwara. It is lifeless in these places. These places are Chiwara cemeteries. The mobile Chiwara is the human Chiwara, and the human is the mobile Chiwara. Moreover, it is neither Chiwara nor the human that is in motion. Both vanish in motion. They are mobility itself. Mobility reigns in everything that is. There is a beat, a rhythm to mobility. Everything that is, is rhythmical. Agricultural work—the work inaugurated by Chiwara—is rhythmical. Generating is rhythmical. Creating is rhythmical. As it is generally said in Africa, nothing is done without music. An African myth of creation states:

> The first thing that man heard after he came into being was music. When he opened his eyes he looked around to see what he had heard, and saw nothing. All his other senses directed him to nothing. Thus, he came to believe that nothing was the source of music and the source of everything else.[66]

In the light of this myth, the visible is musical and, as music is audible, Chiwara is not only visible; it is also audible. The events that surround it are musical. The trotting of Chiwara is musical. It trots rhythmically and, as it does so, human beings are taken in by it and become musical, not by becoming other than what they are, but by being what they are. Human beings do not imitate antelope trotting. Where human beings and antelope have blended into each other, there is no place for imitation. The blending is exhaustively musical.

Previously, it has been asserted that artists, art historians, and social scientists have presented Chiwara as a work of art, and often it was presented as a mask. When presented as such, it dies. It is transformed into what it is not. The word "mask" calls attention to what is masked and appears to be an outer covering of what is covered—the head. The fact that it is worn does not, and should not, covey the idea that it is essentially a thing that is put on the head. Nothing is masked. Chiwara does not mask. In its proper signification, it ceases to be a mask that is worn on the head. It loses its maskly character. If anything, Chiwara exhibits—it brings into the open. There is no outside, and there is no inside. Both inside and inside collapse into one and vanish into each other. The inside becomes the outside, and the outside becomes the inside. As phenomenologists have correctly pointed out, behind the phenomena of phenomenology, there is nothing. If Chiwara is a mask, it is a mask that unmasks itself in being what it is. That is, if it is a mask, it is a mask that is not a mask. Strictly, it is only derivatively that a work of art is imitative. Originally, it is what brings what is imitated into relief. It is precisely what it is—a creative work. A work of art is not a mask—a mask that would tempt one to look at what is masked. It clears and is the clearing from which there arises whatever comes into being. It is in this context that Chiwara is constituted and in which it comes into being. Chiwara draws us into such clearing.

7 Chiwara: The African Antelope Speaks

We are now, hopefully, in a better position to make deeper sense of what Chiwara calls to our attention. In calling attention to itself, Chiwara calls attention to what we are. We are constituted and disclosed in the clearing as the clearing. Chiwara rises from the visible as a part of the visible. It resides in the visible and opens up the world of the visible. It ceases to be a visible object among other objects, and we ourselves thereby cease to be subjects. The visible takes on a form of communism. In this communism, we do not have Chiwara here and the human there, or the human here and Chiwara there. The here is there, and the there is here. What is here and what is there find their being in each other. Each finds itself in the being of the other. But what is shared is more than the visibility of the two. The visible opens up and incorporates all that is visible. Marxist communism falls short of this communism. Marxist communism was, and still remains, human communism. It is a humanist communism. The communism of the visible—the communism that is born out of a work of art—is a more radical humanism, a more elemental communism. It embraces all that is visible, and this includes what we normally think of as things. The human and the nonhuman become expressions of each other. To the extent that the visible is corporeal, we will call this mode of being corporeal communism. The body that capitalism produces is a body that is alienated from other bodies. If, in Marxist language, capitalism is eliminated and alienation is eliminated, the ensuing communism appears to be a communism of disembodied human beings, notwithstanding the Marxist embrace of materialism. Nowhere in the rejection of vulgar materialism do we see the emergence of the communism of the lived bodies, where each of our lived bodies blends into every other lived body. Nor do we see the emergence of the lived bodies with nonlived bodies. Chiwara renders this emergence possible. There is what is communist in Chiwara. Chiwara is the expression of the communism of the body. The visible is the visible of this communism.

The corporeal communism—the communism in which we merge and blend with the corporeal nonhuman—is precisely the humanism that Georg Hegel ignorantly associated with the African to demonstrate the not-yet humanity of the African. It is he who said:

> ... the for the distinction between himself as an individual and the universality of his essential being, the African in the uniform, underdeveloped oneness of his existence has not yet attained; so that the Knowledge of an absolute being, another and Higher than his individual self, is entirely wanting. The Negro, as already observed, exhibits the natural man in his completely wild and untamed state.[67]

He adds:

> What we properly understand by Africa, is the Unhistorical, Undeveloped Spirit, still involved in the condition of mere nature, and which had to be presented here only as on the threshold of the World history.[68]

Hegel was not speaking about Africans, if only because Africans were not, and are not, Negroes. Africans are Africans. The Negro was a fabrication of his own imagination—a fabrication that was, in general, a work of modern European imagination. It was attended by European's self-fabrication. Hegel uses Africans as a resource to construct European identity.

By embracing corporeal communism, we are placed in an environment in which Chiwara, the speaking antelope, emerges naturally. We are also exposed to what speaking is. Here, speaking is not a unique characteristic of human beings. It is not what sets human beings apart from other beings. It is what situates human beings where other beings are situated. It is where speaking has its place. To speak is to usher this situatedness into the open. It is to constitute and reveal this situatedness. Speaking constitutes; it is revealing. Where there is speaking, there is clearing. Speaking clears. We are misled about speaking when we ask, "How can Chiwara—a wooden piece of sculpture—speak?" Here, it is not only Chiwara that is problematized, and it is not only we who are problematized. Speaking is problematized. We are under a mistaken assumption that we already know what speaking is. Chiwara contests this foreknowledge. At issue here is not knowledge narrowly conceived. The knower and the known are at issue. To be at issue is to be brought up into the clearing, to be opened up, and to stand in the clearing.

Hampâté Bâ of Mali, West Africa, has observed that everything speaks. It is also he who tells us that there is a little bit of everything in everything. If he is right, one should not be surprised when one comes face to face with a speaking Chiwara. Chiwara is a thing among other things and is not exempt from speaking. It is also a thing a little bit of which is in us, just as a little bit of us is in it. Let it also be noted that a thing is more than an aggregate of parts, and this includes our own being. When we find our being in the being of others, our whole being is taken up by the being of every other being, just as every other being is taken up by our being. We are Chiwara, and Chiwara is us. We too are things, but not in the normal sense of things. We are speaking things not in the sense of the Cartesian thinking things, but things that do indeed speak—perhaps things René Descartes would never dream of. To be a part of everything is to be open to everything. Here, strictly speaking, openness is not openness of things. Things dissolve in openness, in the clearing. All is clear.

To embrace the view that everything speaks, we have to set aside the view that human beings, and only human beings, speak. But can we do this without setting ourselves apart from ourselves? And in setting aside the view that it is only we who speak, are we not thereby subverting what we are while, at the same time, subverting speaking itself? This latter observation is an observation within an observation and, to understand it, one has to understand that within which it is located. We too are not exempted from the realm of speaking things, for we are things among things. By speaking, we are drawn into the being of the things that speak and stand out as the beings that speak. As if to reaffirm what Bâ says, in her assessment of Frida Kahlo's painted self-portraiture, Raquel Tibol says:

> Someone—something—always protects us from the truth; our own ignorance and fear. Fear of knowing that we are nothing more than vectors—construction, and destruction to be alive and feel the anguish of waiting for the next minute and participating in the complex current of not knowing that we ourselves are headed toward the millions of stone beings, bird being, microbe beings, source beings. We ourselves: a variation of the one unable to escape to the two, to the three, etc.—always returning to one.[69]

Speaking hides itself in us and, in doing so, it hides us from ourselves. To unconceal itself is for us to be unconcealed and to be let out naked in the open—the open where everything else is open. This is the elemental task of the work of art. It is in this work that Chiwara has its place. Chiwara introduces us to the work of sculpture, to what works itself out in the work of sculpture. It draws attention not only to the work of sculpture in general, but to all works of art. All works of art speak and, by speaking and in speaking, they are audible. The visible is the audible, and the audible is visible. What is visible disappears, is swallowed up by the audible so that it can truly reveal itself as the visible. For the visible to be truly visible, it has blended with the audible, and vice versa. The words "visible" and "audible" are to be understood in their elemental sense, a sense that is the ultimate objective of all works of art. What is true of the visible, the audible, is equally true of all other worlds of sensing. Each of these worlds blends into each and every other world in order to be what it is. Clearly, it should be obvious that that we are problematizing sensing. But, strictly speaking, what is at work here is not problematization. If this were the case, would one would succumb to a tendency to look for a solution. What we come face to face with here is not a problem. It is what we have previously referred to as a riddle, as an oracle. It has to remain as such. Chiwara should not be judged in terms of its ability to communicate with us or in terms of our ability to communicate with it. One is not to look at its ability or inability to speak. This looking obscures what language does. Hence, the search for Chiwara's ability to communicate with us or speak to us, and for us to hear it, presupposes what is essential about Chiwara. We too lose the sense of what we are in this expectation.

As a work of sculpture, Chiwara is not a thing, and once it ceases to be seen or viewed this way, the enigma of how it can speak ceases to be an enigma enigmatically. Speaking comes across not solely as a human activity, or an activity of any other being. It is not an activity of anything or any being. It is the necessary condition for the emergence of the bonding of the human and the nonhuman. Speaking is bringing into being. Sculpturing is a creating activity. It is brought into being by an artist, by a creator. But this is a creating where, in creating, the artist or the creator creates himself or herself. Creating is speaking; it is giving birth. Accordingly, to truly see a work of sculpture is to see it creatively. It is to create ourselves as we create it. It is on our side. One creates what one sees, and what one sees is oneself creating. Art bridges the distance between the viewer and the viewed, between the seer and the seen, between the doer and the deed. It transcends the dichotomous mode of being.

The modern project—the project that atomizes us, that sets us apart from each other, and that celebrates our autonomy at the expense of our commonality—violates us. It obscures how, in our being, we are each implicated in the being of other beings. It obscures our being in each other and for each other. We are not strangers to what is corporeal. All that is, is corporeal, and this includes the human and the not human. This is a lesson from sculpture and from all of the arts. This is hidden when and where sculpture is confined to an art gallery, to a museum, or to a space reserved for the display of sculpture. But these places can also be transfigured and indeed have to be transfigured to reveal what is essential about sculpture. What is true of sculpture is true of painting and is equally true of all works of art. We are everywhere where the sculpture is and where any work of art is—not through imposition but by birth. Here too is the place for speaking. Speaking creates this place. The creating is the work of Chiwara. It is Chiwara speaking.

Chapter 8
The Way of Trees in Africa

8 The Way of Trees in Africa

Long time ago a squirrel found itself under the shade of a big tree. He looked at the tree and asked it, "Why do you have such a big belly? It makes you too big to run." The tree asked, "Why must I run?" The squirrel answered, "To escape form danger". The tree responded, "What makes you so sure that you can escape from danger?" The squirrel replied, "I do it all the time. I am light, can run fast, and can climb on a tree to avoid being caught and killed." The tree asked, "How can you avoid the danger of dangers: death?" Here, the squirrel fell silent. The tree said, "No one can run away from death. That is why I am not so foolish to pretend otherwise. No one can run away from death. I am always what I am and where I am. You are a squirrel. You cannot not be other than what you are or be other than where you are. Be what you are and where you are. I am at home in myself and I am a home for all. I offer you a temporary refuge when you are threatened and a place to stay at night. I feed you with my fruits and feed others as well. I provide shade and wood to men. I am a home for insects and birds. To do this, and more, I eat a lot. This is why my belly as big as you say it is. It is not too big for me. And why is your belly so small?? The squirrel said, "I do not know, but I will think of an answer". The tree said, "It is good to think. You can do so under my shade. What I offer makes be what I am". We are all interdependent". (An African tale)

On the face of every tree, there is a story. The story is not on the surface of the tree. It is the tree itself. Every tree tells a story. To see it is to see its story, and to sense it in any other way is to sense its story. Ultimately, botany is tree ontology. To study a tree is to decipher its ontology. Since I am neither a botanist nor a biophysical scientist, there may be a legitimate concern about what I can meaningfully contribute to our understanding of the way of trees in Africa. What can philosophy—my field of study—contribute to the understanding of this way or to the understanding of the way of trees in general? To prepare the way for an answer to this question, it should not be assumed that the physical and biological sciences have a monopoly on helping us understand the way of trees in Africa or anywhere else. Moreover, the understanding of science is not an exclusive domain of physical and biological scientists. Contrary to what may be fashionable, philosophers too have a contribution to make to our understanding of physical and of biological sciences, and to the understanding of science in general. In addition, it should not be forgotten that philosophers are both creatures of nature and a part of the physical and biological world. In seeking to understand nature, they seek to understand themselves in a holistic way. Natural science (physical and biological) is a human science, and where and when human science is at stake, as human beings, philosophers are inevitably implicated and have something significant to say about the nature of this implication.

We have placed ourselves at the center of the living world and have placed other forms of life on the periphery of this center. It is precisely this humanism, this homocentricity, that has brought about the marginalization of trees, as well as the marginalization of other phenomena in nature. In part, it is a rethinking of this state of affairs that is the focus this essay. If the ontological linkage between trees and us is not self-evident, it is because how we stand in relation to trees has not been subjected to a radical investigation or to a radical understanding. Of course, this does not mean that a far-ranging scientific investigation of human beings or that a far-ranging investigation of trees has not taken place. It is also the case that scientific thinking has taken on an imperial aspect and has made strenuous and persistent efforts to bring all thinking under its domain. To this extent, it has adopted a stance similar to monotheism. It has insisted, and continues to insist, that there be no other thinking; consequently, it has sought apostles and disciples to spread this message across the globe. However, regardless of how far-ranging scientific thinking has been, or how far-ranging it will be, it has not exhausted, and cannot exhaust, thinking about what human beings are or what trees are. Richness of thinking is not one of the main products of our current practice of thinking. Even in academic institutions, what passes as critical thinking is a buzzword introduced to sugarcoat crass conformism to a narrow version of thinking. At most, what the academy stresses is scientific thinking. Hesitation in embracing enriched thinking—the thinking that would prepare the way of thinking about our elemental relationship with trees—is imprisonment in conventional conformist thinking about being human and in conformist thinking about trees. In part, it is this—the liberation from either conformism—that inspired my thinking about African trees.

Bringing the way of trees in Africa to bear on the way of being human is not merely a matter of sentimental aestheticism. It is to embrace the openness of our being as an essential aspect of our being. To be what we are is to stand in need of learning what we are; it is to deepen and extend the sense of what we are and, in so doing, to open the possibility that what trees are still remains open. Indeed it makes sense for us to ask ourselves whether, on their side, trees wonder about their being and about how their being relates to our being. This questioning betrays its humanistic prejudice and does violence not only to trees but also to human beings. It presupposes a gap between human beings and trees—a gap that allegedly stands in need of being bridged. Although there is sense in embracing such a gap, it does not eliminate the possibility of a non-gap, a possibility of a realm of being where human being and trees are indistinguishable. Indistinguishability is an experience one has to undergo, but only on the condition that one let oneself go off the superficial attachment to oneself, and also on condition that one lets go the attached to a humanistic understanding of trees. This letting go is the work of the way of trees in Africa, provided we do not stand in its way. It is a releasement that allows us to be what we are and that allows the trees to be what they are. It allows for a unitary mode of being.

To share the experience of the way of trees in Africa requires that we aesthetically find a place for ourselves in this way, conscious of the dangers that we are likely to encounter as we try to find our place. One's place is not a place where one is posited. It is not a container in which one is placed. One's place is where one is constituted as what one is, and it is also where one expresses what one is. Because it is not a container, it has no conceptual or empirical boundaries. And this is precisely how one is to have a sense of oneself. It is in this manner that one's place in the way of trees in Africa is to be experienced. The experience itself is possible because the way of trees in Africa is similarly constituted. It is not a container of African trees, a container of our place, or a container of anything else. It is not a thoroughfare bordered by trees. It is not a path in a tropical forest or a path in the savannah. The way is unconceptualizable. It has no boundaries, just as we ourselves are what we are by not having boundaries. It is indeed the case that without boundaries, definitions would not be possible. But having no boundaries is also a form of definition. But how is one to make sense of one's place in the way of trees in Africa, and how are we to make sense of this way—a way that appears to have no boundaries? How, then, is the knowledge of ourselves, or the knowledge of the way of trees possible? These questions appear to make sense because, normally, boundaries appear to be necessary conditions for making sense. Herein lies our initial predicament. We seek boundaries in what is essentially unbounded. We seek to define the undefinable.

Although I do not want to promise more than I can deliver, I do not know how to restrain myself from doing so. My thinking has a way of running wild, and I must confess that I am not very good at domesticating it. Honestly speaking, there are times when I feel that to domesticate thinking is to do injustice to it, and that wild thinking has a legitimate place in the life of thinking. There is no doubt that some of us have a visceral reaction to undomesticated or wild thinking, but it is precisely such a reaction—driven by the desire to domesticate all thinking and everything that is thought—that ruins not only thinking but also what is thought. Sigmund Freud has already alerted us to this danger when he warns us of the danger of the ego and the superego when, in their struggle to domesticate the id, they leave the id without a safety valve. Without a safety valve, it is condemned to a war against both the ego and the superego, rendering both dysfunctional. Our approach to the way of trees in Africa may encounter major obstacles if cognitive greed is not tamed. When obsessive, the greed to know poses a grave danger to us.

Since the way of trees in Africa is necessarily a sensuous way, to be true to it, it is only as sensuous that it can be thought. But the sensing at work here, like the thinking that is at work here, is undomesticated and has to be preserved as such. But lest one believe erroneously that this does violence to sensing, one must bear in mind that sensing too has the wild as one of its essential features. In sensing the way of trees in Africa, there is what is undomesticated or that which is wild. Here, one wildly senses. It is not that thinking introduces the undomesticated in the way of trees. Rather, the way itself is undomesticated and invites thinking that shares undomesticity. Here, we appear to be immersed in an aesthetic thinking that appears to have no boundaries. The sensorial world is never circumscribed. Its boundaries are perpetually permeable and evanescent. Sensing never freezes the sensed. Were it to do so, it would cease being what it is. Sensing intoxicates, and we, as sensors, become intoxicated and intoxicating.

To the extent that domesticating has something to do with knowing, we run into a problem here regarding the project I am undertaking. The desire to know the way of trees in Africa is a threat to it. Desire is contextual. For the most part, seeking information about it will lead to a dead end. Accordingly, do not expect me to provide information about it, if only because philosophy is the basis of my approach to this way. As I understand it, essentially, philosophy is not in the business of providing information. To be sure, there are professors of philosophy who are in this business and, at times, I must concede, I am one of them. For the moment, however, I will attempt to present myself to you not as a professor of philosophy but as someone who aspires to be a philosopher, which is not the same as someone aspiring to be a professor of philosophy. I take Martin Heidegger seriously when he reminds us that:

> ... the misinterpretation of which philosophy is perpetually beset are promoted most of all by people of our kind, that is by professors of philosophy. It our customary business—which may be said to be justified and even useful—to transmit a certain knowledge of the philosophy of the past, as part of general education. Many people suppose that this is philosophy itself, whereas at best it is the technique of philosophy.[70]

The distinction is not easy to make, especially when one has an audience in view. The audience expects the speaker to say something informative. In this case, there is always the danger of frustrating the audience's expectation. The danger is eased somewhat when the audience is philosophical. Such an audience knows better than to expect the speaker to be nothing more than an information disseminator. Again, I believe that Heidegger is correct when he points out that:

> Words and language are not wrappings in which things are packed for the commerce of those who write and speak. It is in words and language that things first come into being and are.[71]

One needs to know how to listen to a philosophical speech if one is to avoid expecting what is not to be expected. In Africa, this is done proverbially. There is no effective speech that does not contain a proverb. Taken in itself, speech is essentially proverbial.

In what is presented here, I see myself as being in the service of the way of trees in Africa, and it is my hope that this way will address and bring you closer to its neighborhood. Regardless of what may appear to be the case, I am not privileged in what I say about it. I seek to convey what is already within your reach. Although there is nothing new in what I say, what is not new can be more thought provoking if we avail ourselves of it. Availing ourselves is not always easy, especially if what we avail ourselves of initially strikes us as being out of the ordinary. Each one of us is to be addressed by the way of trees in Africa from his or her standpoint. This is the case as long as we bear in mind that the standpoint of each of us is, at the same time, the standpoint of every one of us. It is from this standpoint of standpoints that one truly learns. It is from this standpoint that we are to experience the way of trees in Africa.

What is said above reminds me of the words of Booker T. Washington—an African American. In his notorious "Exposition Address" in Atlanta in 1895, he said, "Cast down your bucket where you are." Despite the controversy that has surrounded this statement, the statement is relevant to us as we try to make sense of the way of trees in Africa. Although our topic is "The Way of Trees in Africa," this way can be accessed from any part of the world. It is a public way. There is what is African in what Washington says. One begins to understand the way of trees in Africa from where one is. But where one is, is always and inevitably out of hand. It is here and not here or, rather, it is here by not being here. As Heidegger has noted:

> ... the frantic abolition of all distances brings no nearness; for nearness does not consist in shortness of distance. What is least remote from us in point of distance, by virtue of its picture on film or its sound on the radio, can a remain far from us. What incalculably far from us in point of distance can be near to us. Short distance not in itself nearness. Nor is great distance remoteness.[72]

A philosophical journey begins at home and ends at home. It is a going away that is not a going away. It seems to me that this is precisely the point that René Descartes was making when he said that:

> It is good to know something of the customs of various peoples, in order to judge our own more objectively, and so that we do not make the mistake of the untraveled in supposing that everything contrary to our customs is ridiculous and irrational. But when one spends too much time traveling, one becomes a stranger at home.[73]

Descartes inadequately and wrongly misconstrued home when he assumed that thinking was the foundation of the human home. To the extent that such a home has a foundation that excludes sensing, it is not the kind of home that could set us on the way to the way of trees in Africa. Since the way is sensuous, divorced from the body, the mind can only lead us away from the way. It is only as embodied that we can find our way to the way of trees. It is only as such that this way can welcome us.

To be sure, one can misconceive one's home and, in so doing, become a stranger to, or at, one's home. The possibility of misconceiving is native to us and to our home. One's home may offer itself in a way that makes one homeless in or at one's home. Moreover, misconceiving of one's home can occur if one confines oneself to a human sense of one's home. One's home has an extra- or nonhuman sense—a sense in which the human sense of home derives its broader and deeper sense. Differently stated, one's home is extra-ordinary. As we think about the way of trees in Africa, let us not forget that trees too have a home—a home that is, at the same time, a human home. When we fail to pay attention to the home of trees, inattention may result in our being kept away from their home, which would equally render us homeless in our home. When and where trees are rendered homeless, we too are thereby rendered homeless. If this is not self-evident, it may be due to our inability to comprehend what a home is. We should not take for granted that what we conventionally believe to be our home is truly our home, and equally, we should not take for granted that what we conventionally believe to be home for trees is truly their home. Convention veils, and it is only in the course of unveiling it that the truth of the interconnectedness of trees and human beings can avail itself to us. If the claim that our home is intrinsically connected with the home of trees sounds fantastic, it may be due to the not-yet-thought-out sense of what it is for trees to have a home or, for that matter, what it is for us to have a home. Philosophy is without convention and thrives in undoing the conventional. It is by being naked that one can truly philosophize. Truth is naked. The pursuit of truth is the pursuit of nakedness. Truth conceals itself when approached by those who are not naked.

Conventional understanding leads us to believe that having a home is exclusively a human mode of being. To be sure, at times, we speak of home for animals, and of animals being homeless. If we speak this way, it is mostly because we believe that animals—unlike trees, for example—are closely related to us. This belief presupposes an understanding of what human beings are, and also an understanding of what trees are. However, in either case, in the presupposition, there lies what remains veiled. A more elemental understanding is veiled. A too-humanistic understanding of the scope of what being at home means may be symptomatic of estrangement from ourselves and from trees. It is important that we preserve the sense of openness of what having a home means if the danger of homelessness is to be held at a distance. It is in the context of such preservation that the way of trees in Africa draws us into itself as belonging to itself. This way preserves this preservation. Such preservation calls for divesting ourselves of what conventionally is taken to be a human being and of what conventionally is taken to be a tree. Accordingly, what is unconventional has a place not only in what a human being is about but also in what a tree is. The way of trees in Africa is where trees have a home. It is where they are what they are. If we follow Booker T. Washington and cast our bucket where we are, the bucket may take us to the realm of the unconventional—a realm of primordial awareness. And we cannot be taken there without undergoing an unconventional transformation of the awareness that we have of ourselves, and that we have of trees.

Washington's advice to drop the bucket where one is has to be taken seriously if there is hope for the right orientation toward the way of trees in Africa. If we are oblivious to the tyranny of convention knowledge, where we think we are may be where we are not, and where we are not may be where we are. The assumption should not be made that one knows where one is or that where one is, is subject to knowledge. There is something African about this advice, but something that is not exclusively African. His advice has an echo, or ought to find an echo, in everyone, for no one can start from where one is not. I will readily admit that this may not have been what was in his mind or in the mind of his audience. But let us bear in mind that to truly hear what others say is to hear creatively.

Booker T. Washington—a descendant of enslaved Africans—was raised in the Southern part of the USA and grew up in the midst of Southern trees. Understanding these trees is a part of understanding him and can be a clue to the African understanding of the way of trees. How this is the case is not self-evident and, to have a sense of why this is the case, let us turn to a student of Southern trees. In speaking about Southern trees, Billie Holiday insightfully and poetically said the following in one of her classic songs:

> Southern trees bear a strange fruit
> Blood on the leaves and blood at the root
> Black bodies swinging in the Southern breeze
> Strange fruit hanging from the poplar trees

Pastoral scene of the gallant South
The bulging eyes and the twisted mouth
Scent of magnolia sweet and fresh
Then the sudden smell of burning flesh

Here is the fruit for the crows to pluck
For the rain to gather for the wind to suck
For the sun to rot for the tree to drop
Here is a strange and bitter crop

    Like Washington, Holiday was an American of African descent, which means that, like Washington, her way was inscribed in the way of trees in Africa, just as the way of trees in Africa was inscribed in the way of her being. Her song teaches us not only what is at stake in being African in America, but also what is at stake in the being of trees in America and in Africa. Accordingly, bringing her song to bear on what is to be said about the way of trees in Africa should not be taken as a diversion or as a digression. She speaks about Southern trees—trees in the Southern region of the USA. Bringing her song to bear on the way of trees in Africa is not a diversion or a digression. It is a key that opens the door to this way. To think of her exclusively as an American, or to think of her sense of the Southern trees exclusively as American, is to misunderstand her and to misunderstand her sense of Southern trees. In addition to having an American heritage, she also had an African heritage. It should not be forgotten that her being and her sensibility were deeply rooted in African soil. It is indeed undeniable that enslaving Africans was accompanied by the process of erasing the consciousness of being African and erasing African perceptual sensibility. Bringing the memory of this erasure to the conscious and reinstituting it was the flesh of her musical botany. Musical botany is a part of the African experience. This experience was playing out in America. It was a part of what she was. She yearned for her African homeland where the being of trees and the being of humans were inseparable, and where one was the site of the other.

    One should not be a prisoner of a narrow interpretation of her musico-botanical geography. Her song has a universal message on musical aesthetics and on arboreal aesthetics, provided that one has an ear and an eye for the message in her song. How this is the case needs to be experienced and understood. There is a depth to musical aesthetics and to arboreal aesthetics that is accessible only to those who have gone through the rite of passage. The elemental in both aesthetics initiates us into such a depth. The surface of the sensuous is what it is by being the flesh of such a depth. It is a surface that is not a surface if, by surface, one has in mind an outer covering.

    I will readily grant that the introduction of Billie Holiday's song creates a legitimate curiosity as to how the message of the song connects with the message that is conveyed by the way of trees in Africa. One can validly ask, what has her African background to do with the way of trees in Africa? What is or should be obvious is that the song is about trees and, evidently, the way of trees in Africa has a bearing on the way of trees everywhere. Despite the reality of the local sense of what is said about trees in her song, what is said about trees anywhere resonates with what is said about trees everywhere, insofar as what is said about them is elemental. The geography of trees is a unified geography. What is said about Southern trees is a lesson about trees everywhere. It is one of the lessons of arboreal aesthetics. The task is to take in and digest this lesson. To be successful in doing so, we are to understand the other aspect of this task—namely, to be taken in and digested by trees.

Billie Holiday can sing about these trees because, in their being, they are open to her as an African descendant. In her song, she also opens up these trees to us. To sing is to open up, just as to poetize is to open up. She herself is open to them, and this is why they can offer themselves to her. They are Billie Holiday's trees and, as such, her way is their way. Moreover, because the way of Southern trees is open and opens up, it is open to the way of trees elsewhere. What is open, insofar as it is open, does not bar itself from what is open. It is this truth that is present in, and is presented by, Holiday's musical aesthetics and by her arboreal aesthetics.

If openness belongs to what is elemental about the way of trees in Africa, in singing about Southern trees, Holiday poetically sings about what is elemental about music and about poetry. In their primordial nature, music and poetry open up. That is, it is in and by opening up that they draw us to what is primordial about them, and in so doing open us up to ourselves. This is what art accomplishes in its elemental sense. However, this takes place only when we ourselves are open. What is uncanny here is that we do not expect music and poetry to teach us about what we are or about what is apparently other than what we are. But music and poetry can teach us not only what we are but also what trees are, and what their way is, provided that we have an ear for them. We can have an ear for them only insofar as hearing is open and dwells in the open. The way of trees in Africa is a musical and poetic way, and it is this way because African trees—and indeed all trees—are musical and poetic. Trees and the way of trees do not only inspire musicality and poesy in us. They are elementarily poetic and musical, and it is only as such that they can inspire. An elemental experience of the way of trees in Africa awakens in us, and brings forth, the musical and poetic nature of African trees and, necessarily, the way of trees everywhere, and the link between trees and human beings.

It is rare that we turn to music or to poetry to learn about trees or their way. For the most part, learning about trees has been reserved for natural and biological science. It is this science that is to guide us in learning about trees, and we rely on it to set limits to what can be said and what cannot be said about trees. Arboreal science—or botany, as it is commonly known—speaks, and we are constrained to listen to what it says. We depend on it to open and to preserve what is known and what is knowable about trees. Bringing music and poetry to bear on our understanding of trees and their way would appear to generate misunderstanding. Commonsense education, reinforced by academic education, leads us to the belief that music is a matter of emotion, and that emotion has nothing to do with the understanding of the real. As for poetry, in our day, Heidegger has reminded us that:

> Poetry is either rejected as a frivolous mooning and vaporizing into the unknown, and a flight into dreamland, or is counted as a part of literature. The prevailing standards, in turn, is made and controlled by the organs for makings public civilized opinions. One of its functionaries -at once driver and driven—is literature industry. In such setting poetry cannot

appear otherwise that as literature. Where it is studies entirely in educational and scientific term, it is the object of literary history. Western poetry goes under the general heading of "European literature"[74]

Professors of arboreal science do not encourage their students to study music and poetry to help them understand trees. Perhaps, when they themselves were students, they were not encouraged to study music or poetry as a part of their study of trees. In the academic environment, generally, students are encouraged to take botany and biology if they are to understand trees. The study and teaching of music are confined to the fine arts, and the study and the teaching of poetry are confined to the humanities. This division of academic labor is taken to be natural, and its abolition threatens the integrity of arboreal science, as well as the integrity of the study of both music and poetry. It is precisely this division of labor that Billie Holiday seeks to subvert in her poetic song, and it is also the division that is imploded in the way of trees in Africa.

Holiday's song teaches us that Southern trees are spatial. They are sites for black bodies—sites where black bodies are displayed in gruesome ways. The bodies are black, in part because they have been torched. They are lynched bodies—bodies that have been blackened, incinerated by fire—fire set deliberately by American Southerners of European descent. Even before they are blackened by fire, these bodies have already been blackened by European thinking and by European sensing. When Africans were forcefully and violently brought to work as slaves in the plantations owned by European descendants, they did not come as blacks, as colored people, or as Negroes, as they were called then. They were Africans—with particular identities indicating the regions and ethnic groups from whence they had come. Their sojourn in the South entailed a process of blackening or negrification. In the South, they became black; they became Negroes. And as they were becoming black or Negroes, European descendants were becoming white. The two becomings were intrinsically tied to each other. None could be successful without the other being successful. Southern trees became the bearers of, and the site of, these strange fruits. This bearing embodied double negation, and perhaps multiple negations. In it, the African ceased to be African, and the European ceased to be European. Violence was also done to trees since, as sites, they did not have to bear these fruits. The trees were transformed into trees of violence. They became a site of violence. They could have given birth to, and could have been the site for, African and European common humanity. Failure to give such a birth resulted in the birth of strange, bitter fruits. Southern trees became a site for paranoia. They gave birth to paranoia—another bitter fruit. Having nightmares about trees and the temptation to flee from trees were also offspring of the Southern trees. What Billie Holiday conveys to us is that trees are a site of sites and, at the same time, these sites are a site that constitutes and displays the site that trees are. Trees are birthing sites. The way of trees in Africa is a site for birthing. The way of trees births.

So far, if there is anyone asking when we will ever get to the way of trees in Africa, patience is in order. The way of trees in Africa is difficult to grasp. One should expect what one ought to expect, and this includes expecting the unexpected.

8 The Way of Trees in Africa

The way of trees in Africa is proverbial. A philosophical journey does not take one away from oneself. To be sure, it may appear otherwise, but otherwise is not otherwise in philosophical life. There is a philosophical way of trees, and there is a nonphilosophical way of trees. The difference lies in the way of trees, if we can be open to it. This possibility of the emergence of this openness lies at the heart of the way of trees. If we pay close attention to the way of trees in Africa, this openness will be available to us.

The way of trees in Africa is the way of trees everywhere. Trees are trees everywhere. In opening itself to what it is, every tree opens what every other tree is. An African tree is a tree of every tree, and so is any non-African tree. This opening up lies in the womb of every tree. This is the teaching of the way of trees. Provided we are ready to learn, being in the way of trees is being in a school where we learn about trees and their way. Here, trees offer themselves to those who want to learn about them. This is not an academic school of today. In the academic school of today, there is little room for the inner teaching of trees. Here, trees withhold their teaching. The academic environment alienates us from what trees are and, when this alienation sets in, we too are alienated from ourselves. It is only when we are at home with ourselves that trees can offer the truth of their being to us. The words of Booker T. Washington drive this truth home when he said that one is to drop one's bucket where one is. In the USA, this African man was accused of embracing racial segregation and of siding with the racists, but he could be understood as exhorting Africans in the USA not to abandon who they are and that it was in their interest not to do so.

In slavery, Africans in the Americas found themselves strangers to what they are, and this was demonstrated in the severance of their intimacy with trees. Trees in the USA were perceived as inimical to their interests. Trees were the property of slave masters and stood for the will of the slave masters. Trees were where Africans who fought for their freedom were hanged. Trees were resources for building prosperity for the slaver masters. Cotton fields, tobacco fields, and sugarcane fields were fields of African degradation. The names for trees were not African names. The name for trees that were a part of the linguistic repertoire disappeared. They were not allowed to take on the Native American names for trees or to take in the Native American meanings that were associated with trees. They were deprived of the Native American wisdom of trees.

Had it not been for slavery, the Africans in the Americas would have made significant contributions to the wisdom of trees in the Americas. The language of trees would have been deepened and broadened. This loss has yet to be recognized, since trees in the Americas have succumbed to the imperial regime in botany. The Native American wisdom of trees could have made it easier for Africans to retain their African botanical wisdom.

For the most part, so far, we have been stalking the way of trees in Africa. One should not lose the existential and experiential aspect of stalking. One does not stalk blindly. One does so on the basis of a sense of what one is stalking. As is well known in hunting societies in Africa, stalking is an art. It is integrated in the process of hunting. Hunting is an art. It requires skills that include a "spiritual" dimension.

One must be in tune with what one hunts and with the environment within which one hunts. One domesticates what one hunts, as well as the environment within which one hunts and, in turn, the hunter is wilded by what he hunts and by the environment within which he hunts. Whether one is hunting, gardening, herding, fishing, or engaging nature in any other way, intimacy with nature is always maintained. The intimacy expresses what one is. To preserve it is to preserve oneself.

What has been said so far has been intended to reinforce the sense that nature is our habitat. The way of trees is the way of nature. Hopefully, now, we are in a position to proceed further toward our goal, and also to deepen our understanding and our experience of what has been said about the way of trees. As we proceed, it may also be worthwhile to bear in our consciousness that, in a sense, we are going toward where we have been and where we are. To deepen the sense of our journey, let us turn to Wangari Maathai, one of the priestesses of the way of trees in Africa.

In her Nobel Peace Prize Lecture, Maathai—a prominent African environmentalist and ecologist from Kenya, East Africa—said:

> When I was a child I would visit a stream next to our home to fetch water for my mother. I would drink water straight from the stream. Playing among the arrowroot leaves I tried in vain to pick up the strands of frog's eggs, believing that they were beads. But every time I put my little fingers under them they would break. Later, I saw thousands of tadpoles: black, energetic and wriggling through the clear water against the background of the brown earth. This is the world I inherited from my parents.[75]

She added that:

> Today over 50 years later, the stream has dried up. Women walk long distances for water, which is not always clean, and children will never know what they have lost. The challenge is to restore the home of the tadpoles and give back to our children a world of beauty and wonder.[76]

When I read these words, they resonated in me, for I had grown up in a similar environment. After being away from Kenya for a long time, immediately after my return, I noticed that the world in which I had grown up had almost disappeared. I noticed fundamental environmental and ecological changes. From what I could tell, natural forces did not exclusively bring about these changes. The drying up of the streams was not solely a matter of the workings of nature. Fellow villagers had contributed significantly to these changes. They had cut down trees in large numbers and thereby contributed significantly to erosion and the drying up of the streams. The grave consequences that followed are yet to be fully understood.

In rural Africa, the cutting down of trees is not primarily a development project, a landscaping project, a beautification project, or a crusade to bring about the extinction of trees. It is not a matter of ridding the environment of the evil spirits that proverbially inhabit African trees. For many Africans, it is a matter of survival. Wood is needed to build shelter. The scarcity of trees and the unbearable costs of stone, bricks, steel, and other fabricated building materials has led many in rural areas to continue relying on trees to provide wood for the construction of shelter. Because the rural areas are not industry intensive, there is little industrial waste to depend on for the construction of shelter. Despite the unbearable poverty that surrounds them, the urban poor have a better chance of accessing urban waste because there is a greater concentration of industries next to where they live. Existing at the margins of cities, and like vultures, they forage for the discarded cardboard, tins, corrugated iron, and other materials to construct shelters.

Increasingly, for the rural poor, the growing scarcity of trees—and hence the scarcity of firewood for cooking and heating—have become unbearable. Natural gas and electricity are prohibitively expensive and are a luxury for a few in the rural areas. Rural electrification does not exist in many rural areas, and even where it is available, the cost is prohibitively high. At one time, one could dream of hydroelectricity, but with the trees gone and the drying of rivers, this dream is painfully nothing more than a dream. The rural areas have become areas of dreamers—fertile ground for parapsychology.

Trees are not only the source of wood. Some provide food for human beings, animals, birds, and insects. With the loss of trees, the development of hunger continues to be a menace for both human beings and other species that depend on trees for food. Some animals, birds, and insects have become extinct. Others have fled and, for some, there is no possibility for a return.

Some trees are home to animals, birds, reptiles, and insects. Having become homeless, these living beings have become extinct or are in the process of become extinct. Some have fled or are in the process of fleeing to more habitable environments. In some cases, in this flight, human beings accompany them, and this accompaniment is a disaster for both. Fierce competition for living space and for food between animals, birds, insects, and human beings has grown fiercer.

Some trees shelter other plants. The sheltered trees, having no trees to shelter them, have become extinct or are in the process of becoming extinct. And whatever depends on these sheltered trees, consequently, has become extinct or is in the process of becoming extinct. Joining those who depend on the sheltering trees, they have taken or are in the process of taking flight to wherever they can find safety, shelter, or food. What is left behind is a cemetery whose perimeter constantly widens.

Some trees have been sources of indigenous medicine and provided important indigenous medical knowledge. Their disappearance has resulted in a substantial disappearance of traditional medicine, as well as the disappearance of indigenous medical knowledge. Whatever remains of indigenous rural medicine, as is the case with rural medical knowledge, is moreover denigrated, thereby contributing further to the neglect and extinction of essential human resources. Practitioners of indigenous medicine are taken to be inferior to modern medical practitioners or are regarded as purveyors of shamanism, or as purveyors of sham medical knowledge. Their patients tend to be indigenous people, are generally poor, and have little formal education.

The distinction between indigenous medicine and modern (scientific) medicine, as is the case with the distinction between indigenous medical knowledge and modern medical knowledge, is a cultural distinction and, as indigenous Africans are compelled to embrace modern medicine and modern medical knowledge, they are inevitably compelled to embrace a new culture—a culture that, in some significant ways, is antithetical to their indigenous culture. The disappearance of their trees is attended by the disappearance of some significant aspects of their culture.

The drying up of streams has brought about disastrous social and cultural consequences. As Maathai indicates, in some areas, there are no more frogs, thus no more strands of frog eggs, and no more tadpoles for children to play with. Other living organisms that have hitherto survived on the vegetation and on each other along the river have also become extinct or are increasingly becoming extinct. Children have been deprived of a play environment—an aesthetic environment that is the environment of their being and that links them with nature. Instead of playing with natural phenomena as toys, or making play toys directly from nature, plastic toys from the urban areas have been introduced to rural children. The toys they play with are largely products of non-African societies and embody the cultural values of those societies. Some human-like toys do not look like Africans; that is, toys that look like children do not look like and do not act like African children. The non-African play environment becomes the instrument of alienating African children from their own cultures. This alienation is more pronounced in urban areas, where the deprivation of the indigenous African play environment is more evident. One sad aspect of this state of affairs is that the alienation that arises from this deprivation is not perceived as alienation. It is perceived as a symbol of modernity. The toys that trickle from the urban area to the rural area are symbols, as well as concrete manifestations, of modernity and thus manifestations of advances in civilization. Unlike their counterparts in the urban area, rural parents are too poor to afford modern toys for their children. The little money they have is used to meet more pressing basic needs. What the national toy world reveals is a rupture in the community of children. Rural children develop a sense of an inferiority complex when they compare themselves with urban children. They see their age-mates in the urban areas possessing toys that they can only dream about. In a world in which the attitude toward money has acquired a religious aura, lack of financial ability has a devastating effect on how rural parents perceive themselves. Lack of money to care for one's children generates low self-esteem. Responsible parents desire their children to have self-esteem. This desire is compromised when the parents do not have the means to meet the needs of their children.

In addition, the loss of the indigenous play environment has had a devastating effect on the knowledge that would have been available to children: self-knowledge, knowledge about vegetation, and knowledge about insects and other organisms that live along the stream. Nature has ceased to be a school where children learn. The vanishing of this school has been, and is, a significant loss to both the local and national community; indeed it is a loss to all Africans and to humanity. The loss of knowledge that has resulted from the vanishing of this school has generated a new form of poverty—a form of poverty that has to be added to the other forms of poverty that afflict Africans today. This poverty is more than poverty of information. It is also spiritual/corporeal poverty—a poverty that cannot be replaced by Christianity or by Islam. The spirituality of this poverty is a spirituality that has deep roots in nature, a spirituality in which humanity and nature are bound to each other, and in which each is the expression of the other. It is poverty that neither the World Bank nor the IMF can comprehend. It is also a poverty to which the pundits of development do not pay attention. It is the poverty that is to be read on the faces of African children. African trees embody this spirituality and, when they are no more, it departs with them. If the children of today are tomorrow's adults, tomorrow adults will embody the poverty of this spirituality. African rural areas are the granaries of indigenous knowledge in Africa. But, driven by the imperative of modernity, the conventional wisdom is that rural areas are granaries of ignorance, granaries of superstition, granaries of savagery and heathenism, and the granaries of everything that is an obstacle to civilization.

As is the case in many others cultures, African trees have religious and spiritual significance. Some trees are religious symbols, some make up ritual and sacred enclaves, and others are memorials to departed elders. When they disappear, such symbols disappear. Sacred enclaves disappear, and ancestral memorials disappear with them. Sites where they once were have become funeral grounds, cemeteries of the departed. That is, the denuded African landscape has become the landscape of the dead. Rural folks have become symbol poor as their land undergoes a metamorphosis. The attempt to replace the lost symbols with foreign symbols renders Africans symbol dependent, making their very own being dependent on others. If the struggle for independence was waged in the name of self-determination, it is clear that the significance of the struggle for the recovery and affirmation of indigenous symbols is yet to be fully recognized. Genuine recognition of this struggle would inevitably bring attention to trees. Those who engage in the recovery process are likely to be viewed as atavistic, as having a morbid and absurd desire to return Africa and Africans to the proverbial Dark Ages. This charge may rest on uncritical worship of the apparent benefits of colonialist and postcolonialist cultures.

On the face of it, the decimation of trees in African appears to be welcome. Economic needs and economic pressures have left Africans with limited options. There has been, and there continues to be, a systematic assault on African trees to make room for cash crops. The colonial economy encouraged Africans to grow cash crops, primarily to help colonial settlers to accumulate wealth, and secondarily to enable Africans to afford the commodities that the colonial powers introduced. To make room for coffee, tobacco, cocoa, sisal, pyrethrum, groundnuts, cotton, sugarcane, and other cash crops, many trees had to be cut down. Shrubs and other vegetation were cleared. This not only resulted in the loss of land for growing food crops, but also curtailed the soil's ability to sustain various forms of life. Old ways of weeding were gradually replaced by herbicides and pesticides. Whenever it rained, these herbicides and pesticides were washed into rivers, streams, and watering holes. Toxic and polluted water was consumed by human beings, by animals, and by other living beings. Trees and other forms of vegetation depended on this toxic and polluted water and, as a result, some have become extinct and others are in the process of becoming extinct. New forms of diseases have emerged.

The cultivation of cash crops replaced the cultivation of food crops, and many Africans assumed and hoped that enough cash would be generated not only to buy food but also to meet other basic needs. Unfortunately, for Africans, cash-crop farming did not generate enough cash to meet their basic needs. It primarily benefited the

European settler communities and their European motherlands. It also benefited a small group of urbanized Africans. To meet the need for food and other needs generated by the demands of modern life, Africans found it difficult, and still find it difficult, to resist cutting down more trees. Tree harvesting for sale also became one of the new economic activities in many parts of Africa. African trees have become integrated into the modern capitalist economy. With the exception of large commercial tree-growing companies, rural Africans could, and can, barely keep up with replacement of the trees that were cut down. Some of the trees are irreplaceable, since they were one of a kind. There has been a death of tree culture, and this death continues. The replacement of indigenous African trees is the replacement of what they meant to Africans, and the replacement trees bring with them their own meanings. Trees are significant, and are significant in ways that are not understood by modern botany. Modern botany carries with it the modern scientific meaning of trees. It is not the only way that trees are significant. There is an African botany that must be considered if one is to make full sense of indigenous African trees.

The split between formal education and indigenous education, and the devaluation of the latter, have gradually transformed the perception of the environmental and ecological environment. The emphasis on modern arboreal science—a science that appears to be the creed of Western European modernity—is gradually replacing indigenous arboreal science at an alarming pace. Trees are at the center of this replacement—a replacement that is not merely physical or mechanical. It is a replacement of a world view in which the nature of human beings and the nature of trees have been radically transformed. Africans have become estranged from themselves and from nature. Rural areas have become the graveyard of African trees and, by implication, the graveyard of the humanity of Africans. African cities have also become a cemetery for African trees. In addition to what has happened to the humanity of Africans, there has been notable destruction and degradation of the environment and of the ecosystem. African rural areas have become the proverbial, actual, and quintessential Heart of Darkness in Africa. Negative ruralism—the belief that rural Africa is the Devil's playground and the negation of modernity and of everything that is associated with civilization—has entered the sphere of religious psychology. It has become an article of faith that is impervious to reason. The notion that I live in the city, therefore I am, or that I live in the rural area, therefore I am not, is a part of this creed. Thus it should not come as a surprise that urban life has become a magnet that irresistibly attracts those who dwell in the rural areas, especially the rural youth. African cities are perceived as the beacon of hope. They are the beacons in the so-called jungles of Africa. They exemplify the best of modernity, the fruit of civilization. The rural areas have become a symbol of shame for urbanized Africans. The urban imperative—the imperative of modernity, the imperative of civilization—has declared war on African rural life. But if one is not dazzled by the apparent city lights and casts a critical gaze on the flight from the rural areas and on the adoration of urban life, to what extent is the city truly restorative or the bearer of African well-being?

Trees are more than instrumental goods for human beings. There are not mere resources for human beings. They have a noninstrumental sense. Thinking about trees and perceiving them exclusively in terms of their usefulness impoverishes not only thinking about them and perceiving them. It also impoverishes our thinking about ourselves and also impoverishes the way we perceive ourselves. It blocks other ways of thinking and other ways of perceiving. In their noninstrumental sense, trees cease being objects for us, and we cease being subjects who come face to face with trees as objects. That is, trees lose their objectness, just as human beings lose their subjectness. With this double loss, there emerges what I have referred to as a primal experience. There is not much information to be conveyed about this experience. Ultimately, it is an experience that one has to undergo. It is an experience whereby what is said about it is indistinguishable from silence. It is the kind of experience that the Western African thinker, Hampâté Bâ, has tried to bring to our attention in his essay "The Living Tradition."[77] There, he claims that, in Africa, a human being is made of every existing element.

The dissolution of subjectness and objectness leaves us in a strange world in which it can be said that trees are us. Hegel would obviously agree with this statement not because he understands it but because he misunderstands it. He would agree with this statement, only to the extent that the "us" refers to Africans and perhaps to some other segments of non-European peoples. It would make sense to him because Africans, he wrote, are yet to cut loose from nature. They are a part of nature and are not conscious of themselves as being apart from nature. In his eyes, Europeans have already severed their ties with nature, and are conscious of themselves as being other than nature. Also, they have thereby severed ties with trees, since they have become fully conscious of their own identity as human beings. For those of us who are non-Hegelians, Hegel was blind to Hegel. He was too humanist to understand himself.

To say that trees are us is to confound the dominant regime of understanding. How could this claim be taken seriously without defying the laws of logic—laws that tell us that a thing is what it is and that it cannot be other than what it is? How can this be the case without violating the ontology of things, without violating the ontological difference that brings intelligibility to the beings of things? The claim that trees are us would appear to be senseless and can only turn our perception and understanding upside down. That is, the claim removes the foundation from both perception and understanding. Evidently, it appears that human beings do not have branches, leaves, stems, roots, or any other feature that distinguishes trees from other beings. Evidently, it also appears that trees do not speak, think, dance, walk, have families, love, build houses, or do other things that human beings do. In either case, none of the features we associate with trees or with human beings exhaust the sense of trees or the sense of being human. It is not that more features need to be added to either trees or to human beings. There is yet a primordial world in which differences vanish without vanishing. This too is a sensorial world, a world that, for the most part, remains closed to us because of the tyranny of the conventional theory of sensing—a theory that legitimizes subject–object sensing as the only mode of sensing. The way of trees in Africa opens this other lived world to us. Our way is thereby also opened up by it. To not find our way in the way of trees in African trees is to not find our way. Conversely, to not find the way of trees in our way is to not find the way of trees in Africa. It is also here that the way of Africa—the way that makes Africa, Africa—is to be found.

They are sites or scents, sites for the birth of strange fruit, sites for the rain to fall, sites for the sun to shine, sites for the wind to blow, sites for the birds to feed on human flesh. To think of Southern trees as a site for multiples sites, is to set aside the view that an understanding of such trees is exhausted when we think of them as things, or as aggregates of leaves, roots, bark, branches, stems, etc. The aggregate that science sums up as the element of a tree diverts us from what is elemental about a tree. A tree is not a thing to which life is added. Plant biology—or, more generally, arboreal science—does not exhaust what is elemental about a tree or what is elemental about the way of a tree. To get to the elemental in either case, one needs to go beneath the arboreal science and uncover what lies there. This takes place if one can attend to memory. Memory recalls the elemental but, for it to do so, it has itself to be elemental. It is as elemental that memory can lead us and secure us in the way of trees in Africa.

They are sites or scents, sites for the birth of strange fruit, sites for the rain to fall, sites for the sun to shine, sites for the wind to blow, sites for the birds to feed on human flesh. To think of Southern trees a site for multiples sites is to set aside the view that an understanding of such trees is exhausted when we think of them as things, or as aggregates of leaves, roots, bark branches, stem etc. The aggregate that science sums up as the element of a tree diverts us from what is elemental about a tree. A tree is not a thing to which life is added. Plant biology, or more generally, arboreal science as understood today, does not exhaust what elemental about a tree or what is elemental about the way of a tree. To get to the elemental in either case one needs to go beneath the arboreal science and uncover what lies there. This takes place if one can attend to memory. Memory recalls the elemental, but for it to do so, it has itself to be elemental. It is as elemental that memory can lead us and secure us in the way of trees in Africa.

Chapter 9
Robben Island Is Not an Island: Introducing No-Geography

9 Robben Island Is Not an Island: Introducing No-Geography

When you are young, you are isolated from others. You are like an isolated island in the ocean or like a lone tree in the desert. When you become old, you realize that you are not isolated. You realize that you are everywhere and nowhere. Then, you are closer to where you are and to where you will be forever.
(An African elder addresses a young person)

By now, Robben Island has captured the attention of millions of people, and there is no doubt that it will continue to draw attention from many more, especially now that that it has been designated as a World Heritage Site. The reason for this historic attention is largely because of the island's association with Nelson Mandela, the first African president of post-apartheid South Africa. It is where Mandela and other African freedom fighters were imprisoned. The significance of this island cannot fully be recognized unless it is recognized that attention is also drawn to those whose attention is drawn to it. The initial attention is directed to the island but, ultimately, if this attention were to follow its natural course, it would lead to paying attention to those who pay attention to it. In other words, this island has a significance that leads beyond it as a way of leading to itself. This island, after all, is an island for us and, as such, it ought to illuminate something about us. The island is an illuminated illuminator. It is a territory that goes beyond everyday geography as a way of being itself. To be under its illumination is to see it as more than a Mandela site. It is a site for each and every one of us. What this implies is not clear. Hopefully, what follows will be a contribution to this intoxicating illumination.

When I was introduced to geography in primary school, I recall how anxious I was when my teacher told us the earth was a sphere. He drew a picture on the blackboard to illustrate what he had in mind. I could not believe that the earth I was walking on—the earth on which gardening took place and the earth where our goats and cows grazed—could be the earth that our teacher was talking about. The earth had to be flat, and I could not imagine this flat earth ever ending. If I walked on it without stopping, I imagined, I could keep on walking forever if I did not fall off. What my teacher said about the earth undermined this confidence. In the light of what my teacher said, my fear was that if I walked far enough I would end up falling off the earth and, if I were to fall off, there would be nothing to fall on, since the teacher did not show anything below the earth. I could not imagine how I or anyone else could fall endlessly. I could not imagine "below the earth." The earth, I imagined, extended endlessly on every side. I could not imagine how anyone could stay on a spherical side of the earth without sliding off, or how one could stand at the bottom of the earth, or how anything could be at the bottom of the earth without falling off. My teacher did not mention anything about gravity and, even if he had, it would not have made any sense to me.

I have to confess that, even today, I am haunted by the idea of nothingness, and I cannot account for why I am haunted, because nothing is nothing and should not cause psychological apprehension for a normal person. There is nothing about me I know of that would lead me to question my sanity. This mood has resonated in ideas I have encountered in the art world, leading me to question the sanity of artists or indeed the sanity of anyone. The earth itself has appeared to me to be enigmatic, especially when it is presented by artists, among whom one must include philosophers. After all, what genuine artists do with paint or with any material they work with, if they are genuine artists, is precisely what genuine philosophers do with words. I often recall the words written by Maurice Merleau-Ponty to describe his sense of an artist:

> The meaning of what the artist is going to say does not exist anywhere—not in things, which as yet have no meaning, nor in the artist himself in his unformulated life. It summons one away from the already constituted reason in which "cultured men" are content to shut themselves, towards a reason that contains its own origins.[78]

Artists too have something to teach us about geography—a geography that may be referred to as no-geography. I use Robben Island to situate this geography. If the title and the passage above generate confusion, it may be worthwhile to bear in mind that confusion is not necessarily a bad thing. It is reasonable to be suspicious of the neighbors who permanently live on the other side of confusion. As Chuang Tzu pointed out, it is indeed true that:

> When the sun and the moon have already come out it is a waste of light to go on burning the torches, isn't it? When the seasonal rains are falling, it's a waste of water to go on irrigating the fields.[79]

But, if I dare say so, for most of us—if not all of us—the sun and the moon have not already come out, and the seasonal rains are yet to fall. It is because of this "not yet" that we are what we are. For us mortals, the sun and the moon are always on the way, and so are the seasonal rains. As Merleau-Ponty observed in his essay on painting, "for painters the world will always be yet to be painted, even if it lasts millions of years . . . it will end without having been conquered in painting."[80] What he says is equally true of all artists and all who are addressed by the artists, which is all of us.

Painting opens the way for our thinking, and it is in a position to do so because thinking itself opens the way for painting. The island is not only subject to painting. It is also subject to thinking. The painter does not dispense with thinking while painting. He or she thinks with his or her brush. The brush thinks. What painting claims for itself, it claims for thinking. Moreover, because painting is the work of the eye and the hand, and because the work of the eye and the hand is the work of the body, thinking itself is to be seen and experienced not only as the work of the eye and the hand but also as the work of the body. Accordingly, thinking is not a stranger to the sensible. It is a part of the sensible and, being so, it is in a position to address Robben Island. This island offers itself to us as sensible. Let us also bear in mind that painting Robben Island is, and remains, a possibility. Painting this island can teach us about this island and, in turn, this island can teach us about painting. It can be painted because it is sensible, and it is so not only for painters but also for all artists. Similarly, it offers itself as such to those of us who are not artists. To think of Robben Island is to think of it from the inside, from the side of the sensible. We ourselves exist inextricably on the side of the island because, like it, we are sensible. It is an extension of what we are, and we are its extension. If this inextricability is the source of confusion, such confusion is to be preserved and nourished. Elemental thinking is oxygenated by confusion. Paradoxical as it may sound, it is the function of authentic thinkers to sow seeds of confusion and to irrigate them with it when they germinate.

One can readily see why the topic would appear to be self-evidently confusing. Logic tells us that a thing cannot be what it is and be what it is not at the same time. Even if one is not carried away by the authority of logic, barring occasional sense deception, sense perception teaches us that what we perceive to be the case is indeed the case. For example, I see that I am what I am and you are what you are. I cannot be what I am and not be what I am. Similarly, you cannot be what you are and not be what you are. One can readily imagine the chaos that would prevail in the world of perception if things were not normally as we perceive them to be. Given this state of affairs, what then can we make of a topic that appears to say what cannot be said meaningfully? How can Robben Island be and not be what it is? How can it not be an island, especially for those who have already been there and know for sure that it is an island? There is a widespread belief that philosophical thinking amounts to nothing more than a play on words—a play that contains nothing substantive. What I have said so far may reinforce this belief. Although it is not my primary objective to dissuade anyone from holding onto this belief, it may be worth bearing in mind that what appears to be a play on words may not be so, and what appears to be substantive may not be so.

To make the claim that Robben Island is not an island flies in the face of geography. It is precisely geography that leads us to conclude that this island is an island, and that it cannot not be an island. But to believe that the authority of geography is unassailable is to embrace an uncritical view of geography. Geography, one must bear in mind, is an anthropomorphic conception of the earth. It is a specific human inscription of the earth. Without such an inscription, there would be no geography, and without geography, there would be no islands. There would be no Robben Island.

The very naming of this island "Robben Island" is human naming—a contingent naming, for one could readily imagine this island being named differently. To be sure, one could argue that regardless of how it is named, the island still remains an island, and how or what it is named does not affect its ontological status. But this argument does not preclude the possibility that this island could be named or be conceived otherwise. This island need not necessarily be named "Island." It could be unnamed or nameless. In short, let us say that the authority of geography is not unassailable. Postmodernity has reminded us that geographical discourse is not a metadiscourse. Like any other phenomenon, it is subject to multiple discourses. In regard to the inscription of the earth, we should be speaking of multiple geographies, a multiplicity that includes the no-geography—the geography that constitutes the soil from which conventional geography arises and from which it receives nourishment.

If we could imagine an earth in itself, it could have a stand on which it could name itself "Earth." And if it could name itself, possibly it could name a part of its territory "Island." Having a stand, however, is a human mode of being. The earth cannot name itself "Earth" and cannot territorialize itself. It is cannot be conscious of itself as having areas, some of which would be islands. We are eternally deprived of the possibility of approaching the earth as it is in itself. In his *Critique of Pure Reason*,[81] Immanuel Kant persuasively argued that a claim that things in themselves are knowable is nonsensical. And it would be equally absurd to claim that things can know themselves. In regard to geography, what we can validly claim is that the knowledge of the earth, or the knowledge of any part of it, is mediated by us. In regard to Robben Island, what we are presented with is an earthly human inscription. We are without the possibility of going behind, above, or beneath this inscription to the sense of this island as it could have in itself. In itself, the island is without sense. Behind, beneath, and above this island, there is nothing. But this nothing is not accidental to the being of this island. It is integral to it if only because as nothing it cannot be separated from it. It sustains it in its being.

The modern conception of the earth and what pertains to it is largely a scientific conception. Crudely put, it is a physicalistic conception, and so is what pertains to it. That is, the earth is a physical phenomenon, and so would be any part of it. This would imply that any island—not just Robben Island—would be a physical phenomenon. Our conception of Robben Island, as would be the case with our understanding of Robben Island, would be subject to physical science. This view of the earth and of its parts tends to be reinforced by common sense. Common sense leads us to believe that there are indeed physical objects that exist independently of us. In addition to offering us a scientific view of the earth, modernity has also offered us the idea of liberty—an idea that not only has come to define who and what we are but also has found its way into our thinking and into our perception, in general. One of the unheralded outcomes of the practice of this idea is that it has led to the questioning of modernity and its offerings. In putting into practice the idea of liberty, we find ourselves attempting to free ourselves from the regime of modernity, or from what has turned out to be the tyranny of modernity. One of the venues for this undertaking is the attempt to free ourselves from the tyranny of scientific conception and from the tyranny of common sense. Edmund Husserl, the founder of modern phenomenology, has brought our attention to the danger of what he calls sensation-monism -a monism that is driven by conventional understanding of natural science. He correctly notes:

> Among non-naturalists, too, there is a widespread tendency to look upon positive science as the only strict science and to recognize as scientific philosophy only one that is based on this sort of science. That, however, is also only prejudice, and it would be a fundamental error to want for that reason to deviate from the line of strict science.[82]

Why, we have found ourselves asking, should the conception of the earth and of what pertains to it be monopolized by physical science and by common sense? Why, in our case, should the conception and the understanding of Robben Island be monopolized by science and by common sense? Science, after all, is our science; it is the science of the human by the human. Similarly, common sense is our common sense. We are not outsiders to science or to common sense. All is up to us. In thinking about the earth and about whatever pertains to it, we are inevitably thinking about ourselves.

Let us then say that Robben Island is the sense that we have of it. Now, the sense we have of it is multiple, and it is in the context of multiplicity that I want us disabused of the notion that the topic of this presentation is absurd or meaningless. The understanding of what we understand is a product of mediation. Mediating what we understand amounts to constructing the meaning of what we understand. This applies to our understanding of Robben Island. Robben Island is what we make of it, and if it is what we make of it, it is because, initially, it is nothing. It is significantly an island for us. It does not exist independently of us. To think of it otherwise is not to think about it at all. It is indeed the case that we think of Robben Island as if it were independent of us. We normally think of it as a physical territory that would be there even if we were not there. This thinking, however, is without foundation, if only because what it claims can never be demonstrated to be the case. Should this be the case, what our task calls for is to articulate how this island derives its sense. I want to focus on this task from an autobiographical perspective. To some of us, this perspective may sound scandalous because we have succumbed to the pressure of a modern sensibility that seeks to socialize us into hearing only what is objective or what is impersonal. This pressure appears to emanate from a prejudice in the understanding of science or from a prejudice in the understanding of reason. Both have been marshaled to build up the ideology of the objectivism and the ideology of the impersonalized. However, being scandalous may have an important role to play in enhancing knowledge and truth, and in enriching our experience. It may enrich our understanding. It may free us and make us ready for the understanding of Robben Island. It must be recognized that during the apartheid era, the meaning of Robben Island was imprisoned with the imprisonment of prisoners. And when the prisoners were freed after the end of apartheid, its meaning was thereby freed.

One day, I found myself at Hiroshima Peace Memorial Park. I had gone there to see and experience the place of mass incineration of human beings by human beings—to see the consequence of the atom bomb dropped by the Americans on the Japanese. On another day, I found myself in a slave dungeon in Salvador, Bahia, Brazil, to see and experience a holding place where Africans were tortured and chained to the wall and to the floor by Portuguese enslavers. On another day, a thought occurred to me that I should go to South Africa and visit Robben Island, to see and experience a place where African freedom fighters were imprisoned and tortured. I have not pursued this thought to the point of physically visiting this island and, at present, I have no intention of visiting it. I find myself questioning this desire—a questioning that haunts me whenever I think of my previous visits to Salvador and Hiroshima. I often find myself asking, why did I ever want to visit these places? I have a feeling that if I could start all over again, I would not want to visit them. And there are times when I do not want even to think about them. But this desire to visit where I did not want to visit will not simply go away. Perhaps, if I squarely face it, it may go away for good. However, we should not be surprised if this turns out to be nothing more than wishful thinking—thinking that tells me more about myself, about what is beyond myself as a part of my being. What is beyond any one of us is still a part of what we are.

What, I ask myself, gave rise to the desire to visit these places? A broader question has presented itself to me: why would anyone want to visit these places? What is it about me that generates this desire? And insofar as I am of the earth, what is it about my earthliness that generates this desire? These questions are interrelated, for I am anyone, and anyone is me. They are questions that call for an attempt to address myself to my self—an address that appears to be intrinsically linked to other human beings if only because I am one of them, and they are of me. The presence of Robben Island in my consciousness forces me to try and come to terms with myself. This presence is not solely the presence of this island; it is also the presence of myself to myself. I am touched by the presence of this island in a way that I am touched by the presence of myself to myself. Differently stated, in a sense, this island is about me. Insofar as I am with you and you are with me as part of being human, it is also about you. This island is my island, and it is your island. This island is ours sensuously, and it is our island not only collectively but also communally. Insofar as this island is not an island, and to the extent that it has a bearing on who and what we are, we are what we are not, and we are not what we are. If this island is what it is not, perhaps I myself am what I am not, and you are what you are not. That is, to be human is to not be. Here, the "not" matters existentially and ontologically.

It should be clear now that in trying to make sense of Robben Island, I will be psychoanalyzing myself, and just to alert you, I will also be psychoanalyzing you. The latter is necessitated because I am you and you are me. I am not sure I am honest enough with myself to psychoanalyze myself, and I may be pretentious in believing that I can be successful in analyzing you. There is a saying among lawyers that it is only a fool who has himself for a lawyer, but it is not self-evident that if a lawyer hires another lawyer, he or she is necessarily better off. Clearly, self-analysis has its pitfalls, but there are also pitfalls when one offers oneself to others for analysis. In either case, there is a possibility for misdiagnosis and, consequently, a possibility of the wrong therapy. It is also worth noting that self-analysis and being analyzed by another are not mutually exclusive, if only because the other is not foreign to what one is.

Robben Island has drawn attention to the students of what have been called dark sites in various parts of the world: Hiroshima, Nagasaki, Ground Zero, the killing fields of Cambodia, Viet Nam, the Americas, Australia, the killing fields of Rwanda, Auschwitz-Birkenau, Treblinka, Leopold's Congo, Jonestown, war sites, and other places of mass annihilation of human beings by human beings. These places have generated what has been called dark tourism or thanatotourism. Evidently, the attraction is not just to a place—it is, rather, to what the visited place symbolizes. Before these places were what they have become, they were not what they have become. It is the sense of the place that attracts. This sense is not inherent in the place. In literature, we also notice plays or novels that attract dark tourists and or thanatotourists. Those who are familiar with classical Greek plays will readily recall, for example, the tragedy that struck the house of Atreus. We have Greek tragedies recorded by Sophocles, Euripides, and other Greek playwrights. What attracts these writers to create these tragic spectacles? And why is there an audience for these compositions? How did the Greeks experience the places where these plays were staged, and how did they experience themselves in this experience? Today, why do we go to the theaters where these tragic plays are enacted? How do we experience the places where they are staged, and how do we experience ourselves in the experience of them? Have we been taken over by sadomasochism—a sadomasochism that is nourished by these plays? What kind of beings are we, beings that are attracted to these plays?

What gave rise to my desire to visit Robben Island has nothing to do with dark tourism or with thanatotourism. I did not think of myself as a tourist. And I did not want to visit Robben Island for artistic inspiration. As is the case with many other individuals, I wanted to go see and experience Robben Island—the island that has come today to be associated with Nelson Mandela. But before Mandela became a central figure in our thinking about this island, I was familiar with it as a prison for those who engaged in anti-apartheid struggle. It was a destination for prominent anti-apartheid South African leaders, especially the leaders who commanded the attention of the masses of anti-apartheid crusaders within South Africa. Because these leaders posed a serious threat to the apartheid regime, they had to be taken to a maximum security prison. Robben Island was an ideal place to send them. It was a place for the forbidden ones. This island was constituted as an island for the unwantables. At one time, the unwantables on this island included the insane and lepers. Except for the wardens, administrators, the inmates, everyone else was restricted to the mainland. But here, we should reflect on this division—a division that was not driven by natural necessity. Robben Island was not inherently a place for the unwantable. Likewise, her inhabitants were not inherently unwantable. There is nothing eternal about the separation between the inhabitants of this place and the inhabitants of the African mainland. The existence of the separation reflects a rupture in our being. How, one may ask, can fellow human beings be wholly other to other human beings? Must we not be trespassers over the boundary that keeps us apart from what or who we are to be ourselves? Must we not have an alternative geography, a no-geography—a geography that unites instead of separating? Isn't the "no" ingrained in the very core of our being an essential mode of our being? Isn't everyone who has been associated with this island, or who is associated with it (all of us), an example of this "no"? Must the island not exist as a "no" to be itself?

My initial attraction to this island was not primarily due the sympathy I had for those who were imprisoned on it or due to the sympathy I had for the antiapartheid struggle. The imprisoned were fellow Africans, fellow human beings, and the struggle was ultimately my struggle, a struggle for myself. I saw this struggle as a part of the overall struggle to overcome European oppression of Africans. I saw it as a struggle to end a violent expropriation of African resources and land, as a struggle to end the exploitation of African labor. I saw it as an attempt to stem a barbaric civilization that Europeans had unleashed on Africans. It was an intimate struggle for me because I was a victim of these processes. It did not matter to me that I was not born in South Africa. What mattered to me is that I was an African and a human being and, as such, I suffered the indignity to which any African was subjected because he or she was an African. It is this awareness of myself that has forced me to rethink my initial desire to go and visit Robben Island. I have a feeling that I have already seen what I wanted to see and have experienced what I wanted to experience. But what have I already seen, and what have I already experienced? What is it

9 Robben Island Is Not an Island: Introducing No-Geography

that was problematizing my seeing? What is it that problematized the experience that I was after? What is it about this place, Robben Island, that called for self-examination? How could I have been there without having been there? What kind of spatiality is at work here? What kind of geography is at work here? What is the geography of self, such that it would lead me to be here and there? Clearly, there is nothing in my previous education in geography that has prepared me for this type of experience. Nothing has prepared me for human geography, for a geography of being human—the geography that brought into relief the awareness that a threat to human dignity is a threat to human dignity everywhere, a geography that would render movement to any place a movement to every place, a movement that would negate itself as movement, since there would be nowhere to move.

On the basis of the way I think about myself, I find myself reflecting on what passes as conventional geography—a geography that is far from lived geography, a geography in which boundaries are intrinsically horizonal and trespassable. In conventional geography, Robben Island is an island off the coast of Cape Town in South Africa. It is an island that is cut off from continental Africa. The Republic of South African has jurisdiction over it. If it falls under this jurisdiction, it is an integral part of the Republic of South Africa. This means that the water that separates it from continental South Africa does not separate. It unites Robben Island with the continental area of the Republic of South Africa. This unification effaces the islandness of this island. As for the boundaries of the Republic of South Africa, we ought not to forget their malleability. What are the geographical boundaries of this republic? Clearly, one can point to political geography, which gives this republic a territory that borders Namibia to the northwest, Botswana in the north, Zimbabwe in the north, and Mozambique in the east, and that surrounds Swaziland and Lesoto. The boundaries of these other countries separate them from other African countries which, in turn, have boundaries that separate them from other African countries, etc. One must not forget that these boundaries are creatures of colonial history. Without this history, one could imagine an alternative configuration of African nations, including the possibility of having the entire continent constituting one nation. The grid that constitutes national boundaries in Africa has not been there from time immemorial, and there is no reason to believe that it will be there forever. This grid is the grid of African selves, and these boundaries are the boundaries of African selves. There is nothing eternal about the selves so constituted. Primarily nothing separates the selves so constituted, and every self is itself subject to endless constitution. Each self is inescapably endlessly haunted by the nothingness of its own being.

Secondly, in Africa today, we have a political geography that is a product of European colonial cartography. It represents a colonialist cartography that, so far, has been spared from anticolonial struggle. There is an illusion, and perhaps a delusion, that the anticolonial struggle for African independence has been won, and that it is now time to engage in business as usual, a part of which is to conduct nation state business. The Republic of South Africa is now a sovereign state, just as are other African nation states. Since Robben Island is under the jurisdiction of a sovereign republic, managing its affairs is an internal affair of this republic. The internal is a political internal. What has been forgotten is that this republic, as is the case with most of the other African nation states, is a product of European political cartography. The African anti-colonial struggle is not over unless this cartography is replaced by an African political cartography. There is a geography-centered anti-colonial struggle that remains to be waged. Robben Island is a part of this struggle. It has a political sense. What is meant by "political" needs need to be fully articulated and freed from the confines of political science, which is a major obstacle in grasping the full sense of the political. It may be worth recalling that in classical Greek thinking, the political defined what it was to be a human being. They study of politics was the study of what it takes to be a human being. Such a study took ethics into account. Ethics appears to have disappeared in the modern study of politics. If Robben Island housed political prisoners, such as Mandela and Sisulu, we cannot fully understand what it means to be a political prisoner until we get a full sense of the political. For the most part, what modernity has bequeathed to us as political is an evasion of the political. It is a flight from the political—the political that defines us in intention and in extension. Until we get a full sense of the political, we will not fully grasp the political sense of Robben Island. Until this happens, we will not grasp the geography that is proper to this island.

To the extent that Robben Island is politically incorporated into the Republic of South Africa, one needs to call on the assistance of political education to understand Robben Island. It is also historically the case that the sense of this island has been, and remains, politically contested. First, we have the Portuguese, who claimed it by "discovery," then it was taken over by the Dutch; after the Dutch, it was taken over by the British, and after the successful war against the British, the European settler community took over. It is under the rule of this community that South African became a republic. Until Africans took over the political leadership of this republic, Robben Island was an island that derived its sense from the Europeans occupiers. The island derived its sense from European colonial and imperialistic politics. It was a part of European political cartography. Today, it appears to be a part of African political cartography. Africans have inherited a legacy of politics that conceals what is essential about being human. The political cartography of this island and, more generally, the political geography of this island—whether European or African—obscures the elemental understanding of this island. What conventional cartography conceals today is that cartography—as the art of making maps—is, at the same time, the art of making self. That is, in cartography, man makes himself, and if he makes himself, it is because to begin with, he is nothing. The Robben Island that European sought to create is a Robben Island whose image of being human excluded Africans. Africans contested this creation and the image of human being that European sought to create. They were set on creating an image of being human than included the humanity of Africans.

Currently, there are ideas that are being floated around as to what is to be done with this island. There is an attempt to determine whether the island should be transformed into a theme park, a tourist destination, a museum, or a living shrine in honor of Mandela. Some decisions have already been made about what this island is to become. The island has been declared a museum, and plans are in place to transform it into a fully developed tourist destination. It has also been declared to be

9 Robben Island Is Not an Island: Introducing No-Geography

a World Heritage Site. This tells us that the assumption underlying the ideas floated around is that, at present, the island is a *tabula rasa* that calls for inscription. To think of the island this way is to think of it as empty. We must pay close attention to the void that this island is, if it is to be understood. The voidness of this island does not lie on its surface. This island is voidness itself. It is this mode of its being that is captured in the topic of this reflection—Robben Island as an island that is not an island. Let us reflect more on what is meant by this claim.

Assuming that this island is voidness, how then do we set boundaries to it? How can one set boundaries to what is not? Can we even call it an island? To call it an island is to recognize that it has boundaries. But if we think of it as voidness, are we not necessarily deprived of such recognition? How does one put a boundary on voidness? Isn't it the very nature of voidness to defy subjection to boundaries? These questions, clearly, indicate the limits of logic and also the limits of geography as a science. As Heidegger noted, in essential matters, science is not very helpful to us, especially when it attempts to venture into what is elemental, insofar as what is elemental brings nothing into relief and wants to think it through. As he points out in his essay on metaphysics, logic and science will avoid dealing with nothing, primarily because nothing is nothing.

Earlier we said that Robben Island is a part of the Republic of South Africa. If we are still governed by what we said in our understanding of what we said, we have a paradox here. In the light of what has been said above, by being a part of South Africa, Robben Island affects the Republic of South Africa with the nothingness that it is. Assuming that it is inherently a part of South Africa, South Africa turns out to be the nothingness that Robben Island is. That is, the Republic of South Africa is a republic of nothingness. Moreover, if it assumed that this republic is inherently a part of Africa, Africa herself meets the same fate: it belongs to nothingness. That is, Africa is nothingness. Let us still go further. Africa is a part of the earth, an inherent part of the earth. As nothingness, Africa will inevitably introduce us to the nothingness that the earth is. What we end up with is an earth that is nothingness. How dare we transform real geography into a geography of nothingness, into a no-geography? But what kind of geography is this, the geography of nothing? But are we merely playing with words here? Have we allowed ourselves to be carried away recklessly by thinking? And what does this say about us? Here, let us not hesitate. Let us open ourselves to what is to come, and let us bear in mind that what is to come is what has been and is what is.

In 1996, Robben Island was declared a World Heritage Site. The geographical sense of this declaration is not obvious. It is not obvious, because how the earth relates to the world is not obvious. The earth is worldly. The earthliness of Robben Island makes this island worldly. Being worldly, the earth is without designatable boundaries. Being earthly, Robben Island is without designatable boundaries. It is not an island—an island that is cut off from anything. In the twentieth century, Heidegger popularized the notion that a human being is a being in- the- world. Had he taken the earthliness of the world seriously or the worldliness of the earth seriously, he would have interpreted and understood the human being as a being- in- the- earth. Just as he made clear that the understanding of what it is to be a being in the world should not lead one to view the world as a container that contains human beings, we are to understand being in the earth in the same manner. The world is not of a thingly character. We need to go further than Heidegger and observe that being human is being of the earth. This observation disabuses us of the temptation to juxtapose our being and the being of the earth. We do not have an external relation with the earth, because we are earthly. The worldly earth is not a container of human beings. Hampâté Bâ, a West African thinker from Mali, refers to an African myth of creation in which it is said that at the beginning, the Maker made man from every element that makes up the earth. That is, man is of the earth. Man is a *Mwananchi* (a Kiswahili word meaning son of the soil, or son of the earth). Worldliness and earthliness are modes of being human, each being the face of the other, and each instantiates our singularity and, at the same time, instantiates our organic unity, our indivisibility. Robben Islandness is earthliness and, as such, it is worldliness. This is an island that is what it is by surpassing itself. There is a song, with lyrics by Woody Guthrie, an American folk singer, that in part says:

> This land is your land,
> this land is my land
> From California, to the New York Island
> From the redwood forest, to the gulf stream waters
> This land was made for you and me
>
> As I was walking I saw a sign
> And the sign said…. No tres passin'
> But on the other side … it didn't say nothin!
> But that side was made for you and me.

We are projected into this other side, the side that didn't say nothin' as a mode of our being. If it is a side that is made for you and me, it is available to us as nothing. This nothing summons us into itself. And because nothin' is nothin', to take heed of this summons is to take heed of nothing in such a manner that we are preserved in it as nothin'. We exist in it as the summoned ones. To be so summoned is to render us available to ourselves. This rendering available is the work of nothingness. This nothingness is internal to us. It makes us be what we are. Moreover, if we pay close attention, the side of the sign that says "no tres passin' " is inseparable from the side that says nothin'. One cannot separate something from nothing or separate nothing from something. The side that says "no tres passin' " is perennially haunted by the side that says nothing. The side that says nothin' is an integral part of the side that says "no tres passin'." The latter contains a "no" that implicates it in the being of the other side. It is only what can be trespassable that can call for a sign that says "no tres passin'."

There is space that separates California from the New York island. This is why California is California and why the New York island is the New York island. But there is no space that separates California from the New York island. Both are parts of the USA—territories of the USA. Lest we forget, the USA is a part of the earth— a territory of the earth. This makes California and the New York island a part of the earth. As the USA is a part of the earth, how could it be so without being a part of Robben Island, which is itself a part of the earth? Many in the USA who sing this song do not have a clue to what this song ultimately signifies. They are held hostages to an alienating sense of this song. They are blind to the claim that the song makes of our situation as human beings—a situation in which all of us are at home, whether we are or are not Americans. Nationalism has been, and continues to be, disastrous for human self-awareness. It sets us apart from each other, alienates us from each other. It is our communal self that constitutes our elemental humanity. One is a human being in communality with all human beings. We are all citizens of Robben Island. Robben Island is our Island regardess of where we live. It is our Island. So far, this remains as the untold story of our being.

Robben Island is a part of Africa, and Africa is a part of the earth. The earth unifies Africa and the USA, and these are united with other territories of the earth. The earth is the mother of all—the mother of us all insofar as we are earthly. A part of what prevents this awareness from coming into relief is our imprisonment in our territories. We are yet to take the walk that Guthrie took. As he tells us, when he was walking, he saw a sign that said "no tres passin'," but the other side of this sign didn't say nothin', and then he says that that side too was made for you and me. This nothingness is for us too. But what does this mean? Here, trespassing is nullified. We are invited to walk into this nothingness—a nothingness that pulls us into itself. It is not a stranger to what we are, for we are of it. Nothingness, too, has a place in geography, and it is in such geography that Robben Island is constituted and in which it is to be understood.

If I did not go to Robben Island, and if my desire to go there is no longer there, perhaps it is because I have realized that there is nowhere to go. Here has become there, and there has become here. This is not to deny that there is a here, and that there is a there. It is a recognition of our geographical rootedness. A painter, as is the case with all artists, calls attention to this rootedness. It is the geography of the artists. The work or art is a geographical work. It teaches us about the earth.

That nowhere from which what the artist is going to say arises is that nowhere from which what has been said about Robben Island arises, and it is where what has been said about it reverts to and dwells. It is a nowhere-geography from which conventional geography arises and from which it derives its essential sense. To get a sense of Robben Island, one must have a dwelling there. It is there, too, that one gets the sense of what one is as a human being.

Robben Island is not only a beacon of light that illuminates Africa and Africans, but also a beacon that illuminates the entire earth, thereby illuminating all human beings, wherever they are and whoever they are. This beacon does not only illuminate all human beings wherever they are. It illuminates itself as such. It has now become fashionable for the United Nations to designate diverse sites as World Heritage Sites. If these sites are to be more than tourist attractions, they must call attention to what Robben Island calls to our attention: recognition and commitment to the living dignity of all human beings. To perform this function, this island must cease being an island and take on a planetary sense. It must be seen and understood as an island that is not an island. This seeing or understanding is both present and ahead of us. Either has an affecting presence. This is a part of what Robben Island illuminates.

Chapter 10
Conclusion

An elderly African sees a young man carrying flywhisk and says to him, "Young man, put down the fly whisk and go wash your hands before touching anything else". "Why", the young man asks. "Is it dirty?' No. it is not dirty. The elder says to the young man, "Your hands are dirty and by touching it you have made it dirty. " Look", the young man says, "I cannot see any dirt where I touched it. Besides, I just washed my hands a few minutes ago. See, my hands are clean". "You are blind", the elderly African says to the young man. Your hands are dirty and

you have dirtied the flywhisk by touching it. In our country, only the elders can hold the flywhisk without dirtying it. They see dirt where young people do not see it. When you get to be an elder, you will be able to see the dirt you cannot see now. By then, you will have clean hands and, with cleans hands, you do not dirt it when you touch it. Until you are an elder you are to stay away from flywhisks. Meanwhile, go on with the business of being young. It just that elders be elders and that the young be young. You have behaved unjustly and this is incompatible with your station in life. The elderly African takes the flywhisk from the young man, brushes the young man's his face with it and spits on the ground. He then informs the young man that the injustice has been removed and now he can resume the business of being young. (An exchange between an African elder and a Young person)

An Africa fly whisk is often encountered in a tourist shop, at an art gallery, in a museum, or in a private collection, where it is exhibited as a tribal or ethnic artifact. It has been transformed into an ethnic or tribal artifact among other such artifacts. It has been researched, and still is being researched, by cultural anthropologists and art historians to add to the stock of tribal or ethnic knowledge. It is now among the items in the landscape of African tourism. Undoubtedly, it is contributing to the national revenue in some African countries and has been an object of export to other countries. What has happened to it is nothing short of transubstantiation. It has ceased to be what it was, and to be what it ought to be. It was not, and it ought not to be, an artifact. It was, and it ought to be, a site where being African is constituted and illuminated. It is the lighting of the African world—a world in which being African is constituted and illuminated. It ought not to be taken exclusively as an object or as an artifact. In a primordial sense, it has no thingly character. Its being is to constitute and to illuminate what is constituted. It haunts those who encounter "it." In an encounter with "it," it ceases being an "it." The encounter is a self-encounter. In the encounter, the materials that make it collaborate with one another in common self-effacement and illuminate this effacement. After the effacement, what emerges and illuminates is comprehensive experience that opens up everything to everything. Here, boundarylessness is experienced and illuminated. Here is the home of the African fly whisk—a home that is, at the same time, the home of justice. Bringing together what ought to be together and maintaining this togetherness is the hallmark of justice. An African fly whisk is a site of justice. As such, it wards off injustice.

An African fly whisk wards off evil. By warding off evil, it illuminates what evil is. It instructs those who are ignorant of evil by opening their eyes to what is evil. Ignorance is evil. The word "evil" has multiple senses. It has a religious sense. It could refer to an offense against a god or against gods. But a religious sense covers more than the gods. A religious offense need not necessarily be an offense against a god or gods. In African and elsewhere, one finds religions without a god or gods. In Africa, the religious encompasses the gods or the goddesses. Ultimately, the religious is ecological. Accordingly, a religious offense is an offense against ecology. It is an offense against being, against life. Consequently, the evil that is warded off by the African fly whisk is an evil that is deemed as such by Africans. Ecological disturbance is an evil. It is an injustice to ecology. Such disturbance is harmful not only to human beings but to all life and to everything that is. In African seeing, what is evil is what threatens life—life not just in an anthropological or humanistic sense but also in the ecological sense. Human life is a part of the ecology of life. When human life is threatened, the entire ecology of life is threatened, and when nonhuman life is threatened, human life is also thereby threatened. For example, an individual is not well if his or her relatives and neighbors are not well. One's neighbors are not only fellow human beings. They consist of all living things in one's neighborhood. When one's chickens, goats, cattle, camels, or pets are not well, one is not well. When one's crops are not well, one is not well, and when plants are not well, one is not well. Even the health of inorganic things affects one's health. They are a part of the overall human well-being. In short, evil is more than the evil that affects human beings as isolated beings. It has a cosmic range. The African fly whisk illuminates this cosmic dimension of evil, and it is the evil that it ultimately wards off. It is precisely for this reason that it is said above that justice is implicated in the life of the African fly whisk. The fly whisk secures justice from the threat of injustice, promotes harmony in life, and secures cosmic order. It keeps injustice and disharmony at life's edge.

The African fly whisk embodies the work of African philosophical illumination. This illumination should guide us to a conclusion that is proper to this book—the conclusion it deserves. It is a philosophy book and, like any other philosophy book, it deserves a philosophical conclusion. As an African philosophy book, its conclusion should be philosophically illuminating in an African way. As if it were by inner necessity, the conclusion is a continuation of what has been said. It should be philosophically illuminating. The conclusion is not a summary of what has been said. It illuminates what has been illuminated. Accordingly, what has been said is not to be placed in the past tense as having been said. What has been said has not been said definitively. To this extent, this conclusion is itself not a conclusion. It is not concluding. Were it to conclude, it would not be philosophically illuminating. One would have a false expectation if one expected to have a closure to a book on African philosophical illumination. A philosophy book is bound by philosophical time. A philosophical time is a time in which the past is in the present and in which the present is in the future. The future itself is both in the present and in the past. This is what should be expected of a philosophy book on African philosophical illumination. What is philosophically African about this book is illuminated in this nonconcluding conclusion. It cannot be stated conclusively. Inconclusiveness permeates every aspect of this book. Nothing is new or added by this conclusion. This is not to say that what has been said has exhaustively been said. As pointed above, what has been said is present in what is said and what will be said. In philosophy, temporal moments are inseparable from each other. This is the nature of a philosophical journey. One knows not where one is going or where one is coming from. One finds oneself on the way. One becomes what one is on the way.

The belief that philosophical illumination is exclusively a matter of the mind, reason, or soul fails to grasp the range of illumination and impoverishes it. It privileges human beings over all other beings insofar as human beings are said to distinguish themselves by having a mind, reason, or a soul. This privileging is a mere human prejudice that obscures the larger world that is shared by both human beings and nonhuman beings. Everything in nature illuminates and is illuminated as such by philosophy, and philosophy is itself illuminated by everything in nature. We are natural beings. Our bodies illuminate. Our feet illuminate, and what they step on illuminates. The hand illuminates, and what it touches equally illuminates. The same can be said about all of the senses and about what is sensed. Sensorial nature illuminates as it illuminated. An incorporeal being, such as the Christian God, cannot illuminate the sensorial world, for it takes what is sensorial to illuminate the sensorial.

What is African is a part of nature. How this is the case is subject to perennial curiosity, for nature is the site of curiosity. Everything in nature is curious. Being curious does not set human beings apart from other beings. Even if one were to believe otherwise, one would have the task of defining what a human being is. Undertaking this task opens a path to the possibility of the linkage that human beings have with other beings. The restriction of illumination to the mind, intellect, reason, or the soul ignores human embodiment. Modern Western philosophers present us with a dualistic understanding of a human being, emphasizing thinking as the essence of what it is be truly human and seeing the body not only as not being essential to being human but also emphasizing the mind as that which illuminates not only itself but everything else. A human being so conceived is not human. It cannot illuminate anything or be illuminated.

During my childhood, I heard a story whose message I have not forgotten. Often, in my village, elders used to sit with young boys in the evening, instructing them on how to conduct their lives. Instead of telling them what to do or what not to do, the instruction took the form of stories. Stories more easily caught the attention of children and were easier to retain in memory. The following story is one of the few that continue to hold great significance to my life.

> Long time ago there was an old man who lived in a forest. He rarely came out of the forest and whenever he did so. He spent only a few hours in the village. Back at home, in the forest he knew about every tree in the forest and his knowledge was such that the villagers said that the trees knew him. To build their huts, the villagers visited him and had him cut trees for them. The village women would come into the forest looking for firewood and he would guide them as to what wood was dry and suitable and cut them for them. Whenever and wherever he was walking about in the forest and whenever he ventured out the light axe that he used for cutting wood always hang on his shoulder. One day, after a hard work, he left for the village. After spending some time with the villages, he was on his way back to the forest when he imagined that he did not have his axe with him. Thinking that he had dropped it on the way from the village, he retraced his steps back to the village but the axe was nowhere to be found. He returned to his dwelling discovered and looked for it everywhere but was not to be found. He decided to return to the village hoping that someone had picked

it up and would not mind returning it to him. A young man in the village recognized him and saw right away that he was disturbed about something. He offered to offer any help that may be needed. The man from the forest informed him that he had lost his axe and had looked for it and could find it anywhere. The young man started laughing and appears to be uncontained in his laughter. The old man asked him why he was so insensitive about his predicament. He did not understand what was so funny about the situation. He turned away in anger but the young man stopped him before he could get away and told him that he knew where the axe was. "Old man, he said, why don't' you look at your shoulder?" The old man looked at his shoulder, and lo behold, the axe was always where he kept it. In astonishment, the old man thanked young man and resumed his way back to the forest. Since then, both have remained friends.

It was rare that the elders explained the sense of the stories. It was left to the children to explore the meaning of the stories on their own. When one is a baby, it makes sense to be fed by an adult. When one is no longer a baby, one must feed himself or herself. Not explaining the sense of the stories was a way for the elders to release the children from the tutelage of the elders so that they could learn to think for themselves, so that they could discover for themselves how to live. What philosophical illumination is cannot be taught, and that it cannot be taught cannot be taught. This is the way of African philosophical illuminations. An African fly whisk is the site of this illumination—illumination that sheds light on what threatens life. It restores the vital balance in life and in nature. It has a medicinal power. It is a part of African medical science. What it is has been covered up by intruders in Africa. As indicated earlier, today it has taken on a permanent place in the tourist art industry. It has been transformed into an ethnic or tribal artifact among other such artifacts. In the academic landscape, it has been researched, and still is being researched, by cultural anthropologists to add to the stock of tribal or ethnic knowledge. What has happened to it is nothing short of transubstantiation to the detriment of African self-awareness, the African sense of nature, and the African's well-being. It has ceased to be what it was and to be what it ought to be. It was not, and it ought not to be, an artifact. It was, and it ought to be, a site where being African is constituted and illuminated. It is the lighting of the African's ever expanding world.

I have found the ever expanding world of the African reciprocated in Taoism, which should not be a surprise once one has recognized and experienced the cosmological sense of one's being. Lao Tzu says:

> Thirty spokes are made one by holes in a hub
> By vacancies joining them for a wheel's use;
> The use of clay in molding pitchers
> Comes from the hollow of its absence;
> Doors, windows, in a house,
> Are used for their emptiness:
> thus we are helped by what is not
> To use what is.[83]

The prominence of emptiness at the heart of beings is not peculiar to Taoism or to Chinese thinking. It is at the heart of all elemental modes of seeing and thought everywhere, and it is at the heart of all beings everywhere. Africa is not an exception. Seeing, thinking, and beings, as understood by Africans, exhibit this mode of being. Moreover, properly understood, emptiness is not internal to beings. It is the flesh of their being. Accordingly, no being can be, or be understood, without taking this element into consideration. If Africa and being African come across as indefinable, it is because of this element. The same must be said about what is to be understood in the expression "African philosophical illumination." One cannot objectify what is expressed in this expression. If one seeks to find out whether what has been said in this book is true, one should not be looking for an object that would make what has been said true. For example, one's Africanness should not be denied because one no longer "scars" his or her body. One's Africanness should not be denied because one does not dress or speak the language of one's ancestors. One's Africanness should not be denied because one does not engage in African social and cultural practices. One cannot mummify Africa, Africans, or African things. It is precisely the project of mummification that was undertaken by the enslavers and colonizers of Africans. Moreover, the mummifiers could not carry out this project without mummifying themselves, without denying themselves as human beings. It is also essential that the notion of Africanness itself be secured from mummification. This can be accomplished by ensuring that it is not immunized against emptiness. There will also be a tomorrow and the day after tomorrow of Africanness. African philosophical illumination oxygenates emptiness and, as such, it serves as an antidote to whatever threatens emptiness. It exhausts itself in doing so.

Emptiness is not interior to beings. It permeates the being of beings. It is what makes what is be what it is. Since this is the case, beings are interrelated. One emptiness is not a barrier to any other emptiness. Emptiness permeates everything that is. Philosophy—African or non-African—is in its service. Whatever philosophy encounters, it awakens emptiness in. It illuminates emptiness in what it encounters. It is able to do this because it is itself emptiness. African philosophy is not an exception. Nothing more or less should be expected of it. It is what must be expected of all philosophy. Enslaving Africans and colonizing them was an attempt to negate the emptiness that is native to them. Today, African philosophy seeks to restore this emptiness if it is truly to be what it is. In this undertaking, it joins not only Asian philosophy but also a reconstructed Western philosophy. One of the tragedies of the European invasion of Africa has been to render Africans blind to what they are and also to what Europeans are. The invasion has also rendered Europeans blind to what they are. It has also rendered non-Africans blind to what Africans are. African philosophical illumination is an antidote to this contagious blindness. It is a call to all peoples of the world to affirm what they have in common in the midst of their differences. What they have in common is the possibility of being what they can become.

At an age where there is tremendous pressure to embrace differences and particularities, and to avoid delusory or illusory universality, how can I say what I have said in this work? Who has made me a spokesperson for Africa and for Africans in the domain of philosophy? Have I accurately presented what is true of the Western or the European domain of philosophy, or have I been indulging in fictitious thinking? In response to either of these questions, I assume that they are raised as philosophical questions and call for a philosophical response. They cannot be understood

10 Conclusion

or answered without paying philosophical attention to what philosophy is. What paying philosophical attention entails is a philosophical issue that I am open to and that every lover of philosophy must be open to. Philosophy flourishes where there is openness. If there is an exaggeration or falsification in what has been said, it is up to others to point out the exaggeration or the falsehood. I have not attempted to circumscribe what is unexaggerated or what is unfalsified. As an African, I am more than what I am as an individual. Being an African is a communal mode of being. One is an African in communion with other Africans. Moreover, being African is a human mode of being, and one cannot be a human being in isolation from other human beings. It is in this sense that I can speak on behalf of fellow Africans and on behalf of fellow human beings. I am inescapably one of them. This mode of being makes it legitimate for fellow Africans and fellow human beings to pass judgment on what I have said, provided that they too recognize their ontological and existential status. What is, is open, and the language that is proper to it is, accordingly, open. To write about philosophy is to welcome others to be cowriters. Philosophy is essentially invitational.

Notes

1. See Maurice Merleau-Ponty, *Phenomenology of Perception*, trans. Colin Smith (New York: Routledge, 2005).
2. Laurence J. Lafleur, *Descartes: Meditations on First Philosophy* (Indianapolis: Bobbs-Merrill Educational, 1960); see Mediations 1 and II.
3. Frantz Fanon, *The Wretched of the Earth*, trans. Richard Philcox (New York: Grove, 2004), lvii.
4. Aimé Césaire, "Discourse on Colonialism," in *Colonial Discourse and Post-colonial Theory: A Reader*, eds. Patrick Williams and Laura Chrisman (New York: Columbia University Press, 1994), 173–174.
5. Paulin Hountondji, *African Philosophy: Myth and Reality*, trans. Henri Evans (Indianapolis: Indiana University Press, 1983); see pages 45 and 67.
6. Ibid, 55.
7. Frantz Fanon, *The Wretched of the Earth*, trans. Richard Philcox (New York: Grove, 2004), 149–150.
8. Ibid, 11.
9. Mogobe B. Ramose, *African Philosophy Through Ubuntu* (Harare: Mond, 1999).
10. Aimé Césaire, "Letter to Maurice Thorez." abahlali.org/files/cesaire_letter.pdf
11. Kofi Awoonor, *Until the Morning After* (Greenfield Center: Greenfield Review, 1987), 4.
12. Chinua Achebe, *Things Fall Apart* (New York: Random House, 1994), 7.
13. Martin Heidegger, *An Introduction to Metaphysics*, trans. Ralph Manheim (New Haven: Yale University Press, 1959), 121.
14. Hampâté Bâ, "The Living Tradition," in *General History of Africa*, ed. J. Kizerbo (Berkeley: University of California, Berkeley, 1981), 170.
15. Ludwig Wittgenstein, *Tractatus Logico-philosophicus*, trans. Daniel Kolak (Mountain View: Mayfield, 1998), 49.
16. See Edmund Husserl, *The Crisis of European Sciences and Transcendental Phenomenology*, trans. David Carr (Evanston: Norwestern University Press,

1970); and Edmund Husserl, *Phenomenology and the Crisis of Philosophy*, trans. Quentin Lauer (New York: Harper Torchbooks, 1965).
17. Kwasi Wiredu, *Philosophy and an African Culture* (Cambridge: Cambridge University Press, 1980).
18. Paulin Hountondji, *African Philosophy: Myth and Reality*, trans. Henri Evans (Indianapolis: Indiana University Press, 1983), 172.
19. Ibid, 106–107.
20. Ibid, 83.
21. Ibid, 98.
22. Edmund Husserl, *The Crisis of European Sciences and Transcendental Phenomenology*, trans. David Carr (Evanston: Northwestern University Press, 1970).
23. Aristotle, *The Basic Works of Aristotle*, ed. Richard McKeon (New York: Random House, 1941).
24. Odera Oruka, *Sage Philosophy: Indigenous Thinkers and Modern Debate on African Philosophy* (Nairobi: African Center for Technological Studies (ACTS) Press, 1991).
25. Martin Heidegger, *What is Philosophy*, trans. Jean T. Wilde and William Kluback, (Albany: New College and University Pres, Inc., 1956), 29–31.
26. Martin Heidegger, *An Introduction to Metaphysics*, trans. Ralph Manheim (New Haven: Yale University Press, 1959), 56–57.
27. Christos C. Evangeliou, *The Hellenic Philosophy: Between Europe, Asia and Africa* (Binghamton: Institute of Global Cultural Studies, Binghamton University, 1997).
28. Placide Tempels, *Bantu Philosophy*, trans. The Revd. Colin King (Paris: Presence Africaine, 1959), 36.
29. Paulin Hountondji, *African Philosophy: Myth and Reality*, trans. Henri Evans (Indianapolis: Indiana University Press, 1983), 72.
30. Francis B. Nyamnjoh, "Relevant Education for African Development: Some Epistemological Considerations," in *African Philosophy: Theory and Practice*, ed. Lansana Keita (Dakar: CODESRIA, 2011), 144.
31. See Friedrich Nietzsche, "Beyond Good and Evil," in *The Portable Nietzsche*, trans. Walter Kaufmann (New York: Penguin Books, 1976).
32. Paulin Hountondji, *African Philosophy: Myth and Reality*, trans. Henri Evans (Indianapolis: Indiana University Press, 1983), 56.
33. Ibid.
34. Bruce Janz, *Philosophy in an African Place* (Lanham: Lexington Press, 2009).
35. Today conversations on race and racism tend to be superficial. They lack in-depth ontological and existential scrutiny—the kind of scrutiny that one finds in Jean-Paul Sartre (*Anti-Semite and the Jew*, trans. George J. Becker (New York: Schocken, 1976)).
36. Malcolm X, *Malcolm X on Afro-American History* (New York: Pathfinder, 1990), 24.
37. Hugh Trevor-Roper, *The Rise of Christian Europe* (New York: Norton, 1965), 9.
38. Jorge Gracia, *Latin American Philosophy* (Amherst: Prometheus, 1986).

Notes

39. Tsenay Serequeberhan, *African Philosophy: The Essential Writings* (New York: Paragon House, 1991), 47.
40. Placide Tempels, *Bantu Philosophy*, trans. The Revd. Colin King (Paris: Presence Africaine, 1959).
41. Kwasi Wiredu, *Philosophy and an African Culture* (Cambridge: Cambridge University Press, 1980), 49.
42. See Walter Rodney's *How Europe Underdeveloped Africa* (Washington, DC: Howard University Press, 1980).
43. Alain Badiou, *Conditions*, trans. Steven Corcoran (New York: Continuum International, 2008), 5.
44. *Hegel's Lectures on the History of Philosophy*, trans. E. S. Haldane (London: Routledge and Kegan Paul, 1892), 1.
45. Maurice Merleau-Ponty, *The Essential Writings of Merleau-Ponty*, trans. Alden L. Fisher (New York: Harcourt Brace, 1969).
46. Friedrich Nietzsche, *Beyond Good and Evil*, trans. Walter Kaufmann (New York: Random House, 1989), 2.
47. Maurice Merleau-Ponty, *The Essential Writings of Merleau-Ponty*, trans. Alden L. Fisher (New York: Harcourt Brace, 1969), 257.
48. Jean-Paul Sartre, *Being and Nothingness*, trans. Hazel Barnes (New York: Washington Square, 1984), 565.
49. Frantz Fanon, *The Wretched of the Earth*, trans. Richard Philcox (New York: Grove, 2004), 182.
50. Wangechi Mutu, *This You Call Civilization*, ed. David Moss (Toronto: Art Gallery of Ontario, 2010), 29.
51. Georg W. F. Hegel, *The Philosophy of History*, trans. J. Sibree (Buffalo: Prometheus, 1991), 93.
52. Georg W. F. Hegel, *Lectures on the Philosophy of the World History*, trans. H. B. Nisbet (Cambridge: Cambridge University Press, 1975), 172–173.
53. Ibid, 44.
54. Georg W. F. Hegel, *The Philosophy of History*, trans. J.Sirbree (Buffalo: Prometheus, 1991), 44.
55. Joseph Conrad, *Heart of Darkness and The Secret Sharer* (New York: Doubleday Bantam, 1981).
56. Georg W. F. Hegel, *The Philosophy of History*, trans. J. Sibree (Buffalo: Prometheus, 1991), 95.
57. Georg W. F. Hegel, *Lectures on the Philosophy of the World History*, trans. Robert F. Brown and Peter C. Hodgson (New York: Oxford University Press, 2011), 88.
58. See Walter Kaufmann, *The Portable Nietzsche*, trans. by Walter Kaufmann (New York: Penguin Books, 1976).
59. Shusaku Endo, *Silence*, trans. William Johnston (New York: Taplinger, 1980), 88.
60. Giorgio Agamben, *The Open: Man and Animal*, trans. Kevin Attell (Palo Alto: Stanford University Press, 2003), 83.

61. See Jean-Paul Sartre, *Being and Nothingness*, trans. Hazel Barnes (New York: Washington Square, 1984).
62. Martin Heidegger, "The Origin of the Work of Art" in *Basic Writings*, ed. David Farrell Krell (New York: Harper Collins, 1993), 141–212.
63. Chinua Achebe, Things Fall Apart, p. 7.
64. Mao Tsetung, *Five Essays on Philosophy* (Peking: Foreign Languages, 1977), 6–7.
65. Maurice Merleau-Ponty, *The Essential Writings of Merleau-Ponty*, trans. Alden L. Fisher (New York: Harcourt Brace, 1969).
66. John Murungi, *African Musical Aesthetics* (Newcastle upon Tyne: Cambridge Scholars, 2011), 1.
67. Georg F.W. Hegel, *The Philosophy of History*, trans. J. Sirbree (Buffalo: Prometheus, 1991).
68. Ibid, 99.
69. Raquel Tibol, *Frida Kahlo: An Open Life* (Albuquerque: University of New Mexico Press, 1999), 27.
70. Martin Heidegger, *An Introduction to Metaphysics*, trans. Ralph Manheim (New Haven: Yale University Press, 1959), 11.
71. Ibid, 13.
72. Martin Heidegger, *Poetry, Language, Thought*, trans. Albert Hofstadter (New York: Harper Collins, 1971), 165.
73. René Descartes, *Discourse on Method and Meditations*, trans. Laurence Lafleur (Indianapolis: Bobbs-Merrill Educational, 1960), 6–8.
74. Martin Heidegger, *Poetry, Language, Thought*, trans. Albert Hofstadter (New York: Harper Collins, 1971), 211–212.
75. Wangari Maathai, "Nobel Lecture" (Oslo: Nobel Media, 2004), accessed January 14, 2017. http://www.nobelprize.org/nobel_prizes/peace/laureates/2004/maathai-lecture-text.html.
76. Ibid.
77. Hampâté Bâ, "The Living Tradition" in *General History of Africa. I: Methodology and Prehistory*, ed. J. Ki-Zerbo (Paris: Heinemann, 1981), 166–203.
78. Maurice Merleau-Ponty, *The Essential Writings of Merleau-Ponty*, trans. Alden L. Fisher (New York: Harcourt Brace, 1969), 285.
79. Chuang Tzu, *Zhuangzi: The Essential Writings*, trans. Brook Ziporyn (Indianapolis: Hackett, 2009), 6.
80. Maurice Merleau-Ponty, *The Essential Writings of Merleau-Ponty*, trans. Alden L. Fisher (New York: Harcourt Brace, 1969), 285.
81. Immanuel Kant, *Critique of Pure Reason*, trans. Paul Guyer and Allen Wood (Cambridge: Cambridge University Press, 1998).
82. Edmund Husserl, *Phenomenology and the Crisis of Philosophy*, trans. Quentin Lauer (New York: Harper & Row, 1965), 82.
83. Lao Tzu, *The Way of Life*, trans. Witter Bynner (Berkeley: Berkeley Publishing, 1994), 39.

CPSIA information can be obtained
at www.ICGtesting.com
Printed in the USA
LVHW051005101119
636873LV00011B/724/P